The Golden Age of Piracy

The Golden Age of Piracy

THE RISE, FALL, AND ENDURING POPULARITY OF PIRATES

Edited by David Head

The University of Georgia Press   Athens

© 2018 by the University of Georgia Press
Athens, Georgia 30602
www.ugapress.org
All rights reserved
Set in Adobe Caslon Pro

Most University of Georgia Press titles are
available from popular e-book vendors.

Printed digitally

Library of Congress Cataloging-in-Publication Data

Names: Head, David, (Historian), editor.
Title: The golden age of piracy : the rise, fall, and enduring popularity of pirates /
edited by David Head.
Description: Athens : The University of Georgia Press, 2018. | Includes
bibliographical references and index.
Identifiers: LCCN 2017052790| ISBN 9780820353265 (hardback : alk. paper) |
ISBN 9780820353258 (pbk. : alk. paper) | ISBN 9780820353272 (ebook)
Subjects: LCSH: Pirates—History—17th century. | Pirates—History—18th
century. | Piracy—Atlantic Ocean Region—History. | Piracy—Caribbean
Area—History. | Atlantic Ocean Region—History—17th century. | Atlantic
Ocean Region—History—18th century. | Caribbean Area—History—17th
century. | Caribbean Area—History—18th century.
Classification: LCC G535 .G54 2018 | DDC 910.4/5—dc23 LC record available at
https://lccn.loc.gov/2017052790

CONTENTS

ACKNOWLEDGMENTS

I would like to thank the contributors, whose hard work, professionalism, and erudition have made the volume possible. They turned in outstanding scholarship, bore my edits patiently, and tolerated my taskmaster dedication to deadlines without mutiny or even demanding an increase to the rum ration. I'm honored to have worked with them. I've enjoyed the support of colleagues at Spring Hill College and the University of Central Florida. In particular, UCF MA student Gramond McPherson served as research assistant and wrangled the notes into shape. Claire Cage, Alan Shane Dillingham, and Timothy Lombardo provided much needed feedback at an early stage. Finally, I want to thank Walter Biggins and the team at the University of Georgia Press for launching the project and carrying it through to the end. It's been a pleasure, once more, to work together.

Portions of two chapters appeared previously in print, and on behalf of the authors I would like to thank the following presses for permission to use that work here: New York University Press for Carolyn Eastman, "'Blood and Lust': Masculinity and Sexuality in Illustrated Print Portrayals of Early Pirates of the Caribbean," in *New Men: Manliness in Early America*, ed. Thomas A. Foster (2011); and University of Massachusetts Press for Guy Chet, *The Ocean Is a Wilderness: Atlantic Piracy and the Limits of State Authority, 1688–1856* (2014).

While the project was underway, my family added a new member to our crew, as my wife, Andrea, and I welcomed a wonderful little girl, Camila. She already has her eye on her sister's pirate outfit—OK, I have *my* eye on it for her. "Ahoy, little matey!"

David Head

Introduction

David Head

When my daughter Carolina was nine months old, she received a navy blue onesie that proclaimed her "Captain of the Pirate Ship!" It had a picture of a large vessel, a three-master, with the various parts labeled, including an ample space in the hold for treasure. "Ahoy Little Matey!" the bottom of the shirt beckoned. It was cute. My little pirate. Adorable.

But why isn't dressing up a baby like a pirate something awful—an act of child abuse even? Pirates were thieves and murderers. They were rapists. They enjoyed torture. They were, to use the technical term, bad guys.

Looking through my daughter's dresser, I see lots of outfits with kitties and puppies, sleepy owls and fun-loving butterflies, and oh so many princesses—but no criminals. Somehow, though, pirates are just fine for kids, like a cuddly cartoon character.

The reason is obvious. Pirates are cool. Sure, adults know they may have been rough around the edges, but that just makes them lovable rogues. Pirates lived free, challenged authority, made their own rules, and drank rum all day and all night under a coconut tree on a white sandy beach by an azure sea. Popular culture tells us so.

Pirates are beloved figures and have been for a long time. The first installment of the *Pirates of the Caribbean* movies, currently the flagship of pirate celebrity, debuted in 2003, and the franchise now numbers five films with no sign of slowing down. *Pirates of the Caribbean* the movie was based on Pirates of the Caribbean the ride, which opened at Disneyland in 1967. Walt seems to have been a pirate enthusiast. His 1950 film version of *Treasure Island* solidified as many images of pirates as the original novel. Its Long John Silver, played by British actor Robert Newton with a penchant for growling r sounds, fixed how we hear pirates talk: "Arrrr!" It might be tempting to say *Treasure Island* the book started the fictional fascination with pirates, but when Robert Louis Stevenson began publishing the story in 1881 he was already heir to a venerable tradition of stories about pirates and buried treasure that stretched back through the nineteenth century and beyond. Stevenson devised the story at first as a rainy-day diversion for his twelve-year-old American stepson, who, like any good boy of his day and class, knew to expect extravagant adventures from pirates.[1]

Though pirates were stylized over the years, the fascination with them grows out of the fact that they were real. Pirates really were dangerous men (and a few dangerous women) who sailed the seas in search of plunder. Pirates really were active in the Caribbean, its islands and adjoining seas, in the sixteenth, seventeenth, and eighteenth centuries. Pirates really did prey on the lucrative trade of Europe's colonizing powers. They may not have buried treasure, jeered a victim walking the plank, or found themselves cursed by Aztec gold, but pirates were a serious problem in the colonial Caribbean. People lost their lives to pirates. People lost their lives as pirates. Anyone who worked or lived by the waters of the early Atlantic world had to confront, as surely as they faced the winds and waves, the danger of pirates.

This volume investigates the real pirates of history and the history of pirates in popular culture. It examines the pirates who accompanied European exploration, empire making, and nation building from the sixteenth century into the nineteenth. It also analyzes how pirates were interpreted by general audiences in the days when pirates were active and how pirates have been remembered in times since. The essays that follow offer a broad picture of piracy. They look at the geopolitical factors that gave rise to piracy, how piracy changed over time, how and why piracy diminished, and what larger lessons about crime and public policy today can be learned from studying pirates of the past. The essays also offer historical context for pirate popular culture. While pirates have long been fashionable, they have played different cultural roles at different times. Seemingly timeless, pirate tales have a history too.

Pirates have probably always existed and probably always will. Homer, Aristotle, and Thucydides wrote about pirates in the ancient world. Today, the International Chamber of Commerce maintains a Piracy Report website (https://icc-ccs.org) where you can find information on the latest incidents of piracy around the world complete with a Google map. Pirates have plundered across the globe. Europe, Africa, the Americas, Asia—all have witnessed piracy at one time or another. No sea has been immune.

This volume has a more specific focus: the so-called golden age of piracy in the Caribbean. Scholars have defined the Golden Age in various ways, sometimes narrowly to indicate only a surge of piracy from 1716 to 1726, at other times more broadly to include the buccaneers of the seventeenth century or to bring in the Elizabethan Sea Dogs of the sixteenth century. In individual chapters, authors advance their periodization as they see fit. Taken as a whole, the work embraces an expansive definition. The essays begin with the origins of Caribbean piracy in the sixteenth century as Spain's enemies attempted to blast their way into the New World that Spain claimed as its own exclusive possession. They continue with the exploits of the buccaneers and famous captains such as Henry Morgan in the seventeenth century that culminated in Spain recognizing the legitimacy of foreign settlement by the 1690s. The work then moves through the ensuing dispersal of the buccaneers from their perch in the Caribbean in the late seventeenth and early eighteenth century and discusses the notorious 1710s and 1720s, the days of Blackbeard and Bartholomew "Black Bart" Roberts, of Anne Bonny and Mary Read. The work further expands the chronology of the Golden Age into the nineteenth century to investigate the timing of piracy's decline and how the popular culture of piracy changed over time. Geographically, the essays are less diffuse. The primary site of action is the Caribbean. Still, the oceans of the world connect and pirates sailed where the winds and currents took them, spilling over into the larger Atlantic Ocean, even around Africa to the Indian Ocean as well. A more global approach over a larger chronology might be possible, but the Golden Age pirates are worth discussing on their own.

The twelve essays presented build on the work of a previous generation of scholars that took the study of piracy, which can easily lapse into rousing, romanticized stories, to new heights of rigor and insight. The contemporary scholarly study of pirates was jolted to life in 1981 when Marcus Rediker, then still a graduate student, published an article that disrupted the traditional understanding of pirates as bloodthirsty criminals. In Rediker's account, reiterated numerous times since, pirates were alienated, class-conscious figures whose villainy was not something to condemn but to applaud because in sailing outside the law, pirates rebelled against the rising power of the state and the emerging dominance of capitalism. For Rediker, pirates were democratic in an autocratic age, anticapitalist in an ocean of merchants, plain, honest men in a world of corrupt, contemptible authorities who truly ruined people's lives and set us on a course we have not yet corrected. In a word, pirates were radicals.[2]

Other scholars worked in a similar vein. Pirates were transgressive in their democratic ethos, plundering together and sharing the proceeds. Pirates were progressive in their racial attitudes and were said to be more accepting of blacks aboard their ships than anyone else of their time. Pirates flouted social norms of gender and sexuality; there were women pirates, and male pirates were said to have been drawn to piracy by the opportunity to engage in homosexual acts away from authorities and stifling social conventions. The radical pirate thesis met stout criticism, especially from scholars who rejected the Marxist and postmodern categories it depended on. Nevertheless, from the 1980s through the 1990s, radical pirates set the terms of debate.[3]

In the 2000s, new scholars challenged the radical pirate thesis with new archival research. Examples of greedy pirates were not hard to find. The explosion of piracy in 1716, to take one instance, had been touched off by a wreck of the Spanish Treasure Fleet in the Bahama Channel that attracted seaborne bandits like, well, like bandits after poorly guarded gold. Examples of pirates abusing black slaves also abounded. When pirates captured slave ships, they sometimes kept the human cargoes to sell; other times, when they wanted a vessel but not more mouths to feed or needed to make a quick getaway, the slaves were thrown overboard or even burned alive. Despite diligent searching, scholars have not found evidence of many women pirates. Anne Bonny and Mary Read remain the most famous—famous because they were apparently so unusual. Even pirates' most distinctively radical practices, such as democratic organization, could be explained plausibly as self-interested, if viewed through a modern economist's distinctive eyes.[4]

Most importantly, scholars of piracy are finding that pirates were not alienated from their land-based communities but rather embedded in them. Like sailors everywhere, pirates may have inhabited a wooden world at sea; however, like sailors everywhere, they eventually came back to land (if they didn't die at sea, of course). Piracy was not necessarily a long-term practice and "pirate" was not an enduring identity. Piracy was something a man might do once, and then go back home. In a similar way, scholars have emphasized that the larger geopolitics and economics of the Atlantic world conditioned the rise, practice, and fall of piracy. Shore-based communities in the colonies, meanwhile, depended on pirates to deliver goods otherwise unavailable in the closed trading systems of the European empires whose edges they inhabited. Colonial communities sheltered pirates as a result.[5]

In yet another connection to the larger world, scholars have changed the conversation about the pirates of fiction and about the fictionalized pirates of reality. Some of the most frequently cited material on pirates has questionable reliability. The well-known *A General History of the Pyrates*, for example, is notoriously slippery, with many of its best stories and quotes too good to be true. But rather than turning away, scholars have embraced the popular culture of pirates. Even fanciful portrayals have a lot to reveal about gender and sexuality, cultural anxieties, the development of capitalism, and how myths are created, altered, and diffused.[6]

The essays that follow collect the latest examples of what might be called the postradical pirate scholarship of Golden Age pirates, and in doing so they advance our understanding of what are now the traditional interests in pirates: who they were, what they did, how they organized themselves, how they lived, how they related to the political and economic systems that surrounded them, how authorities responded, and why and when piracy declined. The essays also join those traditional areas of inquiry to relatively new ones, such as how the image of pirates changed over time and why people liked to consume stories about pirates. As the essays show, we know more about pirates, their victims and collaborators, their supporters and fans, than we did a generation ago. More than embodying the current state of the field, however, the essays also serve as a point of departure, a launching point for new voyages of pirate discovery.

The book is divided into four sections to address a breadth of themes. The first section, "Pirates and Empire," shows how piracy developed out of the European contest for New World empires in the sixteenth and seventeenth centuries and how pirates helped create those empires.

Carla Gardina Pestana begins with the overarching geopolitical context of the Caribbean. Though a site of extensive piracy, the Caribbean was not a lawless free-for-all where crews of would-be pirates lounged on the beaches waiting to swing swords and steal booty. The rise of piracy was bound up with Spain's claim to possess most of the New World exclusively according to the Treaty of Tordesillas (1494), which divided the world for colonization by Spain and Portugal. England, France, and the Netherlands did not agree, however. Drawn by the glimmer of Spanish gold and silver, they harassed Spanish ships and attempted to found their own colonies. By the end of the seventeenth century, the Dutch, English, and French had all won concessions from Spain. The nature of private violence changed and pirates became more marginalized. The early modern Caribbean was a violent place, Pestana shows, but its violence was brought about, shaped, and reduced by specific historic circumstances.

John A. Coakley continues the story of pirates in the imperial contest of the early modern Caribbean. He looks at seventeenth-century Jamaica, a prime site of buccaneering, and how a variety of actors engaged in piracy and piracy-like activities to advance England's larger agenda vis-à-vis Spain. Coakley prefers the term *private seafarer* to traditional labels such as pirate or privateer, since neither term quite captures the murkiness of just what was allowed and what wasn't. Seized from Spain in 1655 during English Lord Protector Oliver Cromwell's Western Design venture in the Caribbean, Jamaica was an English outpost surrounded by none-too-friendly Spaniards. Jamaican governors thus turned to private seafarers for protections, including the offensive first-strike variety of protection in which licensed sea raiders plundered Spanish neighbors. The expeditions of Henry Morgan, carried out between 1668 and 1671, were the most famous operations, with Morgan's sack of Panama the most epic. The raids were examples of private wars, authorized by Jamaica's governor, whose agenda overlapped with, but was not quite identical to, English imperial policy. As Coakley demonstrates, the rise and fall of Jamaica as a port for private raiding tracks the larger history of the Caribbean. Raiders like Morgan were central to the island's strategy of survival next door to enemies and on the edge of England's reach.

Kevin P. McDonald closes the section by turning to the logwood cutters, a group of marginal men who also got themselves branded pirates for engaging in activities contrary to Spain's imperial designs. Operating along the Bay of Campeche, in modern Mexico, and the Bay of Honduras, near today's Belize, the cutters did the hard work of felling logwood trees, prized in Europe as a source of dyes. It was a lucrative trade, and Spain denounced it as illegal, since it pulled resources out of their lands. The logwood cutters provide an example of what McDonald calls the spectrum of piracy—a way of looking at actors defined as pirates that emphasizes how difficult a precise definition could be, how much the definition depended on who did the defining, and how easily the same people could cross from illegal activities, such as smuggling and unauthorized forestry, into more serious illegal activities, such as piracy, and back again.

The next section, "Suppression of Pirates," features three views of the causes and timing of the decline of piracy. Douglas R. Burgess writes about the late seventeenth and early eighteenth centuries and how English authorities came to define piracy and applied that definition through the enhanced jurisdiction of admiralty courts empowered to try and punish pirates. The reforms were easier to implement in England itself than in the American colonies, however, as colonial governments, jealous of their power and liberties, pushed back against more stringent oversight from the metropole. But when the nature of piracy changed, shifting away from its 1690s hotspot in the Indian Ocean and back to the Atlantic and Caribbean, colonists fell in line and accepted the vice-admiralty court officers sent from London to impose law and order. "The results," Burgess writes, "were swift and severe." By the middle 1700s, piracy was controlled.

David Wilson finds that the idea of a coordinated, London-led extermination of pirates in the 1720s is misleading. Yes, governments cracked down on piracy around that time, but they did so acting on their own, in fits and starts, in response to outside pressure as well as to pursue the state's own priorities. Wilson also highlights how different things looked in the metropole and in the colonies. Squeezed by powerful business interests, London officials increased the navy's presence, passed new laws, and offered pardons, although without decisive effect. Colonial efforts appear to have been more effective. Colonists launched their own expeditions against pirate lairs and hired their own pirate-hunting ships, sometimes manned by pardoned pirates out to catch their old booty fellows. The suppression of piracy, according to Wilson, was effected in the third decade of the eighteenth century but it was ultimately not about metropolitan officials imposing order on chaos. Instead, order emerged from a chaotic mix of interests and initiatives coming out of both the center and the periphery.

Guy Chet upends the chronology of pirate suppression. He denies that the 1720s marked anything close to the end of Caribbean and Atlantic piracy. Indeed, he asserts, piracy continued unabated through the eighteenth century well into the nineteenth. After the 1720s, marine insurance rates did not decline as might have been expected with the elimination of a major hazard, courts still heard piracy trials, and officials still complained about depredations. Britain's vaunted naval presence was less effective than often imagined, while officials treated piracy as part of the cost of running an empire. The public's enthusiasm for buying pirated goods remained strong. Piracy did decline by the mid-nineteenth century, Chet writes, but not because of any direct government action. Economic and geopolitical conditions changed and piracy, commerce raiding, and smuggling all became less profitable. And therefore less practiced.

The next section, "Modeling Piracy," takes a step back and asks what larger lessons about human, criminal behavior can be gleaned from the history of piracy and applied to our world today. Virginia W. Lunsford uses the seventeenth-century buccaneers as a case study that has parallels to modern piracy, and she suggests ways that present and future responses to piracy might benefit from a historical perspective. Lunsford identifies six factors that create and sustain piracy: access to recruits, access to goods to steal, a base of operations, sophisticated organization, outside support, and cultural bonds that encourage group solidarity. Attacking these factors was key to breaking up buccaneering and should be a priority for policymakers fighting piracy today, Lunsford concludes.

Peter T. Leeson comes at Golden Age piracy from a different angle. An economist, Leeson applies economic concepts to the work of historians to reveal new explanations for the familiar, if sometimes puzzling, behavior of pirates. Going back to basics, Leeson argues that pirates, like all people, were rational and had to make decisions about scarce resources that have alternative uses. He shows how an economic way of thinking about pirates demonstrates that pirates' democratic organization, use of the Jolly Roger flag, and practice of torture were responses to the incentives they faced as criminals and aided in their attempts to maximize their profits. Leeson's economic approach suggests not only a different way of looking at pirates but also a different way of understanding the operations of criminal enterprises of all kinds.

The essays next turn from the pirates of history to the pirates of popular culture. "Images of Pirates in Their Own Time and Beyond" discusses how audiences at home on shore understood the pirates active out on the deep. Margarette Lincoln writes about Henry Every, an English pirate in the Indian Ocean in the 1690s, and how ballads celebrating his exploits helped create the pirate myth in Britain. Every pillaged a ship belonging to the Indian Mughal, won a fortune, and then disappeared, his fate unknown. He left behind only a vast body of ballads and other literature about his life, fictional or fictionalized, with no easy way to tell the difference. Rather than sleuthing in this literature for clues about Every, Lincoln investigates what the stories themselves tell us about the people who consumed them, what audiences thought about piracy, and what they wanted to see and hear in their tales of pirates. Pirate stories appear, then, as ways to work out different ideas about class and power; gender, sexuality, and marriage; and England and India and the vagaries of empire.

Carolyn Eastman proceeds in a similar vein. She writes about two classic sources on piracy: *Bucaniers of America* by Alexandre Exquemelin (1678) and *A General History of the Pyrates* (1724). Eastman is particularly concerned with the images of masculinity revealed by these accounts of piracy, both in their words and in their pictures. Eastman finds that the interplay between text and image was suffused with messages about masculine sexuality, making pirates into outsiders whose exploits and poses allowed middle-class and elite male readers to imagine themselves in a world where manly men did not need to control themselves as their society demanded.

The volume then moves forward in time to the nineteenth century to look at how pirate myths evolved over time in the changing circumstances of American culture. Matthew Taylor Raffety introduces the pirates of antebellum America, who committed atrocities and then blamed a woman—girlfriend, mother, former plantation mistress—for their fiendish crimes. As Raffety shows, pirate narratives were part of an antebellum confessional literature in which condemned men recounted their deeds according to well-established conventions to give a moral lesson and admonish readers from their sad fate. Pirates were not the only ones to blame women for their sins, but even though their complaints should have generated skepticism due to the lack of women at sea, Raffety finds that the accounts gained plausibility from cultural expectations that women were such moral guardians that any immorality must be traceable to their failing.

Adam Jortner concludes the volume with a treasure hunt. It turns out that hunting for treasure was quite the thing in the early republic, and not just in fiction, although there was a robust folklore tradition of treasure hunting, too. People touched spade to earth and dug up the ground hoping to find gold and silver and a pirate's haul of jewels. Treasure hunting mixed fable, fantasy, esoteric practices, the occult, and a little history to guide seekers, who were cautioned that they might encounter ghosts, goblins, and evil spirits none too eager to give up the valuables of an old buccaneer. Jortner digs through the stories of treasure hunting and discovers that they had a message not about pirates so much as about making yourself ready for capitalism. The moral of the story, Jortner argues, was that thrift and industry were the way to wealth, not getting rich quick from a pirate's lost loot.

The pirates of the long Golden Age discussed in the following pages form an important part of the history of the early modern world as it emerged, expanded, and ushered in the one we live in today. Pirates both facilitated and challenged the expansion of European empires, and it is these pirates whose image has proven so influential on the popular imagination. The following essays help provide answers about just what pirates were and why they are still so fascinating.

NOTES

1. For Newton's performance, see Angus Konstam, *Piracy: The Complete History* (Oxford, UK: Osprey Publishing, 2008), 313. For the composition of *Treasure Island*, see David Cordingly, *Under the Black Flag: The Romance and Reality of Life among the Pirates* (New York: Random House, 1996), 3–4.

2. Rediker's pirate works include: "'Under the Banner of King Death': The Social World of Anglo-American Pirates, 1716 to 1726," *William and Mary Quarterly* 38 (1981): 203–27; *Between the Devil and the Deep Blue Sea: Merchant Seamen, Pirates, and the Anglo-American Maritime World, 1700–1750* (Cambridge, UK: Cambridge University Press, 1987); "Liberty beneath the Jolly Roger: The Lives of Anne Bonny and Mary Read, Pirates," in *Iron Men, Wooden Women: Gender and Seafaring in the Atlantic World, 1700–1920*, ed. Margaret S. Creighton and Lisa Norling (Baltimore: Johns Hopkins University Press, 1996), 1–33; Peter Linebaugh and Rediker, *The Many-Headed Hydra: Sailors, Slaves, Commoners, and the Hidden History of the Revolutionary Atlantic* (Boston: Beacon Press, 2000); *Villains of All Nations: Atlantic Pirates in the Golden Age* (Boston: Beacon Press, 2004); *Outlaws of the Atlantic: Sailors, Pirates, and Motley Crews in the Age of Sail* (Boston: Beacon Press, 2015); "'Under the Banner of King Death'" and "Liberty beneath the Jolly Roger" were reprinted in C. R. Pennell, ed., *Bandits at Sea: A Pirate Reader* (New York: New York University Press, 2001), 139–68 and 299–320, respectively. For historiographic reviews, see C. R. Pennell, "Brought to Book: Reading about Pirates," in *Bandits at Sea*; David J. Starkey, "Voluntaries and Sea Robbers: A Review of the Academic Literature on Privateering, Corsairing, Buccaneering, and Piracy," *Mariner's Mirror* 97 (2011): 127–41; Kris E. Lane, *Piracy: Oxford Bibliographies Online Research Guide* (New York: Oxford University Press, 2014), which is included as "Afterword to the Second Edition" in Lane's *Pillaging the Empire: Global Piracy on the High Seas, 1500–1750*, 2nd ed. (New York: Routledge, 2015), 215–26. For general introductions to piracy, see Peter Earle, *The Pirate Wars* (New York: Thomas Dunne, 2005) and Lane, *Pillaging the Empire*.

3. Pennell, ed., *Bandits at Sea*, includes examples of the major statements of radical pirate historiography. In addition to the Rediker pieces above, see also in *Bandits*

at Sea: J. S. Bromley, *"Outlaws at Sea, 1660–1720*: Liberty, Equality, and Fraternity among the Caribbean Freebooters," 169–94; Kenneth J. Kinkor, "Black Men under the Black Flag," 195–210; and B. R. Burg, "The Buccaneer Community," 211–34. For examples of critiques, see "Roundtable Reviews of Marcus Rediker, *Between the Devil and the Deep Blue Sea: Merchant Seaman, Pirates, and the Anglo-American Maritime World, 1700–1750*, with a Response by Marcus Rediker," *International Journal of Maritime History* 1 (1989): 311–57. Lawrence Osborne's report on the then-emerging radical literature is also helpful; see "A Pirate's Progress: How the Maritime Rogue Became a Multicultural Hero," *Lingua Franca*, March 1998, accessed February 16, 2017, http://linguafranca.mirror.theinfo.org/9803/osborne.html.

4. Arne Bialuschewski has been particularly active challenging the radical pirate thesis. For pirates' motivations, see his "Between Newfoundland and the Malacca Strait: A Survey of the Golden Age of Piracy, 1695–1725," *Mariner's Mirror* 90 (2004): 167–86, and "Pirates, Markets, and Imperial Authority: Economic Aspects of Maritime Depredations in the Atlantic World, 1716–1726," *Global Crime* 9 (2008): 52–65. For pirates, race, and slaves, see "Black People under the Black Flag: Piracy and the Slave Trade on the West Coast of Africa, 1718–1723," *Slavery and Abolition* 29 (2008): 461–75, and "Pirates, Black Sailors, and Seafaring Slaves in the Anglo-American Maritime World, 1716–1726," *Journal of Caribbean History* 45 (2011): 143–58. Pirates also enslaved natives. See Bialuschewski's "Slaves of the Buccaneers: Mayas in Captivity in the Second Half of the Seventeenth Century," *Ethnohistory* 64 (2017): 41–63. On women pirates, scholars are now emphasizing how women were involved in supporting piracy from shore and how they were affected by pirate depredations. See John C. Appleby, *Women and English Piracy, 1540–1720: Partners and Victims of Crime* (Woodbridge, UK: The Boydell Press, 2013); Margarette Lincoln, *British Pirates and Society, 1680–1730* (London: Ashgate, 2014). Peter T. Leeson reinterpreted pirate life from an economist's perspective in *The Invisible Hook: The Hidden Economics of Pirates* (Princeton, N.J.: Princeton University Press, 2009).

5. In addition to Bialuschewski, Appleby, and Lincoln cited above, see also Robert C. Ritchie, *Captain Kidd and the War against the Pirates* (Cambridge, Mass.: Harvard University Press, 1986), and Mark G. Hanna, *Pirate Nests and the Rise of the British Empire, 1570–1740* (Chapel Hill: University of North Carolina Press, 2015).

6. *A General History of the Pyrates* has a fraught publishing history. First brought out in 1724 as *A General History of the Robberies and Murders of the Most Notorious Pyrates* (with a long, long explanatory title following), it was followed by a second volume in 1728. The title page listed Captain Charles Johnson as author. In the twentieth century, it was attributed for a time to Daniel Defoe, then reattributed to the mysterious Captain Johnson, but Arne Bialuschewski discovered it was the work of London printer Nathaniel Mist. See Manuel Schonhorn, "Postscript to the Dover Edition," *A General History of the Pyrates* (Mineola, N.Y.: Dover Publications, 1999),

697–707; Bialuschewski, "Daniel Defoe, Nathaniel Mist, and the 'General History of the Pyrates,'" *The Papers of the Bibliographical Society of America* 98 (2004): 21–38. The classic work on pirate myth versus reality is Cordingly, *Under the Black Flag*. See also Neil Rennie, *Treasure Neverland: Real and Imaginary Pirates* (New York: Oxford University Press, 2013).

Pirates and Empire

Why Atlantic Piracy?

Carla Gardina Pestana

Early modern Atlantic seafaring appears deeply entangled in piracy, with the Caribbean the focal point of such activity. Famous characters fuel the popular association of the Atlantic with pirates, from Sir Francis Drake to Sir Henry Morgan to the notorious Edward Teach (Blackbeard). Our perception of the West Indies as the site of continual, violent seaborne theft is off the mark. In fact, classic pirates—disassociated from the larger society, living by their own code, preying on any and all ships—existed only rarely. Pirates fitting this image became most common as a direct result of an official curb on a variety of activities, such as contraband trade and violence against rival imperial powers, as authorities successfully blocked their access to the coastal communities that had supported them. For much of the two centuries following the advent of Caribbean raiding in the 1520s, pirates worked for European rulers, represented commercial interests, and participated in communities on shore in ways that belie their image as "enemies of all mankind." Only in the early eighteenth century would the tide turn against them in the Atlantic, forcing those who lived by seaborne raiding into the role of the desperate, disaffected pirate. That turn signaled not so much the apex of Atlantic piracy as the beginning of its end.

Piracy came to be associated with the Caribbean for historical reasons. The Atlantic, which we tend to equate with multipronged European expansion in the early modern period, was in fact legally defined as the exclusive purview of the two Iberian powers that would eventually emerge as modern Spain and Portugal. Clearly they did not succeed in keeping out all others, but their efforts to do so shaped not only piracy (and accusations of piracy) but also many other aspects of the Atlantic world. Resisting those exclusive claims made many seafarers into pirates—at least in the eyes of the Iberians they encountered. With the entrée of numerous rivals, the Americas turned into a complex, multinational space, as near constant warfare in Europe, particularly involving the powerful Spanish Habsburg family that ruled Spain from the 1520s, spilled over into the Americas. The great wealth extracted from Spain's American possessions made the Flota de Indias, the fleet that carried Spanish silver to Cádiz, an attractive target in times of war—and at other times as well. The Atlantic thus quickly became and long remained a space of endemic conflict and contested claims, one in which the promise of riches attracted raiders. The combined effect of Spanish exclusionary claims, frequent wars, and vulnerable treasures created Atlantic piracy and sustained it for two centuries. The Caribbean was not simply a violent free-for-all particularly inviting to pirates but a more broadly contested space in which empires fought over access to land, trade, and wealth. Violence in many forms resulted, only some of it purely piratical.

A Sphere for Piracy

The Atlantic—or more correctly sectors of it—became a sphere for piracy because of the peculiarities of its integration into the European world. Entering a space they viewed as unclaimed, Spain and Portugal quickly divided what would turn out to be two additional continents and numerous islands. Within decades, they declared all other governments excluded from these newly discovered spaces.[1] In this, they aspired to act effectively as "a durable and hegemonic regime in a region with the power to define right and wrong." Designating all who entered their space as pirates constituted a part of that effort.[2] Spain's inability to make that exclusion a reality in the Caribbean, in concert with extraction and transportation of great wealth from the region, established the circumstances that made piracy a recurrent problem for two hundred years after the mid-sixteenth century. As in other parts of the world that were not fully controlled by a widely acknowledged authority, incomplete hegemony over the Atlantic opened spaces for illegal trade, poaching, and raids.[3] Most fundamentally, interlopers entered the region because they denied the right of the Spanish or Portuguese to exclude them. Although the Protestant Reformation heightened tensions more generally and encouraged hostilities along religious lines, Caribbean animosities largely ignored religious divisions, with Catholic on Catholic violence nearly as common as Protestant versus Catholic clashes. From the Iberian perspective all interlopers were pirates, but many who were present resisted that definition and even attempted to act in keeping with their own sense of what were legitimate activities. The Spanish practices of deeming all who entered the Caribbean as pirates and treating the relatively harmless with the retribution that true piracy deserved heightened animosities and encouraged the descent into violence.

The European discovery of the Americas, an unprecedented event in world history, led to explorations of these vast areas undertaken by both Spain and Portugal. As new regions opened to European awareness, the two Iberian powers, with the support of the pope, divided ownership and rule of these areas between them—the Americas but also regions in Africa and Asia. In the Americas everything went to Spain save for Brazil, which was Portuguese, while Portugal claimed outposts in Africa and Asia. Both the Portuguese and the Spanish declared their new lands off limits to all other Europeans. Indeed the crown of Castile tried (unsuccessfully) to keep all Spaniards who were not Castilians out of the American kingdoms. The Spanish settlements in the Americas were never as purely Spanish (much less Castilian) as the policy dictated, especially on the Caribbean islands that were settled early and included non-Castilian Spaniards and Portuguese residents.[4] Spain's restrictive policies had a greater impact when it came to blocking trade and settlement. Rival European rulers challenged these rights to exclusive access, particularly those of the Spanish, which encompassed vast swaths of lands they had never visited, much less settled. No one rejected the assertion that discovery brought rights. Rather Spain's rivals focused on the fact that Christopher Columbus only touched at specific places and that the explorers who came after him never visited every bit of the hemisphere. In this thinking, articulated during the first decades of the fifteenth century by French king Francis I, large expanses of the Americas remained open to others to discover, explore, and exploit.[5] This fundamental disagreement, which would not be resolved until the end of the seventeenth century, shaped interactions in the region. Disagreements over access created conditions ripe for clandestine activity and acts of outright violence, as intruders entered the region, undeterred by Spanish claims and indeed bent on challenging them, and the Spanish authorities intermittently attempted to stymie their efforts.

With capacious but controversial Spanish claims dismissed as "contemptible arrogance" in some circles, the unprecedented mineral wealth extracted from Spanish America encouraged Spain's foes to target its American riches.[6] Using native and African labor, the Spanish extracted huge amounts of American silver and with it remade the world economy and cemented Spain's place as the dominant European power. Bullion made the Spanish formidable and allowed them to dominate neighboring states. Rival Europeans feared that Spain aimed at "universal monarchy," that is, control of all the world, and thought they might be able to achieve it given the massive amounts of silver they extracted from the Americas.[7] The Spanish Habsburgs paid for the many wars necessary to extend and defend their extensive domain with American silver. This wealth represented a great temptation. Silver was attractive in and of itself for individuals and states that desired it for their own uses. Snatching it from Spain would undermine its might, which appealed to European states tired of bending to Spain's will. The enemies of Spain fixated on the ships that transported silver to Europe, scouring the sea lanes of the Caribbean and the waters around the Canary Islands in hopes of taking a ship or the entire fleet. Only once in the long history of Spanish mineral extraction did anyone manage the latter feat: Dutch Admiral Piet Heyn in 1626. Other crews grabbed a treasure ship here and there, as did English naval forces dispatched by Oliver Cromwell in 1656.[8] Generally, however, the dream of becoming rich by seizing a ship full of Spanish American silver went unfulfilled.

Throughout these centuries, the Spanish Habsburgs frequently fought wars with one or more European states, wars that increasingly had a Caribbean component. A near-continuous state of warfare meant Spain almost always had enemies ready, from the 1540s, to launch seaborne raids against its Atlantic possessions. Ships that sailed to the Americas in order to fight the Spanish came with authorization or at least under the cover of legitimate war hostilities. In the sixteenth century the ships entering the Caribbean Sea were generally privately owned vessels authorized by a monarch. Francis I sent explorers to North America and to Brazil, as well as corsairs to the Caribbean, the latter from 1542; his son and heir continued the harassment in the West Indies until a treaty was signed in 1559. In the following century, France fought Spain in Europe and the Americas, again using private ships for the latter actions, from 1635 to 1659; Franco-Spanish wars erupted subsequently for some part of each decade thereafter until century's end. The Dutch revolted against Habsburg rule in 1568, fighting a long war to gain their independence, which they achieved in 1648. During that time, the Dutch West India Company pursued the war against Spain in the Americas, sending navies that took the treasure fleet in 1626 and seized part of Brazil in 1630 (then under Spanish rule with the union of the two crowns). England first turned against its longtime ally in the 1580s, when Elizabeth I supported the Dutch Revolt, and eventually went to war openly with Spain. Hence the English sent private vessels with royal authorization (and on at least one occasion royal financial backing) to the Caribbean from 1585 to 1604. During this period Sir Francis Drake and Sir Walter Raleigh gained their reputations as swashbuckling sea dogs. Conflicts pitting Spain against England in the seventeenth century brought private ships again into the region from 1625 to 1630. The English navy first made its appearance in West Indian waters in 1655, in a war that continued until the 1670 Treaty of Madrid, using an increasing number of private men-of-war. Periods of peace were sparse, and the regularity of combat shielded other acts of violence in the West Indies.

Outside of warfare, an age-old practice of raiding as a form of restitution also justified some acts of theft. Individual ships came to the West Indies bent on reprisal in response to previous seizures that their home government had judged illegal. Not all such vessels carried authorization (in the form of a letter of marque and reprisal) from a European authority; some came bent on acts of restitution or retribution without royal support. Seizing ships and cargoes for restitution or retribution predated European expansion into the Americas; before the rise of powerful monarchies, such actions were often conducted under the authority of a local port or a local lord rather than with the permission of the monarch.[9] The early modern period witnessed an effort to rein in local initiative on such matters, but the process proved long and uneven. Reprisal seizures had once been considered entirely justified, and making injured parties see them in a different light demanded a drastic alteration in the thinking of merchants and port communities about how best to protect their interests. The Spanish policy of harshly punishing those caught in the Caribbean resulted in many instances deemed worthy of restitution, creating a vicious cycle. The Providence Island Company ships that raided Spanish vessels in the later 1630s carried authorization gained through a predictable chain of events. The company initially colonized the island off the coast of modern-day Nicaragua on the grounds that Spanish exclusivity was untenable. The Spanish responded to the English presence (which they deemed illegal) by attacking both company vessels and the settlement itself. The company then received authorization to take Spanish property to repay their losses. When Providence Island finally fell to the

Spanish, the English lord high admiral commissioned the privateer William Jackson to exact retribution, which he did on his 1642–1643 tour through the region.[10] Thus efforts to trade peaceably or establish a presence led almost inexorably to violence. As long as the Spanish excluded all other Europeans with force, and as long as other nations rejected that exclusion, confrontation remained inevitable.

The Spanish perspective on all these intruders—whether settlers, contraband traders, or robbers—was that they were pirates. Not only among the Spanish in the Americas but more broadly, *piracy* served as an ugly epithet, for to declare an act to be piracy delegitimized it. Whereas the actors might consider themselves contributing to a war effort or seeking restitution for an earlier wrong, targets of their attacks branded them pirates in order to place their actions firmly outside the law. Labels of piracy occurred far more frequently than actual acts of piracy. When scholars rely on the use of the word to identify a pirate, they privilege accusers' perspectives. Acts of seaborne violence occurred without legitimate cause—simply for personal gain—but such instances were only one part of a highly complex phenomenon. Seaborne warfare, individual acts of reprisal, trade between willing parties that violated imperial policy—all these activities fell under the Spanish rubric for piracy. Even some acts widely held to be piracy fall in a shadowy area, allowing culprits to aver that they believed their actions to have been legitimate. Sir Henry Morgan's devastating assault on Panama (1671) fell in that gray area, permitting him to sue those who printed accusations that he had engaged in piracy. Morgan relied on sluggish and erratic transatlantic communications, which slowed the spread of the news that the Treaty of Madrid had brought a cessation to hostilities, to claim that he attacked under a commission that he believed still to be in force. The Spanish assumed that Morgan knew full well that the war had ended, and they in turn sought retribution against him. Although he spent time imprisoned in the Tower of London, Morgan was also elevated to the post of lieutenant governor of Jamaica, signaling the continued complicity of the government with the sort of depredations that brought him fame.[11] Like the boy who cried wolf, Spain's tendency to cry piracy did not help it to persuade other governments that particular cases represented real outrages. When trading, settling, and even harvesting salt off uninhabited islands could be deemed piracy, the label lost some of its meaning. It behooves scholars to attend to specific circumstances when analyzing piracy accusations. Otherwise, ignoring complexity silently takes sides in debates about legitimacy and rights that are at the heart of accusations and acts.

The Ebb and Flow of Violence

Against a backdrop of numerous wars and many individual acts of reprisal, violence was not continuous but rather ebbed and flowed. The French first came into the region in the 1540s. The Dutch and English followed them some decades later, once wars in Europe propelled them into the Caribbean. Ships with nonviolent intentions—such as exploration, trade, or resource extraction—visited the West Indies. Some quietly went about their business without incident; others were attacked by the Spanish or turned to violence themselves. Certain periods of frequent maritime violence that did not coincide with war displayed a different logic. In the 1570s, the English launched numerous raids against the Spanish, and most of these aimed at retribution for the damage meted out to the captain of a Plymouth ship, John Hawkins, in his 1568 tour of the Spanish Caribbean. Making repeated visits to open a trade in slaves, Hawkins confronted Spanish forces on his third journey, suffering a dramatic defeat at their hands off Vera Cruz. The resulting upsurge in English raiding sought "revenge and reprisal" for Hawkins's defeat.[12] Generally, war's end brought an abatement, as was the case with the English after 1604, the Dutch to an extent during the truce years (1609–21), and the French around the turn of the seventeenth century. Spanish vigilance, although expensive to maintain, also prompted the occasional downturn. Prior to the mid-seventeenth century raiders invariably sailed from Europe and returned there. After that time, communities resident in the Caribbean became sufficiently large and complex to generate local populations of seafarers who could launch or participate in raids. Under those circumstances the later seventeenth century saw more violence and some of the most spectacular individual cases. Among the famous pirates dating from this era were those immortalized by Alexandre Exquemelin in his *Bucaniers of America*, such as Sir Henry Morgan and François l'Olonnais. Other well-known figures of the late seventeenth century include Basil Ringrose, William Dampier, and Bartholomew Sharpe. These late paroxysms of violence arose even as Spain dropped its effort to exclude foreigners, acceding to various foreign activity in a series of treaties: 1648 (Dutch), 1670 (English), and 1697 (French).

By the end of the seventeenth century, the Spanish Habsburg monarchy gave up its claims to exclusive rights to the Americas outside Brazil. This historic change occurred piecemeal, as Spain granted rights to a succession of other governments to have limited access to the Americas. The United Provinces of the Netherlands were the first to receive this boon. In the Treaty of Westphalia (1648), which ended the long Dutch fight for independence, the Spanish acknowledge the right of the Dutch to sail to those places they had customarily had a presence. This concession recognized, among other outposts, the Dutch base on the island of Curaçao. Originally occupied to serve as a naval base during the war against Spain, Curaçao quickly emerged as an important center for contraband trade. The English were next to gain the right to sail Caribbean Seas, after the 1670 Treaty of Madrid gave up Spanish objections to the English colonies there, most notably Jamaica, which had been taken in 1655. That assault, launched under the authority of then Lord Protector Oliver Cromwell, sparked a decade and a half of warfare that resulted in the treaty that finally acceded to English activities.[13] France was last to win these concessions, doing so in the Treaty of Ryswick of 1697. By that time it held not only islands in the eastern Caribbean but Tortuga and a portion of the Spanish island of Santo Domingo. The treaty divided that island, giving France one end as the new colony of Saint-Domingue (today's Haiti). Centuries of pressure from rival European powers finally caused Spain to abandon its exclusive claims to the entire region. Although its implications only gradually became clear, this change also set the stage for a unified opposition to piracy across all these powers. Non-Spanish governments came to oppose piratical activities once raiders no longer targeted an intransigent Spanish enemy who blocked their presence but instead hampered their own ability to profit from peaceful trade. Spanish acceptance of rivals within its American space thus established the conditions for a coordinated campaign against unauthorized seaborne violence.

Sites of Interloping

For two centuries starting in 1500, Spain made grand claims and enacted strict policies but proved unable to enforce them. Counting just the areas they actively held and ruled, the extent of their American empire was truly remarkable. At the same time, it encompassed only a portion of the areas of North America, the Caribbean, and South America outside Portuguese Brazil. In addition to failing to hold all that it claimed, the Spanish Empire in the Americas embraced underpopulated, peripheral locations that saw very little trade or other interaction with the central Spanish settlements and economies. These peripheral regions inclined to open their ports to foreigners, especially if the occasional contraband trader brought much-needed items. Before the Spanish authorities caught up with John Hawkins to destroy most of his ships in the Battle of San Juan de Ulúa off Vera Cruz, he had successfully sold three cargoes of enslaved Africans to willing Spanish purchasers.[14] While central ports and administrative centers followed the trade restrictions more closely, although not uniformly, truck with foreigners occurred more commonly on the periphery. The failure of full Spanish control opened the way to contraband trade. It also permitted interlopers to extract resources, including salt (essential for food preservation) from naturally occurring salt pans on certain islands and later logwood (a desirable product used in the making of furniture) harvested on the Yucatán Peninsula.

Such activities had to be pursued under arms, with the expectation of trouble from Spanish officials who were bent on enforcing the restrictions. As a result, violence always loomed in the background for non-Iberians who sailed American seas. Even when raiding was not the initial aim, frustrated traders might turn to it when they encountered intransigence or threats of violence. Like the eastern Mediterranean after Venice and the Ottomans no longer effectively divided it between them, cracks in the oversight of trade and other interactions left a space open for piracy.[15] The far-reaching but only partially successful Spanish policy overreached, leaving openings for outside actors.

The Spanish policy of exclusion failed most spectacularly not in instances of piracy and other assaults, which must be seen as the price of doing business under the terms they sought to establish, but in the fact of non-Iberian territorial occupation. In the late sixteenth century, Spain's rivals launched efforts at taking American lands. By the first decades of the seventeenth century, all the principal players had achieved a foothold in the Americas, of necessity on lands the Spanish claimed as their own. Prospective colonizers soon learned to stay clear of valuable Spanish-held territory. The fate of the short-lived French colony at St. Augustine, Florida, helped teach this lesson. Determined to protect the treasure fleet's passage home, a Spanish force assailed and massacred the French colonists in 1565. Spain then established a settlement at St. Augustine in order to foil efforts to occupy the strategy chokepoint again.[16] Sir Walter Raleigh sited his colony further north, still intent on using it as a base for depredations against the Spanish but hoping that placing it in modern-day North Carolina might avoid unwanted Spanish attention. Roanoke failed without ever coming under attack by Habsburg forces. In 1641, the Spanish authorities treated Providence Island residents somewhat more gingerly than those in Florida but removed them to the last person all the same. Patrolling the entirety of the Americas presented a too-daunting task, so settlements far to the north were left alone. The French settled Acadia and Quebec, the Dutch moved into the Hudson River region, the English took up Virginia, all out of the way of Spanish activity, but all on lands claimed by Spain. Interloping nations also settled areas on the eastern periphery of the Caribbean, with the French and English establishing outposts on the islands of the Lesser Antilles, which the Spanish had ignored, believing that it offered little of value and that it was well defended by Carib Indians in any event. Yet exclusion remained the policy for many decades after non-Spanish settlement became a reality.

If settlement flourished especially in the most remote locations, piracy proved most common on the immediate fringes of Spanish America. Charting the geographies of seaborne assault must remain incomplete, since incidents were recorded in widely scattered archives. Still, documented cases make clear that some areas attracted raiders far more than others. The Caribbean proved the premier site of piratical (and all other seaborne raiding) activity. As the region that included active local shipping networks, poorly defended coastal towns, and the coveted prize of the silver fleet, the Caribbean offered manifold opportunities for both wartime and unauthorized peacetime seizures. Eventually it came to have a resident population, referred to in English as *buccaneers*, who participated intermittently in assaults, both legal and otherwise.

On the other extreme, locations far from Spanish settlements, unattractive for their lack of high-value exports, might serve as bases, but they seldom served as targets for pirates or other plunderers. Places where other Europeans established colonies, being inherently less valuable, failed to attract Spanish attention initially and offered little to raiders subsequently. New England serves as a case in point. Its settler population grew quickly first through mass migration, then through its unusual demography of low death and high birth rates. Yet its exports were bulky items extracted from forests or agricultural produce. Without mineral wealth or exotic tropical crops, New England remained relatively untroubled by pirates. Early rover

Dixie Bull did modest damage there, and during the eighteenth-century imperial wars, New England shipping, along with other British vessels, faced the threat of privateer or naval seizures.[17] Yet pirates were more likely to visit the region to unload their ill-gotten gains, as William Bradford famously reported in his journal with regard to one sinful marauder, Thomas Cromwell.[18] As Bradford hinted, the region could offer shelter to those seeking to sell illicitly obtained cargoes. Happy to host pirates who infused the local economy with much-needed wealth, Britain's North American colonies proved appealing places to get rid of seized goods or enslaved Africans and to seek shelter among the settler population.[19] Burgeoning northern settler colonies served as bases more than targets because the nature of their economies could absorb wealth and people but generated few high-value cargoes worth taking.

Other Atlantic regional geographies had a more complex relationship to piracy and plunder. The Newfoundland fisheries occasionally received attention from pirate ships that needed to pick up new crew members. Their vessels and their cargoes proved generally less attractive, although hungry raiders might also avail themselves of the available fish to restock their food supplies as well.[20] The West African coast offered attractive cargoes—first ivory or gold, which had ready markets in Europe, and, later, enslaved people who might be sold in the Azores and Canaries or in the colonies of the Americas. African leaders controlled the trade in slaves within Africa itself and at the ports where transactions with European buyers occurred. Raiders could make little headway on land without local arrangements already in place and were reduced to snatching individuals they could enslave, as did a Boston trader in one notorious incident in the 1640s.[21]

More profitable was the prospect of taking a slave ship after it left port. Under most circumstances, captured ships were taken to a friendly port where the enslaved people could be sold. The *Transatlantic Slave Trade Database* lists 1,299 slaving voyages that were thwarted by human agency between the earliest recorded case in 1554 and 1800. Many cases involved seizure of the ship itself or removal of some enslaved individuals. What portion of these thefts arose in the context of warfare, with ship seizures seen as one way to undermine the commerce of the enemy, and what portion resulted from the opportunistic efforts of freelance pirates cannot be determined from the information in the database. Interrupting the trade in slaves represented a lucrative option for raiders so long as they had access to a port where cargo could be sold. Initially with only Spanish and Portuguese Atlantic ports trading in slaves, the sales of stolen slave cargoes had to be conducted as clandestine affairs; later, with more extensive colonization, the options for sales proliferated. Non-Iberian colonies received infusions of enslaved Africans as a result of such seizures long before they had access to the slave trade through official channels. The Dutch ship that sold people in Virginia in 1619, thought to be the first African slaves sold in English North America, stole them off a Portuguese slaving ship rather than trading for them directly in Africa.[22] Piracy and other forms of raiding off the African coast (or in the Caribbean Sea itself) offered one means of furthering war aims, personal profits, or both to those who participated in such seizures.

Although much has been written about it at the time and since, religious animosities played little role in most incidents. That the advent of piracy in the Caribbean dated from the early years of the Protestant Reformation seemed to suggest a causal link, but the fact that only some of the French corsairs who initially raided Spanish shipping and towns identified as Protestant undermined that connection. Most French ships that came armed to the Caribbean to battle Spanish pretension to control most of the Americas or that sailed to Africa to interrupt the slave trade were financed, captained, and crewed by Catholics. Later commentators looking back on Elizabethan seaborne raiding of England often cast it in Protestant and nationalist terms. While it is true that the Dutch who revolted against Habsburg rule were mostly Protestant and that when England's Elizabeth backed them she saw the struggle in part as a Reformed push back against Spain's domineering popery, the Dutch and English reasons to fight Philip II's Spain were never wholly or even centrally religious. To the extent that religious divisions played a role in anti-Spanish depredations, this appears to have been another instance of Spain creating the conditions that realized their own worst fears. Just as they produced pirates out of aspiring traders and prospective settlers, so too did they heighten religious animosities by subjecting Protestant intruders to the Inquisition. Seamen tortured by the Inquisition encouraged a militant anti-Spanish Protestantism in seaport towns where the stories of atrocities circulated, as Kenneth R. Andrews pointed out.[23] Yet when Sir Francis Drake and other marauders attacked colonial churches, they surely did so in search of silver plate and other valuable ornamental objects, not simply to desecrate those spaces.[24] In the Atlantic as in other places, piracy that appears to have been prompted by religious animosities here too proves to have more prosaic roots in issues of profit and geopolitics.[25]

In fact, more than any other factors, geopolitics and the drive for profits influenced who was likely to become a pirate. Spain held most of the wealth and as a result represented the most likely target for those driven by greed. Spain also attempted to block access of all others not only to its wealth but to the entirety of the Americas, a position that made it a target for interlopers of all kinds. Those interlopers were by definition non-Spanish: French, Dutch, and English in particular were drawn to the region. They were the raiders but also the traders and settlers who defied Spanish prohibitions. They came to fight wars against Spain, and they joined pirate crews as well. Under the prevailing circumstances that pitted Spanish authority against intruders of these other nations, Spanish pirates, although not entirely unknown, were thus a rare occurrence. Atlantic conditions encouraged non-Iberian (especially non-Spanish) people to take up piratical activities.

The true pirates of lore (and of much scholarship) did sail these seas, but they did so more rarely than our commitment to their image might suggest. Moreover their rise as a major force occurred only in the early eighteenth century, as the contested geopolitics of the Atlantic underwent a profound shift. After the Spanish acceded to the presence of other colonizing powers, other governments came to join them in their opposition to piracy. Once these groups collaborated to eliminate raiders—after a long period of countenancing them—the men who pursued that livelihood received outlaw status not only in Spanish America but more widely. The multinational pirate crews favored in popular imagination and in the work of such scholars as Marcus Rediker performed their dastardly deeds in the early eighteenth century, after European nations changed the terms of Atlantic engagement. States still fought wars—and did so with the help of privateers who might turn to piracy in peacetime—but they became more seriously committed to ending marauding once it threatened to thwart newly opened markets and to damage their own colonies, shipping, and profits. Under the circumstances, the British and others committed to driving out pirates. Once the Bahamas, which had served as a base for decades, was closed to them, raiders were unable to find other welcoming Atlantic ports. Under the circumstances, they wreaked serious havoc before sailing away. The end of piracy in the Atlantic came about once Spain relinquished its grand claims to all of the Americas and once all European states became invested in peaceful trade and colonization. That shift first fostered the classic pirate outlaw and then curbed all such activity. Like the rise of raiding, its demise came in response to the terms on which European states interacted.

The destructive nature of the era of pirate suppression is well captured in the marauding that occurred on the West African coast between 1717 and 1723. Raiders driven out of the Bahamas in the 1710s visited Africa more interested in the ships than the slaves being transported on them. Whereas ships would serve their need to leave the Atlantic for safer hunting grounds, slaves did them little good if they lacked markets in which to sell them. In this shift, raiders on the African coasts in this period diverged from the practices of the previous century and a half, in which slaves had been seized for sale. That they had no friendly ports where they could sell human cargo indicated how effectively the British and other imperial powers had closed off avenues for their trade. As a result the pirates killed most slaves they took or set them on shore. They forcibly recruited a few African men to join their crews but otherwise had little use for the people and cargoes they seized. This brief period of raiding—which lasted only a few years before the men involved were killed or went on to other regions—demonstrates raiders' dependence on outlets for the goods they grabbed. Without open ports, they could no longer function in their accustomed ways, which had always involved returning to settlements for extended periods. Some of them sought distant oceans where they might return to those ways. By the mid-1720s they left the Atlantic entirely for Madagascar, where for a period they continued practicing piracy.[26]

Conclusion

Rather than ask why Atlantic piracy arose, we might well ask: why not? Piracy and related activities were widespread phenomena in the early modern world. Seaborne plundering represented a common form of warfare; private actors routinely contributed to these actions, either singly or in concert with others under the command of state officials; and theft at sea or on coastal settlements also occurred without official support of any authority. While only taking without sanction conformed to the full definition of piracy, the lines among the various forms of aggression wavered and blurred. Such activities were sufficiently common to make their absence more worthy of remark than their presence. Yet piracy was far from ubiquitous: it did not occur everywhere at all times. Particular conditions made incidents of raiding likely. So the question, framed somewhat differently, demands an answer: What about the early modern Atlantic encouraged acts of piracy and related forms of seaborne violence?

Atlantic piracy and its demise occurred in a particular context, which shaped its distribution over time and space, its participants, and its end. Piracy requires profitable space outside the full control of a widely acknowledged authority. The Atlantic offered both profit and uncertain authority. Other European states and actors rejected Spain's exclusionary claims, creating an opening for them to attempt exploration, trade, resource extraction, and colonization. Spain's efforts to keep them out set the terms of engagement, defining their presence as piratical. Contraband trade, theft, and violence ensued. Only when terms changed—and when other Europeans saw opportunities for peaceful trade as well as undisturbed colonization and resource extraction—did the conditions that had long facilitated seaborne raiding shift. Efforts at suppression defined pirates as enemies of all, cut raiders off from access to the communities that had supported their work, and propelled them into desperate acts of violence and brutality. Earlier conditions had allowed those who committed occasional acts of unjustified theft to be reintegrated into colonial communities. The push toward suppression temporarily encouraged greater atrocities and Atlantic raiders became true enemies of all. This model of piracy was unsustainable, however, without access to land-based communities. The violence of the 1720s represented a last brutal gasp of the piracy that Spain inadvertently promoted by attempting to keep all of the Americas to itself. Almost two centuries after the first raiders came to Atlantic America, the tide finally turned against them.

NOTES

1. Kenneth R. Andrews, *Trade, Plunder, and Settlement: Maritime Enterprise and the Genesis of the British Empire, 1480–1630* (New York: Cambridge University Press), 61.

2. Thomas K. Heebøll-Holm, *Ports, Piracy, and Maritime War: Piracy in the English Channel and the Atlantic, c. 1280–1330*, Medieval Law and Its Practice, 15 (Leiden: Brill, 2013), 3.

3. Sebastian R. Prange's discussion of the Indian Ocean resonates on this point; see "A Trade of No Dishonor: Piracy, Commerce, and Community in the Western Indian Ocean, Twelfth to Sixteenth Century," *American Historical Review* 116 (2011): 1271, 1279, 1291–92.

4. Portuguese mariners came to the Spanish Americas first on Spanish crews and later on slave-trading ships; and Portugal and Spain were united under the Spanish crown from 1580 to 1640, bringing even Brazil under Spain's orbit for a time. With the islands underpopulated and less closely regulated, they tended to have a more diverse population than the mainland settlements.

5. Philip P. Boucher, *France and the American Tropics to 1700: Tropics of Discontent* (Baltimore: The Johns Hopkins University Press, 2008), 41.

6. Kris E. Lane, *Pillaging the Empire: Piracy in the Americas, 1500–1750*, Latin American Realities (Armonk, N.Y.: M. E. Sharpe, 1998), 12.

7. For a long-term perspective on this issue, see "'The Fear of Universal Monarchy': Balance of Power as an Ordering Practice of Liberty," in *Liberal World Orders*, ed. Tim Dunne and Trine Flockhart (Oxford: Oxford University Press for the British Academy, 2013), 121–37.

8. Lane, *Pillaging the Empire*, 69–71. The Cromwellian case involved Blake.

9. Heebøll-Holm, *Ports, Piracy, and Maritime War*, 125, 243, 248.

10. Karen Ordahl Kupperman, *Providence Island: The Other Puritan Colony, 1629–41* (New York: Cambridge University Press, 1993); "A Briefe Journall or a Succint and True Relation," in *The Voyage of Captain William Jackson (1642–1645)*, ed. Vincent T. Harlow, vol. 13, *Camden Miscellany* (London: Royal Historical Society, 1923).

11. The classic accounts of Morgan in Panama include *The Present State of Jamaica* (London, 1683), 55–97; and Alexandre Exquemelin, *Bucaniers of America: Or, a True Account of the Most Remarkable Assaults* (London, 1684), pt. 3, 31–76. For the lawsuits Morgan filed over use of the term *piracy*, see Richard Frohock, "Common Mischaracterizations of Early English Translations of Exquemelin's *Buccaneers of America*," *Notes and Queries* 57, no. 4 (2010): 506–8.

12. Kenneth R. Andrews, *The Spanish Caribbean: Trade and Plunder, 1530–1630* (New Haven: Yale University Press, 1978), 135.

13. The wording of the treaty permitted the English to claim that they also got access to Yucatan logwood harvesting sites, since some crews were there cutting trees at the time of the treaty. See Jesse Cromwell, "Life on the Margins: (Ex) Buccaneers and Spanish Subjects on the Campeche Logwood Periphery, 1660–1716," *Itinerario* 33, no. 3 (2009): 43–71. This would become an ongoing point of friction as the Spanish had not intended to concede that right.

14. For Hawkins's report of the disastrous final voyage, see Richard Hakluyt, *The Principal Navigations, Voyages, Traffiques, and Discoveries of the English Nation* (London, 1599–1600), 3:521–25.

15. For a similar case in the Mediterranean, see Molly Greene, *Catholic Pirates and Greek Merchants: A Maritime History of the Mediterranean*, Princeton Modern Greek Studies (Princeton: Princeton University Press, 2010), chap. 1.

16. Boucher, *France and the American Tropics*, 47–52.

17. *The Journal of John Winthrop, 1630–1649*, ed. Richard S. Dunn et al. (Cambridge: The Belknap Press of Harvard University Press, 1996), 70n, 84, 85, 91; George Francis Dow and John Henry Edmonds, *The Pirates of the New England Coast, 1630–1730* (Salem, Mass.: Marine Research Society, 1923), 20–22.

18. William Bradford, *Of Plymouth Plantation, 1620–1647*, ed. Samuel Eliot Morison (New York: Knopf, 1952), 345–47.

19. Kevin P. McDonald, *Pirates, Merchants, Settlers, and Slaves: Colonial America and the Indo-Atlantic World*, the California World History Library, 21 (Berkeley: University of California Press, 2015); Mark G. Hanna, *Pirate Nests and the Rise of the British Empire, 1570–1740* (Chapel Hill: University of North Carolina Press, 2016).

20. Peter E. Pope, *Fish into Wine: The Newfoundland Plantation in the Seventeenth Century* (Chapel Hill: University of North Carolina Press, 2004) lists piracy as one price of doing business but enumerates relatively few cases, all early seventeenth century (50–52, 418).

21. *Journal of John Winthrop, 1630–1649*, ed. Dunn et al., 602–4.

22. Engel Sluiter, "New Light on the '20. and Odd Negroes' Arriving in Virginia, August 1619," *WMQ*, 3rd ser., 54 (1997): 395–98.

23. Andrews, *Trade, Plunder, and Settlement*, 36.

24. In this light, consider Drake's "alleged" murder of two friars; Emiro Martínez-Osorio, *Authority, Piracy, and Captivity in Colonial Spanish American Writing: Juan de Castellanos's Elegies of Illustrious Men of the Indies* (Lanham, Md.: Bucknell University Press, 2016), 60.

25. Greene, *Catholic Pirates and Greek Merchants*, 231.

26. Arne Bialuschewski, "Black People under the Black Flag: Piracy and the Slave Trade on the West Coast of Africa, 1718–1723," *Slavery and Abolition* 29, no. 4 (2008): 461–75; McDonald, *Pirates, Merchants, Settlers, and Slaves*, chap. 4; Marcus Rediker, *Between the Devil and the Deep Blue Sea: Merchant Seamen, Pirates, and the Anglo-American Maritime World, 1700–1750* (New York: Cambridge University Press, 1987), chap. 6, and *Villains of All Nations: Atlantic Pirates in the Golden Age* (Boston: Beacon Press, 2004).

Jamaica's Private Seafarers

POLITICS AND VIOLENCE IN A SEVENTEENTH-CENTURY ENGLISH COLONY

John A. Coakley

L ong seen as the center of piratical activities in the Caribbean, the English colony of Jamaica hosted many sea raiders in the late seventeenth century, perhaps as many as three thousand at any one time. From 1655, when an English fleet conquered the colony, until 1692, when a massive earthquake destroyed its major city Port Royal, Jamaica was a hub of raiding and illegal trading at sea. The raiders Jamaica hosted, however, worked much more in concert with the colony's government than one might suppose. Most sea raiding activity at this time occurred with the implicit or explicit authorization of colonial governors or other leaders. Because of their connection to government, these men were not consistently called pirates at the time.[1] The more general term *private seafarer*—indicating a sailor who was employed neither by the Royal Navy nor a merchant trading company but who may have chosen to sail for any authority on a contract basis—is therefore more accurate. Jamaica had a higher concentration of private seafarers than other English colonies and used them to a greater extent. Jamaica's governors treated the sailors as, variously, a colonial navy, a police force, and an armed merchant fleet, always to serve island interests in a region they believed to be filled with enemies.

This chapter argues that, by raiding and trading illegally in the Caribbean, Jamaica's private sailors were central to island politics in the period 1655–92, and it details the relationships private sailors had with various local politicians. By and large, it demonstrates the complexity of violence and politics in the seventeenth-century Caribbean. Private sailors attacked heavily fortified cities in the region, ransomed entire towns while burning others to the ground, and boarded ships with sword in hand seeking money and valuable cargo. Thousands of them followed the famous Captain Henry Morgan on four bold raids that netted them a small fortune. Afterward, many returned to the numerous taverns of Port Royal to drink their winnings away. For these actions, they were thought of as both heroes and villains, but ultimately they sailed to make money while serving the interests of their struggling colony.

Gathering the Raiders

Early in 1655, a massive English fleet—on an expedition ambitiously named the Western Design—entered Caribbean waters with orders from England's military dictator, Oliver Cromwell, to wrest the West Indies from Spanish hands. After a stop in English Barbados, in April 1655, nearly eight thousand British and West Indian soldiers and sailors packed into the navy vessels and attacked Santo Domingo de Hispaniola, a rich Spanish port on the southern coast of today's Dominican Republic. They failed miserably. In the next month, the expedition managed one small victory: conquering poorly defended Jamaica, "a consolation prize" that still came with a loss of men and resources. The English invaders quickly took the Spanish capital, St. Jago de la Vega, a few miles inland of Jamaica's remarkable southern harbor, while starting construction on their own fortress and storehouses on a small cay at the great harbor's mouth—soon to become the infamous city Port Royal.[2]

Like most English colonies in the mid-seventeenth century, Jamaica was largely ignored by imperial officials in England, who found it hard to run a military outpost half a world away. Because of its geography, Jamaica was also isolated from other English colonies and lay much closer to Spanish, French, and Dutch holdings. With little communication from England and surrounded by an active theater of war, early English Jamaicans—led by Colonel Edward D'Oyley—took an aggressive stance in the region. With the ships and men available, they launched naval expeditions both to defend their position and to further Cromwell's project of conquering the rest of the Caribbean. Most raids received no direct consent from England but were encouraged by island leadership, and a culture of sea raiding quickly became an entrenched part of Jamaican politics.[3]

The English soldiers and sailors occupying Jamaica embarked on many expeditions from 1655 to 1660. In five major raids, army or navy commanders used state-owned ships and publicly employed soldiers and sailors, but dozens of smaller raids also went out. In 1655, Admiral William Goodson and his fleet attacked Santa Marta, a coastal city in present-day Colombia, securing currency, military supplies, and animal hides to trade for other necessary items. In April 1656, Goodson sacked nearby Rio de la Hacha with ten of Cromwell's ships and 450 men but was unable to acquire much wealth. Commodore Christopher Myngs made a successful raid against Tolú (also in Colombia) in 1658 and followed it the next year by capturing the towns of Coro, Cumaná, and Porto Cabello, all in present-day Venezuela. Later in 1659, D'Oyley himself led an ambitious attempt to capture Spain's annual fleet carrying silver plate but missed the treasure ships by mere hours. Smaller voyages, using private ships and private men, were less documented and typically had smaller paydays but continued the culture of sea raiding on the island.[4]

The island's first sea raids, then, were navy missions or colony-sponsored expeditions, wherein the sailors pillaged Spanish towns or ships and were paid in shares of the proceeds of the goods, currency, or vessels they had looted. This system—called "no purchase, no pay"—came naturally to early English Jamaicans. The English navy boasted a centuries-old tradition of taking such "prizes" during operations and returning them to an admiralty court, which determined their value and parceled out shares to the government, ship owners, captains, and crew. Most recently, Parliament had used this system during the English Civil Wars, and Cromwell had continued it in the 1650s. For example, his Western Design orders authorized Admiral William Penn (father of the founder of Pennsylvania) to plunder Spanish targets and to use the prizes to keep the Design's extensive fleet afloat and sizeable army fed. Although there were commissioners aboard who were authorized to assess the loot and return a portion of it to England at the end of the mission, Penn and his men also frequently followed another naval tradition of not reporting all the loot captured, thereby lining their pockets with stolen goods.[5] Jamaica's private seamen were, therefore, used to taking prizes at sea and to keeping unreported prize goods for themselves.

After the collapse of the Cromwellian protectorate, King Charles II officially took the throne of England in 1660 and set about reforming Jamaica. In an attempt to protect and control the colony, one advisor proposed sending ten English ships to Jamaica as "privateers upon no purchase no pay." The king did not send the ships, but he did try to demilitarize the island, ending the Western Design, cashiering the troops, and appointing civil-ian governors. Even so, the colony lacked a long-term governor until 1664. During those four years, the small island population—some 3,600 white men, women, and children and more than 500 enslaved Africans—lived on roughly 3,000 acres of planted land and sustained their colony through familiar means. They built plantations, hunted wild cattle in the interior, and most importantly, raided at sea.[6] Raiding was arguably more important in this time than it had been previously because D'Oyley and his successors, Thomas Windsor and Charles Lyttleton, sent home most of the navy ships, meaning that the island lacked the maritime protection it had enjoyed during the Cromwell era.

From 1660 to 1664, most Jamaican sea raids were minor affairs using small, privately owned vessels crewed by men out of the public employ. Local officials regulated the process. D'Oyley's council required that captains "upon a private account" have permission from the governor and council to raid or else face a twenty-shilling fine. When D'Oyley left, Governor Windsor called in the raiders but then issued new "instructions to take Spaniards and bring them for Jamaica." William Beeston, a Jamaican merchant and future governor, was surprised at the governor's "war with the Spaniards," and he observed many "privateers" going "to sea for plunder" as a result.[7] The only exceptions to the rule of small-scale raids during this time were two raids led by Myngs in 1662. Since Myngs held a Royal Navy post, his raids had a veneer of imperial authority, but he also enlisted 1,300 mostly private sailors and 15 private boats. They captured Santiago, on Cuba's southern shore, and then Campeche, on the west coast of the Yucatán Peninsula.[8]

Even on smaller raids, Jamaicans claimed royal assent for their actions. When Governor Windsor arrived in Jamaica in 1662, he came with the power to commission men "for the subduing of all our enemies by sea or land." The king's instructions to Windsor also contained an important clarification. "It shall be deemed piracy for any ships to lay wait, or pursue, or take any of our enemies' ships or goods upon those coasts," the instructions read, "but by commission from our high admiral, or authority from him." By separating the criminal act of sea raiding without commission—piracy— from the entrenched Jamaican practice of licensed raiding, the king's words served to increase the practice of raiding overall. Even when the king seemed to desanction Lieutenant Governor Lyttleton's raiders in 1663, Jamaicans interpreted his words liberally. Charles II ordered Lyttleton to cease "such undertakings as have lately been set on foot," but an observer noted that "it [is not] well understood whether his Majesty's order applies to commanding under Lord Windsor's commissions, or prohibiting only wild excursions."[9] Jamaican raiders kept sailing.

Modyford's Private War

In 1664, Sir Thomas Modyford, already one of the richest men on Barbados, sailed to Jamaica to serve as the new governor.[10] Bringing with him hundreds of Barbadian planters, servants, and slaves, his arrival signaled permanence and promised new growth of plantation culture on the island. But he also intensified sea raids. Honing existing practice, Modyford embarked on a series of massive military undertakings. Led first by Deputy Governor Edward Morgan and then by his nephew, Henry Morgan, the raids hit both Dutch and Spanish targets. In addition to these official raids, many smaller "privateers" continued to operate in the region, getting commissions from Modyford and bringing back goods, slaves, and currency to the island. Although he did prosecute as pirates raiders who lacked proper commissions or impeded Jamaican interests, in general, Governor Modyford wholeheartedly supported sea raiders.

He had not set out to do so. When he arrived in Jamaica in 1664, Modyford tried to stop privateers from raiding the Spanish and instead encouraged trading with Spanish subjects. King Charles, arranging peace treaties with Spain, also supported closer relations with the Spanish in the Caribbean. While still on Barbados, Modyford proposed a peace to the governor of Santo Domingo, suggesting that the two "forbear all acts of hostility," and further still, "give each other the free use of our respective harbors." Later, Modyford and the council warned Jamaicans "to treat all the subjects of his Catholic Majesty, wheresoever they shall meet them whether by sea or land, as friends and," the declaration continued, "not to make prize of any the ships or goods." In August, on King Charles's specific orders, the Jamaican Council ordered restitution made to the Spanish and announced that all who attempted "violence and depredation against the said nation [Spain] shall be looked on as pirates and rebels, and proceeded against accordingly."[11] But in time, Modyford's foreign policy grew more bellicose. By 1670, he believed Jamaica "circled in with enemies' countries" and had seen the utility of private sailors on private ships of war.[12]

Under Modyford, island-sponsored raids against nearby foreign colo-

nies began as early as 1665 when England declared war on the Netherlands
in the Second Anglo-Dutch War. Hearing he had authorization to strike
at the Dutch, Modyford reported to England "all the rovers are plodding
[plotting] how to take in Curacao." He immediately sent along his own
proposal for taking the Dutch island and rounding up other Dutch and
French colonies along the way—a sort of second Western Design—which
would "make a clear board, leaving none in these parts but the English and
Spaniards." In April, he began the design by sending Edward Morgan with
ten ships and over five hundred men—"made up chiefly of the reformed
privateers . . . at the old rate of no purchase no pay"—to capture the Dutch
and French. Morgan's grand design temporarily captured the Dutch colonies of St. Eustatius and Saba, in the Lesser Antilles, and won for Jamaica's
planters at least five hundred African slaves. Still, it accomplished little of
lasting import. The Dutch remained in the Caribbean and Morgan died on
the raid.[13]

Henry Morgan then took his uncle's place as the governor's primary
agent at sea. Though relatives, the two Morgans may never have met, a situation made even stranger when Henry married Edward's oldest daughter
(his own cousin) shortly after the Dutch raid. Long viewed as one of the
most infamous pirates of the Caribbean (and the inspiration for a brand of
rum), Henry Morgan first made a name for himself during a 1666 expedition under Captain Edward Mansfield that briefly recaptured Providence
Island from the Spanish. Part of Modyford's private war against Spain, this
expedition proved that Morgan and the privateers were willing to serve
the governor regardless of imperial edicts.[14] From 1668 to 1671, at Modyford's behest, Morgan led a series of four ever-larger raids on nearby Spanish colonies, culminating in the difficult capture of Panama. Sacking Panama brought Morgan notoriety throughout the empire—ever since Francis
Drake's attempt to capture the city a century earlier, Englishmen had imagined it was made of gold—but fame came at a price. At the time the raid
occurred, England and Spain had just signed a treaty, bringing peace after
decades of war. Angered, the king ordered Modyford and Morgan arrested
and brought to England.

Morgan's three raids prior to the Panama expedition—in 1668 and
1669—targeted cities smaller than Panama but still boasted impressive fleets,
large crews, and lucrative prizes. Modyford commissioned each raid based
on intelligence that Spanish forces were massing to invade Jamaica. The first

raid resulted in the ransom of Porto Príncipe de Cuba, netting prizes worth about 50,000 pieces of eight. The second raid, a risky attack on Porto Bello on the Caribbean coast of the Central American isthmus, garnered perhaps 215,000 pieces of eight. The third adventure saw the men spend weeks in the woods surrounding Maracaibo and Gibraltar (also on the isthmus) seeking hidden treasures and torturing the inhabitants for information. Though the payout was nearly as lucrative as the previous raid, they spent much more time acquiring the loot. Morgan's raids were strikes aimed at disrupting the Spanish in the region but not dislodging them entirely. Modyford even tried to convince the Spanish ambassador that letting the seamen raid Spanish targets for the time being benefitted both empires. "I might keep them from joining with mine and your Master's enemies," he wrote. In 1669, Modyford even declared "peace with the Spaniard." It lasted only one year.[15]

Modyford canceled that half-hearted peace as soon as he heard that Spain had authorized its own Caribbean governors to attack the English in the region. This fresh war was the occasion for Morgan's final raid, which resulted in the destruction of Panama. In this case, Modyford and the council commissioned Morgan to make a raid but did not specify a target, instead conceiving of the expedition as retribution for small Cuban raids made on Jamaica's undefended north side. Morgan and his officers decided to attempt Panama, a highly ambitious goal given the city's location on the Pacific coast and its solid defenses. They marched two thousand men over the Central American isthmus. After a hard fight, they invaded the town, desperately sought its riches, and may have even set a fire that burned it to the ground. They were disappointed. Many Panamanians had already escaped with most of the city's treasure, and each of Morgan's men received only about fifteen pounds—hardly a good payday—and Morgan reported only thirty thousand pounds total in plunder. The planters of Jamaica still rejoiced; the raid brought in four hundred slaves.[16]

Morgan's raids have been the stuff of legend, and contemporaries and historians alike have labeled him a "pirate" for his actions. Using Modyford's interpretation of the word, however, he was not. The Jamaican government authorized each raid and Morgan acted as a military leader commanding soldiers and sailors in battle. Although the men were not employed by the government—they made their money only as a share of the proceeds yielded by their plunder—they served the government's interests by enriching Jamaica at the expense of the Spanish.

The Coming of Peace

A year before the Panama raid, English and Spanish negotiators finally nailed down a peace treaty between the nations in the Americas. The 1670 Treaty of Madrid forbade all raiding and optimistically insisted on a clean slate between the powerful empires; it even declared all hostilities "expunged out of remembrance, and buried in Oblivion, as if no such thing had ever past." It recognized English claims to American lands then in their possession and revoked all Spanish claims to the same. It did not, however, allow for easy trade between the empires in America, an ardent desire of the English faction. Instead, a compromise clause provided for limited trading privileges to ports that specifically desired them.[17]

To preserve this new peace, English imperial leaders knew they needed to remove Henry Morgan and Thomas Modyford from the Caribbean and alter Jamaica's relationship with its private seamen. Because Morgan had laid waste to Panama after the treaty was signed, his actions clearly violated the hard-won peace. Modyford had been aware of the treaty negotiations and received a copy of the treaty in December 1670 but never specifically ordered Morgan to abort the mission. Earlier, he had told the admiral to "behave himself with all moderation and civility possible in the carrying on of this war."[18] It was not a bold enough statement against the raid for Modyford to keep his position in Jamaica.

Sir Thomas Lynch took office as lieutenant governor of Jamaica in 1671 with orders to enforce the treaty, reform the island, and arrest Morgan and Modyford and send the two back to England. Lynch's return to the island was a welcome homecoming for him, for he had already lived there for several years. In fact, he had vowed to make Jamaica his permanent home in 1665 but was quickly forced back to England by the newly arrived Modyford. Now, six years later, Lynch could take pleasure in locking up his old rival.[19] Though he did follow through on the arrests, Lynch came to ignore many provisions of the treaty during his tenure as lieutenant governor and during a subsequent term as governor in the 1680s. He used the island's private seamen as a police force to hunt pirates and as armed merchants to run illegal trades in slaves, goods, and logwood.

At first, Lynch ordered strict adherence to the Treaty of Madrid and attempted to decommission Jamaica's private sea raiders. In August 1671, he and the council issued a pardon to any raiders who turned themselves in within eight months, offering the seamen rewards in the form of goods, land, or navy posts. The pardon had little effect. Lynch reported to England that the sea raiders simply started sailing with French commissions they got from Tortuga. According to orders, Lynch then tried to hunt down the raiders with the miniscule naval force available to him. There were never more than two Royal Navy frigates in Jamaica at any one time during this period, and Lynch lacked the authority to countermand orders from English fleet admirals, but imperial officials were optimistic that he could clear the seas of the troublesome raiders. Lynch thought he could, too.[20]

Suppression did not work as well as hoped. Sea raiding activity increased in late 1671 and in early 1672. To add to Lynch's woes, Spanish governors in the region began to seek payment from him for depredations made by rogue Jamaican raiders. In March 1672, he angrily declared that "privateering was the sickness of Jamaica."[21] Lynch realized that he could arrest Modyford and Morgan but that he could not hunt down each one of the thousands of their former seamen. These conditions led him, in 1672, to eschew his imperial orders and hire the private raiders in service of the island, an expedient nearly every governor before him had used.

To help reduce the number of raids Jamaicans made on Spanish targets, Lynch employed the services of several "loyal" private seamen to hunt and capture the "pirates" who remained active. He made a lieutenant out of a man named Prynce, "one of the most famous of the privateers," and put him on board one of the navy frigates. He hired a private frigate to hunt down French and English raiders in the waters near Hispaniola and attempted to fill the ship with private sailors from Port Royal. Finally, he pardoned a captain named Morris—who had been imprisoned for piracy—and ordered him to sail in consort with a navy frigate to hunt down Peter Johnson, a Jamaican raider who had been attacking Spanish ships.[22] Thomas Lynch sanctioned Jamaican sea raiders to capture other raiders. This innovation had a lasting effect. Into the 1680s Jamaican governors kept hiring private sailors to hunt down their former comrades.

Lynch also employed Morgan's former followers to help the island "steal into a trade with the Spaniards." First, he sold African slaves to Spanish colonists throughout the region, thereby making Jamaica a hub of the Atlantic slave trade.[23] Lynch had some success selling slaves and using private seamen to do so. Shortly after his arrival, one of the frigates arranged to sell the black Panamanians whom Henry Morgan had captured to the Spanish colonists of Cartagena. Lynch boasted that he was saving the Spanish money and ridding Jamaica of a potentially dangerous population but he was also profiting from Morgan's raid. In November 1682, during his final term, Lynch hired the famous raider John Coxon to "convey a Spaniard to Havana" after a slave sale.[24] Lynch used Jamaica's private raiders in this role to ensure that the Spanish buyers paid their bills. Coxon had just returned from sacking St. Augustine, and no one was more feared by the small-scale Spanish traders.

Lynch also ran a livestock and goods trade with nearby Cuba. Such trading had been popular before the treaty, but the missions likely ended after Morgan's sack of Panama. Lynch restarted the smuggling runs when he took office, encouraging off-the-books transactions made by captains of small craft in and around Cuba's numerous south cays, which were unpoliced and lay between Cuba and Jamaica. Lynch protected the trade by hiring loyal private seamen to keep the route clear from pirates. Early in 1672, in addition to a Royal Navy frigate, he sent four ships with about five hundred men to take English and French "pirates" who cruised in the cays. Later, after the outbreak of the Third Anglo-Dutch War, he commissioned a captain named Peter Harris to capture a Dutch trader who operated in the cays.[25] Small trades between Jamaica and Cuba would continue even into the next century, and private sailors sometimes operated them or at least prevented other raiders from stealing the goods.

Finally, Lynch encouraged Jamaica's private seamen to cut and carry logwood, a tree found on the Yucatán Peninsula and present-day Belize used to make deep red and purple dyes. This trade provided an employment opportunity for Morgan's former men, and in 1672 the Council of Jamaica found logwood cutting "the only diversion for privateers."[26] But local Spanish officials retaliated. One Jamaican observed that the trade would "occasion a new war," and he was not wrong. The Spanish governor of Campeche hired a former Jamaican seaman named Yallahs to capture English logwood ships in the Bay of Campeche. The next year, the Spanish governor of Havana hired the Irish-born Philip Fitz-Gerald to take logwood ships that neared Cuba; his attacks were particularly vicious.[27] Lynch begged for the authority to commission reprisal raids, but instead the king chose to recall him in 1674, fearful that the Jamaican might start a costly war in the region.

The Final Rise and Fall of Raiding

Starting in the mid-1670s, some private seafarers returned to their old habits of raiding Spanish targets, though they were more consistently prosecuted over the next decade. For the most part, Jamaican raids against Spain increased because of Spanish enforcement against logwood trading. Because of treaty restrictions, Jamaican seamen who did raid chose to do so using commissions that they acquired from French governors on Hispaniola and Tortuga. In 1674, a few hundred Jamaican sailors moved to Tortuga with designs on Spanish targets. In 1677, the seamen of Hispaniola—John Coxon and other Englishmen among them—plundered the city of Santa Marta and kidnapped its high-ranking clergymen. A year later, another mixed force of French and English raiders took Campeche, an act of revenge for ongoing Spanish captive taking.[28]

Even Henry Morgan was involved. Having regained the king's favor while in London, he sailed back to Jamaica in 1675 with a knighthood and a commission as Jamaica's lieutenant governor, serving under the new governor, John Vaughan. Morgan and his brother-in-law Robert Byndloss started "recommend[ing] some of our English privateers unto the French governors to be commissioned by them" and then collected a portion of those raiders' proceeds. Vaughan brought Morgan and Byndloss before the Jamaican Council, but nothing happened. English officials did not pass judgment either, but Secretary of State Henry Coventry warned Morgan that his majesty was incensed about Morgan encouraging English subjects in "serving under foreign Princes at Sea."[29] Morgan and Byndloss's side business seems to have died down at this time.

Some Jamaican raiders kept raiding. In the summer of 1683, up to one thousand men from around the region (including Jamaica) fell on the rich Spanish city of Vera Cruz, situated on the western shore of the Gulf of Mexico. They occupied the town, ransomed the highest officials, and accrued mountains of treasure. The Jamaican sailors on the raid believed they were fulfilling Morgan's legacy from the 1660s, avenging attacks on logwood traders. There was one important difference this time, however: the Jamaican government had not authorized the raid, and returning raiders stayed away from Port Royal. They were afraid of running afoul of a new Jamaican law against piracy that promised strict sentences for those serving a "foreign prince." To prove his loyalty, Morgan had helped write this law as it went through the island assembly in 1681.[30]

Other raiders chose to operate outside the Caribbean in the 1680s, wary of the stricter statutes. Setting out ostensibly on a logwood mission early in the decade, Bartholomew Sharpe and about three hundred others crossed the isthmus overland and raided Spanish ports up and down the South American Pacific coast. Some of them continued around the world, hoping to gain fame or something valuable enough to earn them a pardon in England or the American colonies. In the next few years, more than a thousand English raiders followed them. Hender Molesworth, who took over the Jamaican government when Lynch died in 1684, spent much of his time suppressing these raiders. Luckily for him, the unorganized men failed to capture a Spanish treasure fleet they were awaiting and they drifted back to the Atlantic.[31] But Jamaica was no longer a safe harbor for plunder brought in by raiders.

If the relationship between Jamaica's government and its private seafarers was strained in the 1680s, in the 1690s it ended nearly completely. Due to a new war with France in 1689, islanders feared the seamen would take commissions from French colonies to invade Jamaica. In fact the French did attack Jamaica in 1694, but that was mostly the result of natural disaster. A massive earthquake nearly destroyed the city of Port Royal in 1692, killing and dispersing the city's seafaring inhabitants and leaving the colony vulnerable to enemies.

Jamaican planters and merchants had long feared that the French would invade their island. Since the 1670s, they had also believed that the colony could find itself attacked by its own private seamen because Jamaican sailors had close relations with the French in the region. "If the privateers were forced away from Jamaica," an English report warned, "their company would not only be very acceptable to, but probably courted by most of the French Plantations." Such an alliance, the report continued, would "subject all our Plantations as that to be preyed upon at the pleasure of the said Rovers."[32] In 1689, war broke out between England and France, a result of the Glorious Revolution that brought King William III and Queen Mary II to the English throne, ousting the French-allied James II. Jamaicans grew very nervous, but the Earl of Inchiquin—the island's short-lived governor in the early 1690s—used naval and local resources to strike at nearby French colonies.[33] Nature intervened and the governor suffered an early demise in 1692. And before his successor, Sir William Beeston, could reach Jamaica, the colony fell prey to one of the worst natural disasters in early modern history.

On the morning of June 7, 1692, the ground started shaking in Port Royal. Buildings collapsed and residents disappeared in the rubble, swallowed whole by the sandy soil the city had been built on. The Port Royal earthquake claimed around five thousand lives, shaved off two-thirds of the city's land mass, and toppled most of its standing structures. Even the buildings in Spanish Town, several miles inland, collapsed. Residents as far as the north side lost their houses that day. In Port Royal itself, the harbor side area where sailors gathered—for work and for tavern merriment—sunk into the sea completely.[34]

The French took advantage of Jamaica's weakened state. In June 1694, a well-manned fleet from Saint-Domingue invaded Jamaica. Governor Beeston could not respond effectively, for Jamaica had lost thousands of its own private seamen in the earthquake. Not all had died; many just chose to leave for better harbors, and he could convince few to return. The French attack was therefore devastating, but the attackers did not attempt to conquer. Instead they wreaked havoc across the island until a hastily organized Jamaican militia could confront them on land and force them back to Saint-Domingue.[35] Beeston's desperate letters to England during the attack convinced the Royal Navy to send out their own massive fleet in retaliation, but its presence made Beeston lose control of the Jamaican war effort that governors had been waging since 1655. Thereafter, the Royal Navy—which did not take orders from colonial governors—maintained a consistent presence in the Caribbean. Moreover, monarchs commissioned their own raiders directly from England to supplement the navy's work. Colonially licensed private seafarers working in the Jamaican government's interest had little room left to operate.

Conclusion

As soon as it was conquered in 1655, the English colony of Jamaica developed a local political culture that relied on private seafarers to raid Spanish targets and acquire capital, slaves, and goods for the colony. Modyford and Morgan perfected these plundering raids during a private war against the enemies that surrounded the island, culminating in the sacking of Panama.

After Anglo-Spanish peace came to the Caribbean in 1671, Jamaican leaders like Lynch found alternate employment for the private seamen of Port Royal, but most of those opportunities faded in the 1680s. Private raiding of this sort enjoyed a surge during its last decade, as the men enlisted this time in French ships in order to plunder Spanish targets. The sailors' relationships with the French panicked the politicians and merchants who had once supported them, and they found themselves unwelcome in Jamaica. Finally, the 1692 Port Royal earthquake killed or dispersed those seamen who had remained on the island, making Jamaica vulnerable to a devastating French invasion. In the process, Jamaican governors lost power over the navy in the region, and local seamen lost jobs to crown-regulated privateers.

For forty years, at least two generations of private seamen inhabited Port Royal and sailed in support of Jamaican government interests using a standard payment system of prize shares and unreported stolen loot. They defended the colony, carried its numerous illegal trades, and hunted noncommissioned raiders. They represented a unique period of colonial control over sea raiding and embodied a connection between politics and violence that marked the early modern Atlantic world. They were praised and pilloried for their actions, sometimes heroes and sometimes pirates. Jamaica's private seafarers lived on the margins but were central to building a colony.

NOTES

The author would like to thank David Head for his organizational and editing expertise, the history department at the University of Wisconsin–Madison (where some of these ideas first appeared as a dissertation), and Katherine Hollander for constantly reading and talking about this work.

Abbreviations

CO	Colonial Office
CSPC	Calendar of State Papers, Colonial Series
PRO	Public Records Office
TNA	The National Archives of the United Kingdom, Kew

1. From the late seventeenth century to today, international law has treated pirates as stateless vagabonds operating for their own gain and has marked them *hostis humani generis* (enemies of all). The word *privateer* arose in English during the seventeenth century and has come to mean a sea raider operating under state license during wartime. The actions of Jamaica's private seafarers lie between these

two poles, pirate and privateer, and took place at a time when neither word had a so-lidified meaning. See Daniel Heller Roazen, *The Enemy of All: Piracy and the Law of Nations* (New York: Zone Books, 2009); N. A. M. Rodger, "The Law and Language of Private Naval Warfare," *Mariner's Mirror* 100 (2014): 5–16.

2. S. A. G. Taylor, *The Western Design: An Account of Cromwell's Expedition to the Caribbean* (London: Solstice Publications, 1969), 35; see also C. H. Firth, ed., *The Narrative of General Venables, with an Appendix of Papers Relating to the Expedition to the West Indies and the Conquest of Jamaica, 1654–1655* (1900; repr., New York: Johnson Reprint, 1965). The latest telling is Carla Gardina Pestana, *The English Conquest of Jamaica: Oliver Cromwell's Bid for Empire* (Cambridge, Mass.: Harvard University Press, 2017), and Mark G. Hanna, *Pirate Nests and the Rise of the British Empire, 1570–1740* (Chapel Hill: University of North Carolina Press, 2015), chap. 3.

3. See S. A. G. Taylor, "Edward D'Oyley's Journal, Part 1," *Jamaican Historical Review* 10 (1973): 33–110; "Edward D'Oyley's Journal, Part 2," *Jamaican Historical Review* 11 (1978): 62–117. The only English territory that had come close to matching Jamaica in location and size was Providence Island, but it had been captured by the Spanish in 1641. Its loss helped motivate Cromwell to launch the Design. See Karen Ordahl Kupperman, *Providence Island, 1630–1641: The Other Puritan Colony* (Cambridge: Cambridge University Press, 1993).

4. John Lambert, April 29, 1656, Manuscript 986 (National Library of Jamaica, Kingston); William Goodson, TNA:PRO CO 1/32/63; PRO, *Calendars of State Papers, Colonial Series, America and West Indies: Volume 9, 1675–1676* and Addendum 1656, (London, 1893), nos. 266–70, 275. C. H. Firth, "The Capture of Santiago, in Cuba, by Captain Myngs, 1662," *English Historical Review* 14 (1899): 536–40; Stephen Saunders Webb, *The Governors-General: The English Army and the Definition of the Empire, 1569–1681* (Chapel Hill: University of North Carolina Press, 1979), 188–94.

5. B. S. Capp, *Cromwell's Navy: The Fleet and the English Revolution, 1648–1660* (Oxford: Clarendon Press, 1989); N. A. M. Rodger, *The Safeguard of the Sea: A Naval History of Britain, 660–1649* (New York: W. W. Norton, 1998), 127, 321, 423; Firth, ed., *Narrative of General Venables,* 114–15.

6. Unknown, May 1660, TNA:PRO CO 1/14/4. Population statistics from "An Accompt of the Inhabitants of the Island Jamaica," October 28, 1662, Rawlinson A Collection, vol. 347, fol. 35 (Bodleian Library, Oxford University, UK).

7. D'Oyley, "By the Governor and Council &c," June 26, 1661, TNA:PRO CO 140/1/4; "The Condition of the Island of Jamaica at the Lord Windsor's Departure," Rawlinson A Collection, vol. 347, fol. 30; William Beeston, "A Journal Kept by Col. William Beeston," in *Interesting Tracts, Relating to the Island of Jamaica* (St. Jago de la Vega, Jamaica: Lewis, Lunan, and Jones, 1800), 276–77.

8. Firth, "The Capture of Santiago," 9; Beeston, "Journal," 278; "An Accompt of

the Private Ships of War Belonging to Jamaica and Turtudos in 1663," Rawlinson A Collection, vol. 347, fol. 33.

9. *Journals of the Assembly of Jamaica*, vol. 1, 1663–1709 (Jamaica: Alexander Aikman?, 1811), appendix, p. 5. TNA:PRO CO 1/27/23; unknown, 1664?, CSPC 1661–1668 (London, 1880), no. 811.

10. By 1671, Modyford held at least nine thousand acres of land outright and four hundred slaves; see Richard S. Dunn, *Sugar and Slaves: The Rise of the Planter Class in the English West Indies, 1624–1713* (Chapel Hill: University of North Carolina Press, 1972), 68, 81, 154.

11. "By His Excellencie the Governour and Councill," June 11, 1664, TNA:PRO CO 140/1/92; Joseph Martyn to Sec. Bennet, June 26, 1664, TNA:PRO CO 1/18/80; Col. Edward Morgan to Sec. Bennet, June 28, 1664, TNA:PRO CO 1/18/82; Council Minutes, August 19, 1664, TNA:PRO CO 140/1/123.

12. "The Governor of Jamaica's Answers to the Inquiries of His Majesty's Commissioners," *Journals of the Assembly of Jamaica*, appendix, p. 23. Morgan to Bennet, TNA:PRO CO 1/18/82.

13. Thomas Modyford to Bennet, February 1665, TNA:PRO CO 1/19/27; Modyford to Sec. Arlington, April 1665, TNA:PRO CO 1/19/29.

14. E. A Cruikshank, *The Life of Sir Henry Morgan; with an Account of the English Settlement of the Island of Jamaica (1655–1688)* (Toronto: Macmillan, 1935), 4, 40; Dudley Pope, *The Buccaneer King: The Biography of Sir Henry Morgan, 1635–1688* (New York: Dodd, Mead, 1978), 67; Council Minutes, February 22, 1666, TNA:PRO CO 140/1/168.

15. The piece of eight was a unit of Spanish currency very common in the Americas. For Porto Príncipe, see "Information of Admiral Henry Morgan," September 7, 1668, TNA:PRO CO 1/23/53, and Alexandre O. Exquemelin, *The Buccaneers of America*, trans. Alexis Brown (Mineola, N.Y.: Dover, 2000), 127–33; for Porto Bello, see Exquemelin, *Buccaneers of America*, 140. For Maracaibo and Gibraltar, see Charles Leslie, *A New History of Jamaica from the Earliest Accounts, to the Taking of Porto Bello by Vice-Admiral Vernon. In Thirteen Letters from a Gentleman to His Friend. . . . With Two Maps* (London: Printed for J. Hodges, 1740), 121–32, and Exquemelin, *Buccaneers of America*, 141–63; Thomas Modyford to Spanish Ambassador, June 16, 1669, TNA:PRO CO 138/1/41; James Modyford to Andrew King, June 29, 1669, Westminster Abbey Muniments 11929, in Thornton, "The Modyfords and Morgan," *Jamaican Historical Review* 2 (1952): 56.

16. "Copy of a Commission of Warre," February 5, 1670, TNA:PRO CO 138/1/46; "Copy of an Order of Sir Thomas Modyford," June 29, 1670, TNA:PRO CO 138/1/47–48; for the attack, see Peter Earle, *The Sack of Panamá* (New York: Thomas Dunne, 2007), 223, 229, and Exquemelin, *Buccaneers of America*, 207.

17. *A Treaty for the Composing of Differences, Restraining of Depredations, and Establishing of Peace in America: Between the Crowns of Great Britain and Spain* (London, 1670), secs. 7–9.

18. Modyford to Sec. Arlington, August 20, 1670, TNA:PRO CO 1/25/55; December 18, 1670, 1/25/103.

19. Lynch to Sec. Bennet, February 12, 1665, TNA:PRO CO 1/19/23. Though Modyford's arrest was immediate, Lynch waited a year before sending Morgan to England. See Cruikshank, *Life of Sir Henry Morgan*, 217–19.

20. Council Minutes, August 12, 1671, TNA:PRO CO 140/1/223. Lynch reported that "the privateers are all divided"; see Lynch to Sec. Arlington, August 20, 1671, TNA:PRO CO 1/27/22.

21. CSPC 1669–1674 (London, 1889), nos. 697, 729, 733, 777, 785, 789, 796; Thomas Lynch to Council for Trade and Plantations, March 10, 1672, TNA:PRO CO 1/28/27.

22. Lynch to Sec. Arlington, December 17, 1671, TNA:PRO CO 1/27/58; CSPC 1669–1674, no. 726; TNA:PRO CO 1/28/3; Lynch to Sec. Williamson, January 27, 1672, TNA:PRO CO 1/28/7; CO 1/29/37.

23. Lynch to Sec. Williamson, July 5, 1672, TNA:PRO CO 1/29/6.

24. Lynch to Arlington, August 20, 1671, TNA:PRO CO 1/27/22; Lynch to Williamson, January 13, 1672, TNA:PRO CO 1/28/3; Lynch to Sec. Jenkins, November 6, 1682, TNA:PRO CO 1/49/91.

25. J. Modyford to A. King, May 11, 1668, Westminster Abbey Muniments 11917 and 11940, in Thornton, "Modyfords," 46; Lynch to Council for Plantations, April 4 and 28, 1673, TNA:PRO CO 1/30/19, 29; Lynch to Don Francisco Rodrigues, April 5, 1672, TNA:PRO CO 1/28/35; CSPC 1669–1674, nos. 1/28/885, 1/28/887, 1/28/940.

26. On logwood, see Mavis Christine Campbell, *Becoming Belize: A History of an Outpost of Empire Searching for Identity, 1528–1823* (Kingston, Jamaica: University of the West Indies Press, 2011), and Nuala Zahedieh, "The Merchants of Port Royal, Jamaica, and the Spanish Contraband Trade, 1655–1692," *William and Mary Quarterly* 43 (1986): 585; Council Minutes, March 20, 1672, CSPC 1669–1674, no. 786.

27. R. Browne to Williamson, July 6, 1671, TNA:PRO CO 1/27/6; Lynch to Arlington, December 25, 1671, TNA:PRO CO 1/27/66; Petition to the King, February 27, 1674, TNA:PRO CO 1/31/12.

28. Lynch to Williamson, November 20, 1674, TNA:PRO CO 1/31/77; newsletter, February 9, 1677, TNA:PRO CO 1/39/30; Vaughan to Williamson, July 18, 1677, CSPC 1677–80 (London, 1896), no. 347; Carlisle to Sec. Coventry, October 24, 1678, TNA:PRO CO 138/3/277–84.

29. Vaughan to Williamson, May 2, 1676, TNA:PRO CO 1/36/58; "An Accompt of Sir Henry Morgan," *Correspondence and Papers of Henry Coventry*, A.C.L.S. British Manuscripts Project, vol. 75, fol. 51; see also CSPC 1675–1676 (London, 1893), nos. 998, 657, 1129; Henry Coventry to Henry Morgan, June 8, 1676, "Correspondence from

Henry Coventry to the Residents in Portugal and to the Governors of the Plantations, 1674–1679," Additional Manuscript 25120 (British Library), 76.

30. *London Gazette*, October 26–November 1, 1683, http://www.thegazette.co.uk/London/issue/1873/page/1; "Captain Van Horn's Taking of la Vera Cruz," in Philip Ayres, *The Voyages and Adventures of Capt. Barth. Sharp and Others in the South Sea* (London: Printed by B.W. for R.H. and S.T., 1684), 115; see also CSPC 1681–1685, nos. 1163, 1249, 1261, 1563, 1759; Francis Hanson, *The Laws of Jamaica* (London: Printed by H. Hills for Charles Harper, 1683), 46.

31. "Narrative of a Voyage from Jamaica to Porto Bello," 1679, Sloane Manuscript 2752 (British Library, London, UK), fols. 29–35; see also Derek Howse and Norman J. W. Thrower, eds., *A Buccaneer's Atlas: Basil Ringrose's South Sea Waggoner: A Sea Atlas and Sailing Directions of the Pacific Coast of the Americas 1682* (Berkeley: University of California Press, 1992), 1–26; Molesworth to Blathwayt, February 3, 1685, TNA:PRO CO 1/57/9; Molesworth to Sunderland, April 24, 1685, CO 1/57/100; Molesworth to Blathwayt, August 29, 1685, CO 1/58/44; Molesworth to Sunderland, August 4, 1686, CO 1/60/20.

32. "Mr. Worsley's Discourse," BL, Add. MS 11410, 623.

33. CSPC 1689–1692 (London, 1901), nos. 1041, 1325, 1353, 1368.

34. Matthew Mulcahy, "The Port Royal Earthquake and the World of Wonders in Seventeenth-Century Jamaica," *Early American Studies: An Interdisciplinary Journal* 6 (2008): 391–421; Michael Pawson and David Buisseret, *Port Royal, Jamaica* (1974; repr., Kingston, Jamaica: The University of the West Indies Press, 2000), 165–68.

35. After the earthquake, the council estimated it could raise two hundred men for defense, as opposed to the two thousand it could have raised prior, Council to Sec. Nottingham, September 20, 1692, CSPC 1689–1692, no. 2499. Beeston to Lords of Trade, November 18, 1694, TNA:PRO CO 137/1/223; David Buisseret, "The French Invasion of Jamaica—1694," *Jamaica Journal* 16 (1983): 31–33.

"Sailors from the Woods"

LOGWOOD CUTTING AND
THE SPECTRUM OF PIRACY

Kevin P. McDonald

L ogwood cutting was arguably the most profitable illicit activity in the history of the Atlantic world. This chapter highlights the contested nature of the practice and examines the loggers, who operated as both interlopers and marauders along a continuum of piratical activities. Historians of British Honduras have discussed the significance of the logwood cutters in political and diplomatic terms; it is the logwood cutting itself as an alternative maritime practice that has eluded the attention of many scholars. As a result, chroniclers have missed a number of key points regarding the settlements. That pirates were part of the story is not always a given, and greater attention must be paid to the multifaceted role of pirates and piracy as a process by which the English empire emerged from its embryonic form.[1]

Though most of the hundreds of pirate cutters remain nameless, the roster of buccaneers and pirates connected to the logwood-cutting settlements is a veritable rogues gallery, including François l'Olonnais (Jean-David Nau), Christopher Myngs, William Dampier, Henry Every, John Plantain, John Lewis, Edward Low, and George Blacketer, among the most notorious.[2] Dampier, who engaged in "piratical escapades" for nearly a decade of his life, spent two different seasons in the logwood settlements and is perhaps the best contemporary informant.[3] If historians have ignored, downplayed, or dismissed the notion of pirates as multifaceted maritime laborers, contemporary observers were more cognizant, as another observer noted: "The wood cutters are generally a rude drunken crew, some of them have been pirates, and most of them sailors."[4] Elsewhere, in reference to listless crews residing at Jamaica, the London newspapers reported a similar sentiment: "the men being therefore left at liberty to shift for themselves, engaged themselves in such service as they could get."[5] Perhaps most directly on point, the logwood cutters, as one historian has recognized, were "former or resting privateers, some five or six hundred being engaged in the business . . . a pool of men ready to join in any nefarious and potentially profitable activity."[6]

As these contemporaries and some few historians have suggested, a useful way of examining piracy is to view it as one of many alternative maritime practices along a continuum. The continuum itself might shift, based on changing perceptions, definitions, and practices. The spectrum of piracy operates on multiple levels, from the individual to community and state-sponsored practices involving maritime marauding. In the early modern era, in the absence of fully developed navies, states used the privateering system, in which privately owned merchant vessels were sanctioned to convert to men-of-war. Public officials granted legal commissions to privateers: letters of marque during wartime, and in times of peace, letters of reprisal, which allowed injured subjects to retaliate against losses. Though regulated, this system was rife with abuses and allowed adventuresome merchants, captains, and seamen opportunities to exceed the boundaries of their instructions. An English privateer might attack a Portuguese-owned vessel captained by a Frenchman, even if the commission stated it could attack only a French-owned vessel; or the capture of a French vessel might occur after the commission expired. Such attacks, beyond the bounds of the legal letters, would thus constitute an act of piracy. However, the colonies, in particular, were not inclined to parse these legal niceties, especially if the privateers brought in lucrative prizes.

A broader argument can be made regarding piracy and early modern European colonialism in general. The Iberians, even under state sponsorship, operated in a piratical manner when coming into contact with non-Europeans, and much the same when northern Europeans began to challenge Iberian hegemony. As early as 1341, the Portuguese began kidnapping and enslaving natives from the Canary Islands.[7] The conquest and colonization of these Atlantic islands provided a model for the Columbian voyages that followed. Though on a state-sanctioned voyage in 1492, Columbus seized a Taino trading canoe, terrifying the native women and children aboard, before capturing additional natives and returning to Spain. Most of the natives died on the transatlantic voyage. Ten years later, on his fourth and final voyage, while cruising off the coast of Honduras, Columbus captured another large trading canoe, plundered its cargo, and captured the indigenous captain and other native passengers and crew.[8]

European challenges to Iberian hegemony began with maritime marauding: in 1523, the French corsair Jean Florin captured a portion of Moctezuma's treasure at sea, the beginning of Protestant French (Huguenot) raids against the Spanish in both the Atlantic and Caribbean. These raids would eventually lead to *boucanier* settlements in places like northwestern Hispaniola and Tortuga, which in turn became the foundations of the French colony of Saint-Domingue. A privateer colony was also established by the French but destroyed by the Spanish at La Florida in the 1560s, and English privateers founded but lost Roanoke in the 1580s. Successful colonies, too, openly embraced the use of privateers and pirates, especially in their early stages of development, both for military defense and economic aggrandizement. The most conspicuous example might be Jamaica, but New York, Rhode Island, and other North American colonies were deemed "pirate nests," especially in the 1690s.[9]

Slave trading and raiding were foundational features of Atlantic world colonization, and English privateers and pirates were instrumental in this process. Sir John Hawkins, the original English privateer slaver, seized three hundred slaves in Portuguese custody off Sierra Leone in 1562, then illegally sold them to Spanish settlers in northern Hispaniola. On a second privateering voyage, accompanied by Francis Drake, Hawkins raided the West African coast, taking four hundred slaves, then forcefully compelled Spanish settlers in the Caribbean to purchase them. On the third and largest Elizabethan expedition in 1567, six English vessels captured nearly five hundred African slaves, most of whom died during the lengthy two-month Middle Passage to the Caribbean.[10] In the first half of the seventeenth century, the newly established colonies of Bermuda, Virginia, New Netherlands, St. Christopher's, Barbados, Providence Island, and Association Island (Tortuga), as well as Anglo-Dutch settlements in South America (Amazon and Pará river basins) and Dutch Brazil (Pernambuco and Bahia), received their first generations of slaves by Anglo-Dutch pirates and privateers, who pillaged the human cargoes from Portuguese slave ships.[11] At the end of the century, pirates were instrumental in delivering Malagasy slaves to colonial New York.[12]

Colonial officials and merchants often condoned, if not outright supported, piratical practices. The maritime world of the port town, with its docks and wharves, slips and warehouses, taverns and grog houses, thus figures prominently in the historical rise and fall of pirate cycles and communities. But it was also the amphibious world of mangroves and marshes, liminal spaces, where communities of maritime marauders were often situated, that led to their significance as "transfrontiersmen," cross-cultural brokers and middlemen connecting European merchants and colonizers with various local indigenous populations.[13] The logwood settlements along the Bays of Campeche and Honduras were one such space, and the logwood cutters, hence, were transfrontiersmen—or as one contemporary observer colorfully termed them, "sailors from the woods."[14]

Piracy was not a fixed classification, and many different activities and actors might find themselves defined as pirates. On one end of the spectrum, persons defined by law as pirate might spend their lives among like-minded individuals, assembling as maritime marauders, regularly pillaging vessels on the high seas. These are the "hardcore pirates" most readers associate with piracy. On the other end, an individual, or even an individual crew, might commit a single act of piracy with no intention of embracing a criminal way of life. Specific circumstances, such as the temptation of opportunity or the compulsion of desperation, drove their actions, not a desire to "turn pirate" as a career. By legal definition, however, both the hardcore crews and the single-incident individuals were deemed "pirate." Likewise, piracy was only one of a host of interchangeable maritime activities undertaken by individuals and crews in similar historical patterns, depending on economic and social circumstances in the local, regional, and global contexts. So-called pirates raided for slaves and traded slaves they captured. They engaged in wrecking and salvage. They hunted turtles, cut logwood, and sailed privateers. In addition, and despite close association with piracy, trading in proscribed goods (contraband) and smuggling were not deemed to be piracy in Anglo-American law, though the Spanish considered them to be piratical activities on their face. Individuals that authorities classified as pirate might be found anywhere along the spectrum of piracy, with most "pirates" falling somewhere in between the two extremities, neither hardened criminals nor one-time plunderers. Wherever they fell, individuals called "pirates" most likely did not exclusively practice robbery at sea but rather combined many different activities as needed. Logwood cutting was an alternative maritime practice that helps further illuminate the spectrum of roles hidden by the label *pirate*.[15]

Logwood as a Commodity

The logwood, known by various appellations, is a tropical genus of bushy and thorny trees, well known as the source of important dyes. Obtained from the heart of the logwood, the dyes produce a range of colors including black, gray, red, purple, blue, and green. The original habitat has been a matter of some dispute, but it undoubtedly grew in the littoral regions of the Bay of Campeche and the Bay of Honduras. The tree is small, rarely fifty feet high, attaining a maximum diameter of two feet.[16] The logwood was used as a coloring agent in the pre-Columbian era by the Maya, who called it *Ek*.[17] By the middle of the sixteenth century, *palo de campeche*, as the Spanish called it, had become a profitable segment of the growing commodities exchange with Europe. By 1753, when the cycle of violence between the Spanish and English interlopers reached a fever pitch, the logwood tree received a most appropriate appellation in the Linnaean system of classification: *Haematoxylum campechianum*, or, the bloodwood of Campeche.

Though the Spanish were the first to introduce logwood to Europe, it was well enough known in Elizabethan England to be opposed by an Act of Parliament (1581) prohibiting its use. Because of inadequate knowledge regarding its chemical properties, it attained status as a "fugitive dye," as it often bled, or faded.[18] The prohibition was repeated again under James I in 1622. The ban was repealed under Charles II in 1662, as improved methods in the use of coloring agents gained traction. In the early years of cultivation, Spain had a monopoly on the market, charging one hundred pounds per ton for the debarked wood. The Spanish supply, described as an occasional shipload, never caught up with the increasing European demand, especially in the textile and furniture industries.[19]

The topography where the logwood grew was difficult and dangerous, and while Spain claimed the entire region under the Treaty of Tordesillas (1494), it never completely conquered nor settled the region. The logwood trees grew along rivers and lagoons: an amphibious landscape alternately marked by mangroves, marshes, creeks, and savannahs. The terrestrial and maritime worlds were indivisible and overlapping in these jungle regions—a potential advantage to those groups, such as pirates, predisposed to such watery realms. English traders observed that the coastline was "a great part drowned," while Dampier remarked that "all the Savannahs for many Miles, seem to be but part of the Sea." Native fishermen were likewise aware of the advantages to operating in this watery realm and would sink their *canoas* (canoes) to the waterline to avoid being observed and snapped up by privateers.[20] Difficult to colonize and clear, the challenging topography instead provided a refuge for two renegade groups: the local Indians, hostile to Spanish settlement and control; and the ambitious and adventurous sort like Dampier and others of the buccaneering and maritime communities, who arrived at first seasonally to cut and ship the wood and later as permanent settlers.

Like slave trading and raiding, the cutting of logwood was a quintessential Atlantic world activity. The cutters arrived from various colonies and were sponsored and provisioned by merchants from Jamaica, New York, New England, Carolina, and Bermuda. Once cut, the logwood was re-exported via these same colonial outposts to European markets. By the middle of the eighteenth century, the cutters were using enslaved African laborers, further solidifying the process as quintessentially Atlantic in nature. The tools of the trade included hatchets, axes, machetes, saws, and wedges; a gun, powder, and shot for hunting; and a raised pavilion for each man for sleeping above the creeks and wetlands.[21]

The cutting process was strenuous and involved companies of three to ten men. Unlike many other types of wood, the logs were too heavy to float downstream: the closer the trees grew to the creek, the easier went the work: the trees had to be cut, felled, chipped, carried, and then loaded first onto the canoes in the creeks, and from the canoes to the ships at anchor in deeper water. A settlement, often consisting of hundreds of men, was abandoned once it was cleared beyond "1,500 paces," or one league, from the creek.[22] Dampier provides perhaps the richest description of the process, including the reason for debarking: "We always chuse to cut the old black-rinded Trees; for these have less sap, and require but little pains to chip or cut it. The sap is white, and the heart red . . . therefore we chip off all the white sap, till we come to the heart; and then it is fit to be transported to Europe." The largest trees, which Dampier says were 5–6 feet wide, were more challenging: "these we can scarce cut into Logs small enough for a Man's Burthen, without great Labour; and therefore are forced to blow them up." As many of the cutters were also buccaneers, they had ample experience with gunpowder. Dampier esteemed logwood for more than its commercial value as a dye: "[It] burns very well, making a clear strong fire, and very lasting. We always harden the Steels of our Fire-Arms, when they are faulty, in a Logwood fire."[23] Thus, the pirate-cutters used it to hone their weapons when it came time to shift from one alternate maritime practice (cutting) to others: hunting feral game and targeting Spaniards.

Though the living conditions were more uncomfortable in the wet season, when even the savannahs were flooded, it might also be the most productive, as the cutters could literally roll out of their raised sleeping pavilions into knee-deep water and begin their tasks: felling, cutting, chipping, and carriage. The crews were often of multiple generations, and the division of labor was based on seniority—the chipper was "the principal man," and carriage, being the most onerous and least-skilled task, fell to the newest arrivals, who were often but not always apprenticed to their seniors. In addition to the prearranged crews, carriage work was also done on an individual "for hire" basis. Because of the nature of the work, the cutters were "sturdy, strong fellows," according to Dampier, capable of carrying enormous burdens of wood.[24]

Over time, many thousands of men took part in logwood cutting. Given the strenuous labor requirements, uncomfortable conditions, environmental dangers, and hostile Spaniards, the logwood-cutting business was not for everyone. Even the most dedicated cutters enjoyed a break from the heavy work; as Dampier discovered when vessels arrived with fresh provisions, especially liquor, production came to a standstill. Dampier further commented that some new arrivals, "not liking either the place or employment," would depart at the first opportunity. But others, like the older men in Dampier's company, were clearly drawn to the adventurous lifestyle. One such cutter, "Daniel the Irishman," was attacked and nearly devoured by an alligator. He departed the settlements, "in deplorable condition, and not able to stand on his feet," but after convalescing in New England, he returned, with a limp, to cut logwood the next season.[25]

Though dangerous, the pay was good, and an industrious servant or apprentice could rise up quickly through the ranks to become a captain of his own crew. Dampier made five pounds per month for the ton of logwood he agreed to haul, almost double the monthly wage of a second mate or a Newfoundland fisherman, and three to four times as much as laborers working in England at the time. Even as the price of logwood dropped, individual profits could be enormous: over an eight-week period in 1749, the shares of fourteen "sailor-loggers" came to twelve pounds per week, or forty times an average sailor's wage.[26] For an enterprising cutter, the provisioning aspect could also be lucrative: beer, flour, and other "necessaries" (read: rum) were often resold at considerable profit. The commercial value of logwood was undeniable. One scholar has stated that it was the second most valuable colonial American export.[27] For the first generation of Jamaican merchants, in particular, logwood was a critical commodity and has been calculated to have accounted for over half of Jamaican exports before 1680.[28] Even wreckers could turn an enormous profit: when a Spanish ship laden with logwood wrecked at Bermuda in 1637, the salvagers netted ten thousand pounds, or twice the value of the island's entire tobacco crop that year.[29]

In the English closed commercial system (mercantilism), the distribution of logwood was problematic, as it was frequently re-exported through Jamaica, Boston, and New York, and it often went directly to England's continental competitors. In 1682, Governor Lynch of Jamaica, for instance, railed against the illicit practice. "I have forbidden our cutting logwood in the Bay of Campeachy and Honduras," he wrote, "your Lordships having justly declared that the country being the Spaniards' we ought not to cut the wood." Lynch noted that "there is not the least pretence or reason for it," concluding that "it is now become a greater drug than fustic [a yellow dye], and is almost all carried to Hamburgh, New England, Holland, &c, which injures us and the customs and trade of the nation."[30] The Baymen, as they became known, were wedged between English mercantile laws and Spanish *guardacostas*: they were either "robbers" stealing from the Spanish, or smugglers, dealing in proscribed goods.[31]

By 1701, however, the re-export practice was no longer illicit, as the Privy Council ruled that direct exports did not violate the Navigation Acts. In this ruling, the Lords Justices declared the Campeche region "was not an English colony (and) logwood might be cut there by any nation," hence, logwood could not be an enumerated good.[32] Despite the decision, legal disputes continued between logwood merchants and customs officials in various colonies. In 1707, Lord Cornbury seized and condemned an English logwood vessel in New Jersey for illegal trading, and while the judgment was reversed on appeal by the High Court of Admiralty, Cornbury still refused to pay over the required moneys to the owner.[33] In 1714, the British merchant ship *Triv-*

erton was seized and condemned in Nantucket on the grounds that logwood was an enumerated article under a 1660 act and that the duties imposed by the 1673 act on logwood shipped between colonies had not been paid. The judge, Sir Edward Northey, ruled in favor of the owners, deciding that both acts referred to English colonial products, the logwood was foreign, and thus the vessel and cargo were not liable to forfeiture.[34] The situation was still contested in 1724: "There is annually a great many vessels goes from [Boston] to the bay of Honduras to cutt and load logwood a great part whereof is brought into this port and it [is] practised to load logwood from this part for Holland, Hamborough, and the Streights, which I humbly presume to be very prejudicial to the trade and manufactories of Great Brittain if not timely prevented."[35] The issue would eventually fade away in the last quarter of the century, with the transition to mahogany, and perhaps more significantly, the loss of the North American colonies.

Logwood Cutters, Piracy, and Sovereignty

The logwood trade itself was illicit on a number of levels, not just from the English imperial/mercantilist view, but more significantly, by the Spanish. From the time of Tordesillas, and in numerous *ordenes* and *cédulas* written thereafter, the Spanish were clear in stipulating that English cutters, and the merchants who supported them, were engaged in "clandestine" trade and so, by definition, were pirates.[36] Furthermore, many of these interlopers did, in fact, engage in maritime marauding, targeting Spanish vessels and towns, as well as natives, who regardless of their intransigence, were considered subjects of the Crown. That the region itself suffered numerous English attacks from the sea, both official and semiofficial, further tainted any Englishmen in the region with the piratical brushstroke. But it was the continuous attacks emanating from the logwood cutters themselves that firmly established the cutters as pirates, or at the very least, privateers. The violence was cyclical, and once the Spanish evicted the cutters from one area, the cutters would shift, with their arms, and reappear in a new region—for example, the shift from the Bay of Campeche to the Bay of Honduras (Belize). Gradually, the Spaniards reduced the settlements to three: the Moskito Coast, south of Cabo Gracias a Dios; the Bay Islands in the Gulf of Honduras; and the eastern coast of the Yucatán Peninsula, centered at the Belize River.[37] The logwood-cutting settlements at Belize

River endured and expanded to become the colony of British Honduras, and later, the independent nation of Belize.

The first generation of English pirates, the buccaneers, were directly tied to Caribbean hinterlands. Indeed, it is no small irony that the Spanish supplying the Caribbean with hogs and cattle gave rise to the first *boucaniers*, in places like northwestern Hispaniola and the island of Tortuga, in the first decades of the seventeenth century. These transplanted herds continued to nourish the interlopers well into the eighteenth century. The irony was not lost on Dampier, who commented that, "had it not been for the great care of the Spaniards, in Stocking the West Indies with Hogs and Bullocks, the Privateers must have starved. But now the Main, as well as the Island, is plentiful provided; particularly the Bay of Campeachy, the Islands of Cuba, Pines, Hispaniola, Portarica, &c. Where, besides wild Hogs, there are abundance of Crawls or Hogfarms; in some of which, I have heard, there are no less than 1500. *This was the main Subsistence of the Privateers*."[38]

While the buccaneering community subsisted on wild Spanish herds throughout the western Caribbean region, the Yucatán region itself remained relatively untamed. While the region was nominally conquered by the Spanish, native resistance was persistent with extended periods of open rebellion throughout the sixteenth and seventeenth centuries. To protect from external aggressions, beginning in 1573, the Spanish created a coastal defense system of *vigías*, or lookouts, consisting at first of wooden and thatch-roofed outposts, and later, more formal stone watchtowers placed in strategic locations along the shoreline. By the late seventeenth century, there were fourteen *vigías* on the northern coast of the Yucatán Peninsula, with eight more added by 1766. This system of coastal defenses proved to be ineffective against a number of maritime assaults. In 1659, English buccaneers under the leadership of Sir Christopher Myngs sacked Campeche, and two decades later, in 1678, English privateers again captured the town.[39]

These formal invasions were not the only incidents of marauding in the region, and the Spanish had long considered construction of an overland route from northeastern Yucatán south to Honduras, both to avoid the troubles of the sea route—especially English pirates—and to better control the natives of the interior. In 1677, on an expedition along the course of the proposed highway, Father Delgado, a Dominican priest, was informed by local natives at various stages of recent English depredations in the region. When he reached the "Rio de Texach," Delgado himself was taken prisoner by English pirates. As a telling example of the harsh and isolated conditions, the pirates appropriated his shoes and his clothing—as well as the priest's boy servant.[40]

Piracies could be well planned, retaliatory, and/or random, as the attack on Father Delgado makes clear. But a direct connection of logwood cutting with piracy is clearly outlined by its contemporary practitioners and observ-ers. Dampier notes that if the logwood cutters came across any vessels, they would turn to piracy: "Either light or laden, they made bold to take and sell both the Ships and the Indian Sailors that belonged to them." Even Damp-ier, a participant, recognized the questionable legality of these seizures: "This they would tell you was by way of reprizal, for some former injuries received of the Spaniards; though indeed 'twas but a pretence: for the Governours of Jamaica knew nothing of it." Dampier further commented on the cycli-cal nature of the activity, stating, "Neither durst the Spaniards complain; for at that time they used to take all the English Ships they met with in these Parts, not sparing even such as came laden with Sugar from Jamaica, and were bound for England; especially if they had Logwood aboard. This was done openly, for the Ships were carried into the Havanna, there sold, and the Men imprisoned without any Redress."[41] Dampier thus provides a clear ex-ample of the cycle of violence and informal methods of redress as practiced by the pirate cutter community.

It was not just against the Spanish, however, that piratical acts were made manifest. The logwood-cutting crews, on occasion, might turn against their own captain and English officials, as an incident in 1682 makes plain. The governor of Jamaica, Sir Thomas Lynch, dispatched Captain Coxon and a fleet of ships to collect English logwood-cutting crews from the Bays of Campeche and Honduras. At that time, London officials declared that the region in question belonged to the Spanish, and logwood cutting was thus forbidden. When Coxon arrived, however, his crews mutinied and plotted "to go privateering." Instead of fulfilling his official task of clearing the log-wood cutters, Coxon instead joined them in their transition to becoming "privateers."[42] This pattern was perhaps best explained a generation later by John Atkins, himself a privateer surgeon turned pirate, who stated, "The transition being easy from a Buccanier to a Pyrate, from plundering for oth-ers to do it for themselves."[43]

As the multigenerational commentary suggests, pirate cutters had been using both the Bay of Campeche and the Bay of Honduras for over a century. The Spanish gradually evicted them from the former, but the English pirate cutters stubbornly clung to the Honduran littoral like barnacles on a whale. The origins of the English settlements are murky. The first Englishmen arrived in the early seventeenth century, and varying dates of origin include 1603, 1617, and 1638. The last date is perhaps most intriguing, as it coincides with a Spanish expulsion of the buccaneers from Tortuga. The settlements along the Belize River (Rio Valis) have been attributed to an English or Scottish pirate named Wallace (spelled variously as Wallice, Willis, or Wallis). Tradition has stated that the name "Belize" itself was derived from the Spanish corruption of this name: Peter Wallace or Willis was a notorious buccaneer and ex-governor of Tortuga. Like many traditions, this was likely a modern invention, in this instance, from the British Honduran era. But there is little doubt the region served as a base for privateering, especially around the mouth of the Belize River, which was relatively concealed with challenging approaches, and yet was near enough the customary sea routes.[44]

In addition to Tortuga, other nearby privateer bases supplied the logwood region with English settlers. The logwood settlements received a boost in population in 1641 when the Puritan privateer colony on Old Providence (Santa Catalina) was recaptured by the Spanish.[45] Logwood cutters from Jamaica provided the most consistent flow of settlers. Indeed, it was the Jamaican buccaneer community itself, which had previously plundered Spanish vessels containing logwood, that formed the nucleus of these settlements. These settlers, as once and future buccaneers, connect the logwood settlements directly to piracy and maritime marauding. Indeed, the centuries-long Anglo-Spanish diplomatic tussles often centered around these very issues.

That the Bay of Honduras region, and the logwood itself, were disputed for over two centuries by Great Britain and Spain adds further to the layers of illicitness. Indeed, no formal English authority organized nor authorized English settlement in Belize until 1763. On the other hand, the Spanish claims of sovereignty dated to 1494, under the approval and authority of the Vatican. The English response came a century later, when Queen Elizabeth unleashed her Sea Dogs upon the Spanish Main.[46] Spanish complaints of English ravages "beyond the line" led to Elizabeth's famous boast that "the Spaniards by their hard dealing with the English . . . had drawn these mischiefs upon themselves," and further, that neither the pope's gift nor Philip

II's claim could prevent her subjects from trading and settling "into those parts . . . where the Spaniards do not inhabit."[47] With this opening gambit, the queen thus struck at the heart of the legal and diplomatic disputes that would occupy the logwood settlements for the next two and half centuries. The Spanish based their claims on the right of discovery, while the English argument centered around occupation and improvement.[48]

The Treaty of Madrid (1670) forbade the English from taking logwood from Spanish ships, but this did not hinder the development of the settlements, nor the trade, as Dampier well attests in his 1676 account. In 1670, Sir Thomas Modyford, the governor of Jamaica, urged formal recognition of the logwood cutters and assistance for "these new sucking colonies" (that is, the logwood settlements). Modyford argued that two-thirds of the English privateers would take up the logwood trade following the peace with Spain and that "these soldierly men would be kept within peaceable bounds, and be always ready to serve His Majesty in any new rupture." The military value of the logwood-cutting pirates was thus well understood, at least in Jamaica. Their economic and mercantile potential was likewise comprehended; Modyford further informed London that "about a dozen logwood vessels, formerly privateers, [were] selling the wood at £25 and £50 a ton, and making a great profit." Addressing the sovereignty issue, he further informed "that they go to places uninhabited or inhabited only by Indians." Connecting these activities to broader mercantile and colonial policy, Modyford remarked, "if encouraged, the whole logwood trade will be English and be very considerable to His Majesty, paying £5 per ton custom."[49] Modyford's successor, Governor Lynch, stated in 1672 that England might become "the store house of the logwood for all Europe which may be worth £100,000 per annum to the trade and customs."[50] The English loggers were harvesting more than two thousand tons of logwood annually.[51]

Governor Lynch wrote numerous letters regarding the issue, as a cycle of Spanish attacks on the settlements, followed by piratical English reprisals, ensued during the 1670s. The Council of Plantations in London was typically silent on the matter, causing great consternation from Lynch: "for God's sake to give your commands about the logwood . . . certainly the Spaniards cannot suffer it, but may take some of them which will occasion a new war."[52] The Spanish at this juncture, with considerable success, outsourced their *guarda-costa* duties to Dutch and Irish buccaneers, who seized seventy-five English vessels between 1671 and 1674.[53] By 1675, Governor Lord Vaughan of Jamaica was urging London to annex the logwood settlements to protect both the English settlers and the lucrative trade.[54] This was never accomplished, and in 1680, the Spanish destroyed many of the English camps at Trist Island, capturing and enslaving eighty woodcutters.[55]

During the early 1700s, several proposals were made to fortify the settlements and to establish a government led by John Lewis, described as "a planter and merchant from Jamaica" (but who may have actually been a notorious pirate). The proposals went nowhere.[56] The Spanish attacks on the logwood camps were proving effective but did little to dampen the Baymen's spirits over the long run. Following Queen Anne's War, hundreds of unemployed privateers and seamen arrived to form new settlements, creating a postwar logwood boom that actually drove down prices to historic lows.[57] While Spanish and British diplomats continued to tussle over the issue in Europe, the cycle of violence continued in the western Yucatán coast, and by 1716, the last two hundred cutters negotiated a surrender and safe passage to Jamaica: the Baymen had been expelled from Campeche, but not from the Bay of Honduras. Despite eight major Spanish assaults on Belize from 1724 to 1754, the population remained in the thousands, and exports rose to eighteen thousand tons of logwood (1756), carried to market annually by a fleet of forty to seventy vessels.[58]

With the shift to Belize came a dramatic change in the social and racial structure of the settlements, as the Baymen came to increasingly use slave labor. Rather than cross-cultural communities of Euro-Americans and Indians, the settlements began to mirror other frontier slave societies of the Atlantic world. As soon as 1745, the numbers were dramatic: a British official reported the number of white men at Belize to be 50, "and 120 Negroes."[59] African and Creole slaves would continue to comprise 75 percent of Belize's population. By the 1760s, there were two hundred white and seven hundred enslaved inhabitants.[60]

Pirates and Indians

Before the "*irrupciones de bucaneros*," the local indigenous populations, descendants of the Maya, reluctantly cut logwood for the Spanish.[61] After the pirate cutters arrived, an interesting and complex cross-cultural milieu emerged. Many natives were disinclined to acquiesce to the Spanish demands on their time and labor. Upon encountering a grove of tropical fruit trees, Dampier remarked that they were "but lately planted here by a colony of Indians, who revolted from the Spaniards and settled here [Laguna de Terminos, Bay of Campeche]. It is no new thing for the Indians in these Woody Parts of America, to fly away whole Towns at once, and settle themselves in the unfrequented Woods to enjoy their Freedom; and if they are accidentally discovered, they will remove again; which they can easily do."[62] Natives, like pirate cutters, used the amphibious environment to their advantage.

Not just pirate cutters, but English officials recognized the native presence. Governor Modyford of Jamaica, for example, reported that English vessels extracted logwood only in areas where there were no Spaniards, only Indians.[63] Dampier adopted another useful term for the natives, calling them "fugitive Indians,"[64] a community that shared many things in common with the logwood cutters, not least their status as renegades. In particular, the native dugout *canoa* was the vessel of choice for buccaneering and logwood cutting. The natives and pirate settlers also shared a communal, hunter-gatherer lifestyle. By all accounts, the region was bountiful in fish, oysters, deer, and after the Spanish arrival, feral bulls, which could be deadly. Among the most challenging constraints was finding a steady supply of fresh water, especially during the dry season, when the freshwater ponds dried up. The logwood cutters cleared their own paths, dug their own wells—carefully, so as to not reach salt water—and tapped the wild pines, which might hold up to a quart of water, an example of the kind of local environmental knowledge critical for survival.[65]

The pirates and Indians also shared a healthy wariness of the Spanish. The Indians' trepidation might date to 1502, when the Admiral of the Ocean Sea, Christopher Columbus, seized a great indigenous trading canoe, "long as a galley," in the Bay of Honduras. Further contacts with the Spanish came in 1511 following a shipwreck, when the castaways were either sacrificed or enslaved by the Maya, among whom was Gerónimo de Aguilar, a Franciscan friar, and Guerrero, the *"renegado"* who lived and fought with the Maya against his former fellow Castilian invaders.[66] The Spanish conquest of the Yucatán Peninsula progressed ambivalently after 1527, as Governor Francisco de Montejo and others found the terrain and the local Amerindians uninviting and the region unsuitable for settlement. Montejo's lieutenant, Alonso Dávila, journeyed by canoe along the unceasing rivers, lagoons, and swamps, frequently raiding native villages for food. Dominican priests had some limited successes in the 1550s, but the natives remained relatively "unsubdued" for another century and a half. There were some sizeable "Indian towns" like Summasenta and Chucquebul, the latter reported to have two thousand families with a few churches and priests.[67]

The presence of substantial indigenous populations not only raised the question of sovereignty beyond European entities alone. As a practical matter, the native inhabitants also established alternative market systems that were often used by the pirates and loggers. Buyers and sellers convened along known intersections of the major rivers and creeks used for travel, and the pirates could supplement their hunting and gathering with yams, plantains, potatoes, sugar, fowls, and eggs. The cacao beans, used as currency at the time of Columbus's maritime raid in 1502, were still in circulation when Dampier visited the region in 1676. Pirates were well aware of the beans' value, often, he said, targeting the "caravan of mules laden with cacao," headed toward the major Spanish town of Vera Cruz, "taking away as much as they could carry with them."[68]

Many natives of the Yucatán region maintained a measure of independence from the Spanish, as indicated by their "fugitive" status at Beef Island (Laguna de Términos) in 1676. The Yucatecan Indians, in particular, were fleeing the onerous *repartimiento*, or labor and tribute obligations, demanded by the Spanish.[69] Dampier suggested that they were encouraged to join the logwood settlements by female kinfolk who had already joined the English as mistresses. "Besides gaining their Freedom from the Spaniards," Dampier wrote of the Indians, "they might see their Friends and Accquaintances, that had been taken some time before by the Privateers, and sold to the Logwood-Cutters, with whom some of the Women lived still though others of them had been conducted by them, to their own Habitations." Dampier continued by noting that "it was these Women after their return made known the Kind Entertainment that they met with from the English; and perswaded their Friends to leave their Dwellings near the Spaniards, and settle on this Island." Dampier further suggested a common communal space of cross-cultural interactions. "They were not very shy all the time I lived there," he wrote, "but I know that upon the least disgust they would have been gone."[70]

Dampier reveals, in addition to the mutual Spanish enemy, a fascinating cross-cultural community of pirates and Indians. As in many such transfrontier groupings, indigenous women appear to have played the key cooperative role as cohabitants with the Euro-American settlers. At the same time, a sense of unease or angst emerges from Dampier's telling: "[the Indians] had been here almost a year before they were discovered by the English, and even then were accidentally found."[71] The natives' anxiety is more clearly understood in the beginning of the quote, where Dampier reveals that the Indians were enslaved and traded among the privateers/logwood cutters. Thus, an uneasy mixing of pirates and Indians emerged in the mangroves. Though a different community of natives, it is worth further mention that a century later, during treaty negotiations in 1784, the British settler subjects protested "any suggestion of abandoning the [Moskito] Indians."[72] Perhaps there is no more clear a statement on the value of the cross-cultural relationship, one forged by pirate cutters a century earlier.

Conclusion

The spectrum of piracy allows us to view pirates as multifaceted historical agents and piracy as a complex, multilayered historical activity and process. From the native perspective, the arrival of Columbus signaled the beginning of European piratical practices, which often targeted them, though other times looked to incorporate them into cross-cultural communities. The logwood regions themselves—the jungle littorals of the Bay of Campeche and the Bay of Honduras—connect directly to the broader history of Indo-Atlantic pirate settlements, such as Tortuga, Port Royal, Old Providence (Santa Catalina), New Providence (Bahamas), and St. Maries in Madagascar. Like the Red Sea Men who raided from Madagascar in the 1690s, the Baymen were important cross-cultural brokers operating in illicit yet significant alternative economies, far from the prying eyes and ears of imperial agents and customs officials.[73]

   The posturing of Queen Elizabeth notwithstanding, the logwood settlements sprung up from below by English pirates, often with the assistance and alliance of the local natives. Writing in 1931, Major Sir John Alder Burdon, the governor and commander-in-chief of the colony of British Honduras, proclaimed, "the utmost credit on the race of adventurers to whom Great Britain owes her Colonial Empire ... their daring, their tenacity, their fundamental desire for and achievement of British law and order."[74] Rather than following Burdon, as one scholar has further suggested, by "bringing [the buccaneers] more closely into the fold of civilized statehood ... as objects of its disciplinary control . . . and reformed, re-civilized sovereign subjects," it was instead the pirate cutters who led the state to incorporate their own distinctive brand of sovereignty, based on common consent, that was eventually enshrined and codified by Royal Authority in 1765. It was not imperial law and order but instead Burnaby's Code, derived directly from the pirate cutters, that became one of the oldest written constitutions in the world.[75] The story that the word "Belize" originated from a pirate's name is apocryphal and contested, but it is fitting. The British Empire itself was arguably founded not in a fit of absence of mind but instead in a flurry of purposeful if messy and contingent piratical enterprises.

NOTES

Portions of this chapter were presented at the ACH Conference in Havana in June 2016. The author would like to thank the conveners and participants for their comments, in particular Anne Macpherson of CUNY–Brockport, who provided extensive commentary and critique.

1. A worthwhile study is A. M. Wilson, "The Logwood Trade in the Seventeenth and Eighteenth Centuries," in *Essays in the History of Modern Europe*, ed. Donald C. McKay (1936; repr., Freeport, N.Y.: Books for Libraries Press, 1968); see also Gilbert Joseph, "British Loggers and Spanish Governors: The Logwood Trade and Its Settlements in the Yucatán Peninsula, Part 1," *Caribbean Studies* 14 (1974): 7–37, and "Part 2," *Caribbean Studies* 15, (1976): 43–52; Michael Jarvis considers the logwood region to be part of "the forest commons of the Americas," though at one point, he does call the Baymen "perpetual imperial trespassers"; see Michael Jarvis, *In the Eye of All Trade* (Chapel Hill: University of North Carolina Press, 2010), 218, 221.

2. Plantain apprenticed as a logwood cutter as a boy; Every was captain of a logwood crew; see Charles Grey, *Pirates of the Eastern Seas (1618–1723): A Lurid Page of History* (London: Low, Marston, 1933), 57, 151, 286; Marcus Rediker, *Villains of All Nations* (Boston: Beacon Press, 2004), 46.

3. The quote is from William H. Bonner, *Captain William Dampier: Buccaneer-Author* (Stanford: Stanford University Press, 1934), 11. See also Phillip Edwards, *The Story of the Voyage* (New York: Cambridge University Press, 1994), chap. 2; Anna Neill, "Buccaneer Ethnography: Nature, Culture, and Nation in the Journals of William Dampier," *Eighteenth Century Studies* 33 (2000): 165–80.

4. Quoted in Peter Earle, *The Pirate Wars* (London: Methuen, 2003), 97, 161. Jarvis identifies the observer as Nathaniel Uring. See Jarvis, *In the Eye of All Trade*, 226.

5. The *Post Boy* (London), January 27, 1700 (British Library).

6. Earle, *Pirate Wars*, 97.

7. David Abulafia, *The Discovery of Mankind* (New Haven: Yale University Press, 2008), 38, 66.

8. Christopher Columbus, *Journal of Christopher Columbus (during His First Voyage, 1492–93)*, trans. Clements Markham (London: Hakluyt Society, 1892), 74–75; Inga Clendinnen, *Ambivalent Conquests: Maya and Spaniard in Yucatan, 1517–1570* (New York: Cambridge University Press, 1987), 3. See also Abulafia, *Discovery of Mankind*, 126, 128, 145, 230. On the consideration of these acts as "piracy," at least one prominent contemporary Spanish intellectual, Bartolomé de las Casas, the famous Dominican friar, criticized these episodes as a breach of the law of nations.

9. See Kris E. Lane, *Pillaging the Empire: Piracy in the Americas, 1500–1750* (Armonk, N.Y.: M. E. Sharpe, 1998); Karen Ordahl Kupperman, *Roanoke: The Abandoned Colony* (Lanham, Md.: Rowman and Littlefield, 2007); Mark G. Hanna, *Pirate Nests and the Rise of the British Empire* (Chapel Hill: University of North Carolina Press, 2015).

10. See, for example, Philip D. Curtin, *The Rise and Fall of the Plantation Complex* (New York: Cambridge University Press, 1990); Barbara L. Solow, ed., *Slavery and the Rise of the Atlantic System* (New York: Cambridge University Press, 1991); Kenneth Morgan, *Slavery, Atlantic Trade, and the British Economy, 1660–1800* (New York: Cambridge University Press, 2000); Lane, *Pillaging the Empire*, 34–40; George Francis Dow, *Slave Ships and Slaving* (New York: Dover, 1970), 19–30.

11. See Vincent Harlow, *The Voyages of Captain William Jackson (1642–45)* (London: Royal Historical Society, 1924); Linda Marinda Heywood and John Kelly Thornton, *Central Africans, Atlantic Creoles, and the Foundation of the Americas, 1585–1660* (New York: Cambridge University Press, 2007), 27–28; Karen Ordahl Kupperman, *Providence Island, 1630–1641: The Other Puritan Colony* (New York: Cambridge University Press, 1993), 172, 191, 197, 278, 283.

12. See Kevin P. McDonald, *Pirates, Merchants, Settlers, and Slaves: Colonial America and the Indo-Atlantic World* (Berkeley: University of California Press, 2015), 47; Gregory E. O'Malley, *Final Passages: The Intercolonial Slave Trade of British America, 1609–1807* (Chapel Hill: University of North Carolina Press, 2014), chap. 2. While pirates were often instrumental in delivering enslaved cargoes to developing colonies, the pirate crews themselves were often multinational and might include black sailors. Pirates came from all nations and ethnic backgrounds, and the composition of a single pirate crew could range widely. However, pirates were not necessarily egalitarian in their outlook, and it was arguably more likely for pirates to use African slaves as forced laborers on their own ships than it was for African slaves to be welcomed into the pirate crew. See Alexandre Exquemelin, *The Buccaneers of America*, trans. Alexis Brown (Mineola, N.Y.: Dover Publications, 2000), 164, 170, 172, 181, 215; Jeffrey Bol-

ster, *Black Jacks: African American Seamen in the Age of Sail* (Cambridge, Mass.: Harvard University Press, 1998), 15.

13. The term *transfrontiersmen* is found in Curtin, *Rise and Fall of the Plantation Complex*, 92, 95–96.

14. Anonymous memorial, June 1738, in Sir Herbert W. Richmond, ed., "The Land Forces of France—June 1738," *Publications of the Navy Records Society* 63 (London, 1928): 65–68.

15. For further discussion of this concept, see McDonald, *Pirates, Merchants, Settlers, and Slaves*, 6–7.

16. Samuel J. Record and Robert W. Hess, *Timbers of the New World* (New Haven, Conn.: Yale University Press, 1943), 276.

17. Alan K. Craig, "Logwood as a Factor in the Settlement of British Honduras," *Caribbean Studies* 9 (1969): 53.

18. "Restoration of an Ancient Manuscript," *Quarterly Journal of Current Acquisitions* 10 (1952): 15; "The Development of the Textile Industries," *Journal of the Royal Society of Arts* 64 (1915): 133.

19. Joseph E. Stevens, *A Tale of Two Trees: Logwood and Quebracho, 1798–1948: An American Dyewood Company* (n.p., 1948?), 2–3; "Proclamation for the Preventing of the Exportation of Woolles, Woolle-fels, Yarne, Fullers Earth, and Woad-ashes, and for the Better Vent of Cloth, and Stuffe Made of Wooll, within This Kingdome" (London: Bonham Norton and Iohn Bill, 1622), Huntington Library.

20. "Copy of an Account of the Sea Ports Belonging to the Spaniards in America," September 1705 (CO 137:51), cited in Sir John A. Burdon, *Archives of British Honduras: From 1801–1840* (London: Sifton, Praed, 1931), 60; William Dampier, *Voyages and Descriptions*, 3rd ed. (London: James Knapton, 1705), 2:7, 55.

21. Dampier, *Voyages*, 2:41.

22. Ibid., 2:42.

23. Ibid., 2:56–57.

24. Ibid., 2:80, 83.

25. Ibid., 2:78, 88.

26. Jarvis, *In the Eye of All Trade*, 222, 228.

27. John H. Andrews, "Anglo-American Trade in the Early Eighteenth Century," *Geographical Review* 45 (1955): 99–101.

28. David Eltis, "New Estimates of Exports from Barbados and Jamaica, 1665–1701," *William and Mary Quarterly* 52 (1995): 641n.

29. Jarvis, *In the Eye of All Trade*, 219.

30. "Answer of Edward Randolph to Several Heads of Inquiry Concerning the Present State of New England," October 12, 1676, in Calendar of State Papers (hereafter CSP), 1675–1676, no. 1067; Lynch to the Lords of Trade and Plantations,

August 29, 1682, in CSP, 1681–1685, no. 668, cited in Michael A. Camille and Rafael Espejo-Saavedra, "Historical Geography of the Belizean Logwood Trade," *Yearbook. Conference of Latin Americanist Geographers* 22 (1996): 79–80. In 1699, thirty tons of logwood were shipped direct to Venice, in Burdon, *Archives of British Honduras*, 58.

31. "Robbers" is a quote from "Lt. Gov. Molesworth (Jamaica) to William Blathwayt," December 17, 1686, CSP, 1685–1688, cited in Burdon, *Archives of British Honduras*, 58. Andrews remarks that of the logwood re-exported to England from North America, two-thirds came from New England and one-sixth from New York. Boston alone imported twenty-five cargoes from Campeche in 1715, Andrews, "Anglo-American Trade," 101.

32. Jarvis, *In the Eye of All Trade*, 223; Council of Trade and Plantations (hereafter CTP) to Lords Justices, September 3, 1701, CSP, in Burdon, *Archives of British Honduras*, 59.

33. The owner subsequently petitioned Queen Anne for recovery of losses sustained by the seizure of his vessel; the resolution is unknown. CTP to Earl of Sunderland, October 23, 1707, CSP, 1706–1708, in Burdon, *Archives of British Honduras*, 61.

34. "Opinions of Council in Customs Cases," 1708–1717, 1714, BL, Add. MSS 8832, cited in Burdon, *Archives of British Honduras*, 62–63. The *Triverton* was leaky and was forced to transfer its cargo, bound directly for the Mediterranean market.

35. Mr. Cummings to the CTP, December 22, 1724, in CSP, 1724–1725, no. 439, cited in Camille and Espejo-Saavedra, "Historical Geography of the Belizean Logwood Trade," 80.

36. José Antonio Calderón Quijano, *Belice 1663(?)–1821* (Seville: Escuela de Estudios Hispano Americanos, 1944), 65; Joseph, "British Loggers, Part 2," 46.

37. Burdon, *Archives of British Honduras*, xiv.

38. For the early history of the *boucaniers*, see Exquemelin, *Buccaneers of America*; Dampier, *Voyages*, 2:98; italics added for emphasis.

39. On native resistance, see especially Grant Jones, *Maya Resistance to Spanish Rule* (Albuquerque: University of New Mexico Press, 1989); Matthew Restall, *The Black Middle: Africans, Mayas, and Spaniards in Colonial Yucatan* (Stanford, Calif.: Stanford University Press, 2009); on the *vigía* system and the formal English invasions, see Restall, *The Black Middle*, 170 and 214, respectively.

40. D. A. G. Waddell, *British Honduras: A Historical and Contemporary Survey* (London: Oxford University Press, 1961), 3–7, quote found on p. 6; "Memorandum of Fr. Joseph Delgado," June 7, 1677, in Doris Stone, *Some Spanish Entradas, 1524–1695* (New Orleans: Tulane University of Louisiana, 1931), 264–69. The priest was not left naked but instead garbed in a "torn shirt and some shorts."

41. Dampier, *Voyages*, 2:43–44.

42. Lynch to Lords of Trade and Plantations, August 29, 1682; and Lynch to Sec. Sir Leoline Jenkins, November 6, 1682, in Burdon, *Archives of British Honduras*, 57.

43. John Atkins, *A Voyage to Guinea, Brasil, and the West Indies in His Majesty's Ships, the* Swallow *and* Weymouth (London: Ward and Chandler, 1735), 226.

44. See Quijano, *Belice*, 7, 20, 33–35, 46–47, 53; Waddell, *British Honduras*, 7. The "Wallace/Belize" theory has recently been discredited as an origin myth in Victor Bulmer-Thomas and Barbara Bulmer-Thomas, *The Economic History of Belize: From the Seventeenth Century to Post-Independence* (Benque Viejo del Carmen, Belize: Cubola Books, 2012).

45. Burdon, *Archives of British Honduras*, 3; Waddell, *British Honduras*, 7; Craig, "Logwood as a Factor," 55.

46. For an overview of Elizabethan piracy, privateering, and contraband trading, see Lane, *Pillaging the Empire*, chap. 2.

47. "Queen Elizabeth's Reply to the Spanish Ambassador's Complaint," 1587, cited in Burdon, *Archives of British Honduras*, 48.

48. See Eva Botella-Ordinas, "Debating Empires, Inventing Empires: British Territorial Claims against the Spaniards in America, 1670–1714," *Journal for Early Modern Cultural Studies* 10 (2010): 142–68.

49. Modyford to Lord Arlington, Sec. of State, October 31, 1670, CSP, 1669–1674, cited in Burdon, *Archives of British Honduras*, 49–50; Nigel O. Bolland, "The Social Structure and Social Relations of the Bay of Honduras in the Eighteenth Century," *Journal of Caribbean History* 6 (1973): 25.

50. Lynch to Sir Charles Lyttleton, January 28, 1672, in Burdon, *Archives of British Honduras*, 52.

51. Figure cited in Jarvis, *In the Eye of All Trade*, 220.

52. Lynch to CTP, July 2, 1671, CSP, 1669–1674, cited in Burdon, *Archives of British Honduras*, 52.

53. Lynch to CTP, April 4, 1673; and Lynch to CTP, April 28, 1673, in Burdon, *Archives of British Honduras*, 54–56.

54. Vaughan to Secretary Sir Joseph Williamson, September 20, 1675, CSP, cited in Burdon, *Archives of British Honduras*, 55–56.

55. Jarvis, *In the Eye of All Trade*, 221; seventy-one woodcutters were eventually released in 1687. See Burdon, *Archives of British Honduras*, 57.

56. Burdon, *Archives of British Honduras*, 59–60.

57. Logwood still sold for ten pounds a ton in Kingston; see Jarvis, *In the Eye of All Trade*, 224.

58. Ibid., 226.

59. Major Caulfield, Ratan, to Mr. Trelawny, August 2, 1745, CO 137:48, in Burdon, *Archives of British Honduras*, 73.

60. Jarvis, *In the Eye of All Trade*, 227–28.

61. Quote from Quijano, *Belice*, 5.

62. Dampier, *Voyages*, 2:94–95; the fruits mentioned were guava, limes, oranges, sapodillas, all loaded with vitamin C, the key protection against scurvy.

63. Modyford to Secretary Lord Arlington, October 31, 1670, in CSP, 1669–1674, no. 310, cited in Camille and Espejo-Saavedra, "Historical Geography of the Belizean Logwood Trade," 78.

64. Dampier, *Voyages*, 2:96. Dampier is perhaps the best contemporary English source on the logwood settlements. John Atkins visited them in 1735.

65. Ibid., 2:56.

66. Columbus, *Journal of Christopher Columbus*, 74–75; Clendinnen, *Ambivalent Conquests*, 3; Abulafia, *Discovery of Mankind*, 126, 128, 145, 230; McDonald, *Pirates, Merchants, Settlers, and Slaves*, 15; Columbus named the bay on account of its great depths, see Waddell, *British Honduras*, 3.

67. Dampier, *Voyages*, 2:51; Waddell, *British Honduras*, 3–7, quote on p. 6.

68. Dampier, *Voyages*, 2:120–21.

69. Joseph, "British Loggers, Part 2," 47n, citing the *Consejo de Indias* (1677). For a book-length study on the subject, see Jones, *Maya Resistance to Spanish Rule*.

70. Dampier, *Voyages*, 2:96–97.

71. Ibid., 2:97.

72. "Memorial of His Majesty's Subjects, Settled on Yucatan in the Bay of Honduras, to Lord Sidney, Sec. of State for the Home Dept.," November 11, 1784, CO 123:3, cited in Burdon, *Archives of British Honduras*, 149.

73. On the Red Sea Men, see McDonald, *Pirates, Merchants, Settlers, and Slaves*, 82–84, 87, 90, 125, 129.

74. Burdon, *Archives of British Honduras*, 1.

75. The scholarly quote is Neill, "Buccaneer Ethnography," 166; Burnaby was a British admiral who arrived at the scene and subsequently recorded the preexisting customs of the pirate cutters. "Burnaby's Laws," April 9, 1765, can be found in Burdon, *Archives of British Honduras*, 100–106.

Suppression of Pirates

Trial and Error

PIRACY TRIALS IN ENGLAND
AND ITS COLONIES, 1696-1723

Douglas R. Burgess

In July 1723, famed Boston preacher Cotton Mather ascended the pulpit in Newport, Rhode Island, to offer a jeremiad on his favorite subject: the wantonness of the people before him. The occasion was propitious. That very afternoon the town had turned out in force to witness the execution of sixteen men convicted of piracy; hangings and speeches took the better part of the day. Now, at last, it was Mather's job to provide the moral lesson behind it all. He did not hesitate. Having laid the blame for the pirates' behavior squarely on the shoulders of his listeners—their sloth had bred wickedness! their greed invited disaster!—he turned, finally, to the children. "Among the dolorous ejaculations of the dying pirates," he bellowed at them, "how often do you hear them confessing '*My grieving & leaving & scorning of my parents has been that which brought the vengeance of GOD upon me!*' Shall this confession make no impression on you, O wicked and woeful children, who break the hearts of your parents with your ungodly ways?" One can imagine the sniffles and sobs from the front row.[1]

Such was the common view of piracy by the second decade of the eighteenth century. Pirates were outsiders, men who had cast their lot against society and came, inevitably, to a bad end. They were also, paradoxically, products of that society: their avarice and depravity magnified the more venial sins of the community as a whole. But was it always thus? Older parishioners in Mather's audience—perhaps even Mather himself—would remember a time not long past when pirates were welcomed in that very harbor, along with nearly all other ports in the English colonial world. Perhaps that explains the vinegar in Mather's speech.

The image of a pirate dangling at the end of a gibbet is as ubiquitous as it is misleading. Only for a relatively brief time in the history of England

and her colonies were pirates effectively hunted, captured, prosecuted, and hanged; for the rest, their depredations went largely unanswered. The legal aspects of piracy may seem dry compared with tales of swashbuckling and hoards of gold, but the law was of paramount importance. Until England and other nations defined the crime, they were effectively powerless to stop it. Definition seems like an easy matter compared with the laborious business of pirate hunting. Yet such clarity in the law took centuries, and when it finally arrived—in the second decade of the eighteenth century—the pirate wars that followed were short, bloody, and effective. We must, then, understand the nature of a pirate trial in order to better understand piracy itself.

Little Treasons: The Development of English Piracy Law

The history of piracy trials is one of a centuries-long battle over meaning. Who were these criminals, and what was the exact nature of their crime? Ostensibly there were simple answers to both questions. The first legal definition was coined in the Roman Republic and has remained viable—more or less—ever since. Pirates, according to Marcus Tullius Cicero, were *hostis humani generis*, "enemies of the human race," a sweeping caste of criminality that was invoked countless times since antiquity, including in Sir Edward Coke's seminal 1628 work *Institutes of the Laws of England*.[2] As such, they were presumed to have "made war against the entire world," as Daniel Defoe described it. Every nation was tasked with rooting them out, and the challenge their crime posed to free societies would be unequaled until the rise of organized terror in the late twentieth century. Yet they were also ordinary robbers, no different than "highwaymen at sea," as seventeenth-century Lord Chief Justice Sir Charles Hedges described them. The gulf between these two concepts is immense and would be the source of legal headaches for centuries.

In England, petit treason, or launching a private war against the state and its citizens, was not a common law crime. The Magna Carta provided defendants a jury of their peers, but when the victim was England itself, it was understood that only a judge could properly determine guilt and punishment. Hence for much of its history England sought to try piracy cases in admiralty court. They were never entirely successful. First, the burden of proof was too high: treason demanded either a confession from the accused or sworn testimony of "witnesses indifferent."[3] Neither was easy to come by in a piracy trial. Second, there were political factors. Parliament, which disliked granting more legal prerogatives to the sovereign, vested the common law courts with full authority to try pirates in the reign of Henry VIII, even going so far as to replace the loaded term *pirate* with a more ordinary-sounding *confederator*.[4] But common law juries were notoriously reluctant to convict. In most cases juries were composed of pirates' friends and family: courts were convened in the same seaside communities where the defendants had grown up. As long as the pirate confined his depredations to foreign vessels (as most did), juries were inclined to look the other way. Most instances, in fact, never even reached the threshold of a trial.

James I was the first English sovereign to mount a serious challenge to the courts' prerogative, and the circumstances were singular. Ascending the throne in 1603, James inherited an empty treasury and a stale war with Spain that neither side wished to continue. He also inherited scores of privateers that sailed under Elizabeth I bearing letters of marque, prize commissions entitling them to plunder the Spanish at will. These corsairs had been a vital part of English military strategy under the late queen but had by now become something of an embarrassment. James had them recalled (few heeded him, as it turned out) and enacted sweeping legislation designed to quash them once and for all. Jurisdiction was wrested from the common law courts, and special courts of admiralty were to be convened throughout the kingdom. Cases, the king proclaimed, "shall be heard by the Judge of the Admiralty without admitting unnecessary delay, and no appeal shall be allowed to the defendant."[5] Yet this abrupt volte-face—privateers one day, pirates the next—was self-defeating. James lacked the resources and manpower to do anything more than threaten. With no one to bring the pirates to trial, the admiralty courts languished. After James's death, the next generation of pirates simply transferred their base of operations to the Caribbean and the American colonies, placing themselves beyond the reach of the Crown. The record of prosecutions tells the story: between 1605 and 1696 there were only a handful of successful piracy trials in England or its dominions, in an age when piracy flourished as never before.[6]

"The Sword Shall Maintain Me": The Every Trials of 1696

The stark and unworkable divisions between admiralty and common law came into sharp relief in 1696, during one of the most celebrated trials of the century. In late 1694 Henry Every, first mate of the merchant ship *Charles II*, led a mutiny and sailed for the Indian Ocean. He knew what he would find there: East India Company ships laden with silks, spices, precious stones, and other luxuries, all bound from Bombay to London. In fact, Every had missed such a convoy by only a few hours and discovered instead an even greater prize: the private yacht of the Great Mogul, King Aurangzeb, which carried a fortune in gold specie and the Mogul's own daughter. Every took both for himself, though he later released the princess. The treasure was the single largest ever seized from a seaborne piratical raid, then or after. When news of Every's coup reached India, Aurangzeb responded furiously by closing down all trade with England until the pirate Henry Every was caught and hanged.[7]

Despite the first worldwide manhunt in modern history, Every was never found. Six members of his crew, however, were apprehended at various English ports and transported to the Old Bailey for trial. With the Great Mogul waiting in the gallery, as it were, this trial assumed dimensions far greater than the norm. Nor was he the only intended audience. In their eagerness to capture Every and his crew, the English Board of Trade unwittingly uncovered scores of other pirates living throughout the Atlantic world, many with the explicit knowledge and consent of colonial governors. The colonies had made a tidy profit off goods purloined from the East India Company—a fact that, if known by the Great Mogul, likely would have ended Indian trade forever. The trial, therefore, would also serve as the means whereby the English colonies were put on official notice that the Crown was cracking down on corruption.

Even the English people themselves needed a salutary reminder. Not long before the trial began, a small pamphlet of doggerel appeared in London booksellers' shops. Titled "The Ballad of Henry Every" and written allegedly by the pirate himself, it exhorted other young Englishmen to abandon their mundane jobs and join him in a life of adventure and ease: "Come all you brave boys, whose courage is bold / Will you venture with me? I'll glut you with gold."[8] In the anxious and class-conscious days of William and Mary, any attempt to transcend one's station—by legal or illegal means—was understood as a serious threat to the established order. Every's call was thus revolutionary in every sense and demanded the chilling response that a trial—and hangings—would provide.

The problem was how best to frame the trial narrative. There was nothing preventing the admiralty from convening a court and trying Every's crew in camera, but the optics (as we would call them) were unsatisfactory. It was not enough for Every's crew to be tried and condemned; it must be done by the English people themselves. That meant a jury trial. But a jury came with its own pitfalls—namely, the jurymen themselves. In admiralty the verdict was never in doubt. The common law held no such assurance.

Some form of compromise was clearly in order. The Crown arrived at one by convening a jury trial under admiralty jurisdiction, an odd arrangement that melded civil procedure with common law. The most imposing courtroom in the Old Bailey was engaged, festooned with flags and a great crest bearing *Dieu et Mon Droit*, the English sovereign's motto "My divine right," underneath which sat the chief justice of admiralty. The Crown threw all its weight into establishing the majesty of the law, and the result was impressive. The jurymen must have been overwhelmed, to say nothing of the defendants. Sir Robert Newton opened for the prosecution in a snow-white jabot and powdered wig. Every's crewmates, deprived of their stolen wealth and thus indigent, represented themselves. The lopsidedness was almost comical. The pirates knew nothing of the intricacies of procedure and frequently invoked the judge and even the prosecution for guidance. "This man is a prisoner for piracy, my Lord!" one objected when a witness came forward. It was actually a perfectly good point: a pirate fearful for his life would hardly qualify as a "witness indifferent." But the chief justice lowered his brow and answered, "What if he be?"

"I do not understand Law," the defendant answered, "and hope your Lordship will advise us."

"I will do you all right," the judge assured him. "If he be so, that is no objection against him; he may be a good witness for all that."[9]

The prosecution's closing statement laid out a case that barely had to be explained: by turning mutineer and attacking a vessel belonging to His Majesty's good friend King Aurangzeb, Every and his men had jeopardized foreign relations and put the Crown in danger. Their petit treason had, according to Sir Robert Newton, brought about "the total loss of Indian trade, and thereby the impoverishment of this kingdom." The jury retired to consider their verdict on October 30, 1696. Several hours later they returned and acquitted all six defendants.

Who knows why they did it? The pirates' guilt was beyond question. Perhaps the pomp and majesty of the surroundings had backfired and made the humble jurymen feel kinship with the accused. Perhaps they had sympathy for the pitiful figures in the dock, confused and bedraggled with so many powerful forces arrayed against them. But most likely it came down to a rejection of Newton's final address. "Suffer pirates," he thundered at them, "and the commerce of the world shall cease!"[10] The men in the jury box were not financiers nor ministers of state. Such highfalutin appeals left them cold. What they *did* understand was that Henry Every had stolen from a "heathen," however highly placed. In a kind of inverted logic, it was the English state that had betrayed its own ideals by becoming involved in such trade to begin with. Or as the verses attributed to Every put it:

> French, Spanish, and Portuguese, the Heathen likewise,
> He has made a War with them until that he dies . . .
> My false-hearted nation, to you I declare,
> I have done thee no wrong, thou must me forgive,
> The Sword shall maintain me as long as I live.[11]

One might also spare some sympathy for the Board of Trade and all those at Whitehall whose careers hung—so to speak—on a successful prosecution. So it was that on October 31, All Hallow's Eve, the six pirates, who expected to be released onto the streets of London, found themselves once again in the dock, facing a new jury. Which was just as well, as the judge snapped, "If you have returned any of the former Jury, you have not done well, for that Verdict was a dishonour to the Justice of the Nation."[12] Thus framing the narrative, the second trial began.

The law of double jeopardy meant the pirates could not be tried for the same crime twice. Consequently, the Crown connived to indict them for mutiny, not piracy. The pirates boggled at this, and little wonder. "I am ignorant of these proceedings," one of them bemoaned. In the end it was the chief justice himself who put the crime in its proper perspective, one far more palatable to a jury of shopkeepers and tradesmen. "Now Piracy is only a Sea term for Robbery," he told them, "Piracy being a Robbery committed within the Jurisdiction of the Admiralty; if any man be assaulted in that Jurisdiction, and his Ship or Goods violently taken away without Legal Authority, this is Robbery and Piracy." Not a word was said about the commerce of the world, or the king's dear friend the Great Mogul. His words must have done the trick, for the jury came back shortly thereafter and convicted the pirates—"mutineers"—on all charges.[13]

Rarely has one trial so encapsulated the divisions within both law and public perception. As "enemies of the human race," tried in the full majesty of admiralty, the pirates went free. Only when they were reduced to good old-fashioned common law brigands did the conviction stick. The Every trial did not resolve the longstanding conflict between these two versions of the crime, nor did its ad hoc compromise between civil and common law achieve any lasting success. Yet it was, in its way, instructive. The Crown learned that a great gulf existed between itself and its subjects. Across the Atlantic, in the American colonies, the gulf was greater still.

"Bondage and Slavery": Piracy Trials in the American Colonies

The issue of admiralty jurisdiction had always been a sore spot for colonial governors. In theory, an English governor acted *in loco regis* and was thus vested with all the powers and duties of the sovereign. Governors could raise militia and make war, levy taxes, imprison subjects, and regulate trade. This last included, necessarily, the functions of admiralty, at least so far as collecting customs duties and hiring vessels to act as a private coast guard. In time of war, it also meant the governor had the power to commission privateers. But the long delay of communication between Crown and colony meant wars that had long since ended on the European continent might carry on for months, even years, by proxy in the colonies.[14] In Jamaica, for example, Governor Thomas Modyford felt secure enough in his position to commission Henry Morgan's devastating raid on Panama in 1671, despite there being no state of war between England and Spain. Modyford's example was followed in the American colonies in the 1690s, resulting in a paradoxical situation worthy of a W. S. Gilbert libretto: Anglo-American colonial governors commissioning Anglo-American pirates to attack Anglo-Indian trade in the Red Sea, with a resultant boom for American (but not Anglo) colonial commerce. The English Crown received hints of this subterfuge during the inquiries following Henry Every's piracy, but the full extent would not be known for some time. Nor did the Board of Trade ever fully understand why colonial governors would so eagerly betray the Crown. Simple greed, they assumed, or outright wickedness.

The truth is more complex. Governors zealously guarded their prerogatives; in charter colonies, distinguished by the presence of a legal document not unlike a bill of rights, those prerogatives were intertwined with "sacred" liberties guaranteed by the sovereign in perpetuity. Among them was the exercise of admiralty jurisdiction. Thus it fell to the colonies—and their governors—to define the crime of piracy and prosecute it accordingly. Not surprisingly, they defined it as narrowly as possible to allow administrators a free hand in granting privateering commissions. In Rhode Island in 1684, at the insistence of the Crown, the colony enacted an antipiracy statute that promised pirates would suffer "the pains of death, without benefit of clergy." This sounded severe, yet closer reading of the statute revealed that it limited the crime of piracy to those who "contrary to his Majesty's Proclamations . . . have and do continually go off from this colony unto foreign princes' services."[15] This absurdly narrow definition absolved an entire generation of pirates; the first successful prosecution for piracy in the colony would not occur until the next century.

The English crown was not entirely unmindful of the colonies' attempts to protect the pirates under their jurisdiction. Months after the Every trials, the Board of Trade wrote the governor of Rhode Island: "His Majesty has also received complaints that the entertainment given to pirates . . . has occasioned many ill-minded persons, seamen and others to desert their habitations and apply themselves to such wicked and destructive courses to the great weakening and dispeopling of the colonies."[16] Yet this was couched in the form of a grievance to be remedied; the Crown still had faith in its governors.

Nevertheless, the stunning record of colonial nonprosecution gave the Crown pause. As early as the 1670s there were proposals raised in Parliament to establish vice-admiralty courts in the Atlantic colonies, wresting the power of admiralty jurisdiction from the governors altogether. For a brief time when the New England colonies were reorganized as the Dominion of New England, governors lost admiralty jurisdiction (as part of a larger disfranchisement of colonial governments), but after the dissolution of the Dominion in 1688 the colonists demanded, and received, all the rights and privileges they had heretofore enjoyed—including admiralty. A decade later, following the revelations of the Every case, the Board of Trade was willing to reconsider the matter. They began by demanding of a copy of the laws from the most recalcitrant colonies—Massachusetts, Rhode Island, and New York. Then the long wait began. Over a year later a copy of Rhode Island's laws arrived but were nothing more than "a blind copy of their laws," according to the board, "full of incoherence and nonsense jumbled together and confused. The Government themselves cannot tell when they have the whole: how then can the people be supposed to know what is Law amongst them?"[17]

Actually, by all accounts the colonists had a very good idea indeed of the law among them and were zealous in defending it. Confronted with lists of known pirates inhabiting their colonies, governors blithely denied having seen any of them and wrote leisurely answers, trusting the long interval of transatlantic communication to protect them. To a great extent, it did. Relatively few were removed from office: Governor Samuel Cranston of Rhode Island, whom the Board of Trade accused of open treason, served a record thirty years. When colonial surveyor Edward Randolph wrote a critical letter to the Board of Trade charging that "neither Judges nor Juries nor witnesses are under any obligation so that all things are managed there [Rhode Island] according to their will and interest," Governor Cranston's reply was mildness itself.[18] "Several informations," he wrote, "have been forwarded to you that Rhode Island is a place where pirates are entertained. . . . These things have been misrepresented to you. We have never countenanced such proceedings."[19] The board's response still blisters paint some three hundred years later: "We observe what you say upon the subject of privateering commissions granted. We cannot but esteem this willful neglect, and we must tell you, that unless you reform all such shuffling in your correspondence with us, you will unavoidably find it turn no less to your prejudice than the miscarriages themselves that you would conceal. . . . These answers are so contrary to truth and to your duty that we wonder how you could write them."[20] Yet Cranston served on, unscathed.

The solution advocated by colonial surveyor Edward Randolph had the virtue of precedent and simplicity: just as James I had done in England, the Crown must now send admiralty judges to the colonies. Only then, Randolph cautioned, could justice be done. The Board of Trade hemmed and hawed; it was an expensive proposition, and one certain to raise colonial ire. Finally, in January 1698, it was decided. Dozens of judges departed England for the colonies, each bearing a vice-admiralty commission signed by the king himself. Dozens more were deputized within the colonies, with the strict understanding that if they failed to find pirates to prosecute they would soon lose their places. As expected, the vice-admiralty judges outraged colonial sensibilities. But the colonists' response was canny. Presented with one such judge, Governor Walter Clarke first denied the validity of the commission, then prevaricated by claiming he could not endorse it before consulting the colonial assembly. Appearing before them, he warned that the commissions were nothing less than an assault of the colony's sacred rights under the charter, and "we had better like men spend one half of our Estates to maintain our privileges" or they might find themselves "brought into bondage and slavery." The judge, Peleg Sanford, was never confirmed. Such resistance, covert and open, paid off: the century rolled over without a single new piracy trial occurring anywhere in the English Atlantic.[21]

Then, suddenly, everything changed. The second decade of the eighteenth century saw significant growth in the number of colonial piracy trials: modest at first, ultimately becoming a deluge. What happened? Most historians point to (as one described it) a policy of "strict, centralized control" at Whitehall: the establishment of the Board of Trade, replacement of amateur aristocrats with career bureaucrats at the highest levels of government, and active engagement by the Crown in all aspects of antipiracy legislation and implementation.[22] Yet while these factors were undeniable, the greatest change occurred thousands of miles away. The East India Company began convoying their ships. Almost instantly, the lucrative Red Sea trade disappeared. The pirate colony at St. Mary's off the Madagascar coast closed up shop, its titular "King" Adam Baldridge summarily deposed. American pirates had to make the difficult choice of whether to return to their former occupations—many were slave traders or merchantmen—or continue their present one under vastly changed circumstances. The majority simply dissolved back into the fabric of the colonies. A small but vociferous minority chose to rebel. These few formed the nucleus of a deadly surge in piracy, a brief and bloody time from 1713 to 1725 that witnessed the careers of such notables as Edward Low, Jack Rackham, Mary Read, Anne Bonny, and of course Edward Teach, alias Blackbeard. The sad truth, however, is that for all the dark luster of their reputations, this last generation of pirates fought for scraps. Denied the riches of the Indies, they haunted the Caribbean and the American coast, hoping to pick up stray merchantmen. It was a brutal life and rarely a profitable one.[23]

More importantly, it radically altered the relationship between the pirates and their erstwhile colonial protectors. With pirates lurking offshore instead of thousands of miles away, and launching their attacks on local rather than "heathen" trade, it did not take long for colonial attitudes to harden. This new generation of pirates was considerably rowdier than the last, and even if they kept their depredations confined to other colonies, they still swaggered back every few weeks and raised riot in the town. All the money they spent on drink and other pleasures hardly compensated for their loud, odiferous presence. Nor were these men cut from the same dignified cloth as Thomas Tew or William Kidd. They were, with some notable exceptions, the dregs: ordinary seamen that took up piracy to escape a life of drudgery before the mast. Their navigational skills were hazy at best, a far cry from the kind of advanced knowledge needed to pilot a vessel halfway around the world to the Red Sea.

For the first time, the English colonies were now just as committed to stamping out the pirate menace as the Crown was. The results were swift and severe. Following the Peace of Utrecht in 1713, when a brief resurgence of privateering was abruptly cut short, the Board of Trade sent a circular letter to the colonial governors that read in part: "I am hereby to acquaint you in that in case any of H.M. Governors or any others concerned in the surrender or pardon of any of the pirates, shall receive any sum of money or any other gratuity or any other advantage whatsoever on account thereof, it is H.M. intention that he or they so offending shall be prosecuted with the utmost severity of the law."[24] In previous years, warnings like this would have lain unheeded under a paperweight on governors' desks, but with the pirates thrown back on the colonies, colonial administrators were only too willing to round them up. Governor Francis Nicholson of Virginia even outfitted a vessel out of his own pocket and became pirate hunter himself. Other, less athletic governors were content to simply put out word: no further commissions or protections were forthcoming, and the pirates had best make themselves scarce.

Nowhere was this sea change more evident than in the piracy trials occurring during this period. In Boston in 1718 eight men were tried for piracy. They produced in evidence a grimy commission bearing the seal of Queen Anne, doubtless left over from the late war. A few years earlier this would have sufficed, however thin a reed. Now the court answered tersely that "the commission of the late Queen Anne was of no force after Her Majesty's demise . . . it having died with the Queen."[25] As if to punctuate the passing of an era, the presiding judge also instructed his jury in terms that could have been borrowed directly from Cicero, by way of Sir Edward Coke and Sir Robert Newton: "The pirate can claim the protection of no prince, the privilege of no country, the benefit of no law; he is denied common humanity, and the very rights of nature . . . and is to be dealt with [as a] wild and savage beast, which every man may lawfully destroy."[26] The jury agreed; all the men were hanged.

Denied the traditional cover of a commission, friendly jury, or sympathetic government, accused pirates fell back on more traditional defenses. Nearly all claimed they had been pressed into piracy against their wills, and trials tended to degenerate into endless squabbles of accusation and counteraccusation. This hardly helped defendants' chances. Piracy trials and executions became allegorical plays reinforcing community morality. At the same Newport trial where Cotton Mather appeared in 1723, the condemned pirates themselves were given the opportunity to speak from the scaffold. "Live soberly, and let not yourselves be overcome with strong drink," one admonished the crowd. "Alas! It is a sad thing, a too-reigning vice among men, the inlet of numberless sins and evils, the ruin of a great many families."[27] These words appeared in a pamphlet published later, along with Mather's sermon. Did the pirate actually deliver them as recorded? Possibly not; the diction is a little too polished, the rhythmic cadences not dissimilar to Mather's own. Yet, true or not, pirates' dying speeches are an accurate barometer of public attitudes. Far from Henry Every's taunting exhortations in verse, these men pleaded with the crowd not to follow them astray. Having once been heroes, and later respected members of the community, they were now objects of pity and scorn, living embodiments of the wrong path. "I beg that it may be a warning to all young people," one allegedly wrote his mother, "to keep themselves from all bad courses, especially Sabbath breaking, drinking to excess, and blaspheming the name of God." As if reinforcing public morality were not enough, he closed by defending the very caste system that made piracy so tempting: "And I beseech all that are servants to keep faithful to the Masters, for if I had been dutiful to mine, tis likely I had not been brought to this untimely end."[28] In the highly stylized pageant of an eighteenth-century trial, it was vital that the condemned criminal acknowledge his or her own guilt. Only then was the community's decision justified. Here, the pirate is the metaphorical scapegoat, bearing all the community's sins—venial and mortal—and transmuting them into forgiveness through his own sacrificial execution.

Conclusion

By the middle of the eighteenth century Atlantic piracy had all but disappeared. The intervening centuries up to the present offer only a handful of piracy trials, and very little of note. One might thus regard the colonial trials as a kind of punctuation mark at the end of a long era, and a resolution of that centuries-old question over the meaning of the crime. Were pirates enemies of the human race, or ordinary criminals? Case law seems to favor the former, though prosecutors were not shy in invoking the old idea of "highwaymen at sea" if it helped ensure a conviction. Ultimately, however, *hostis humani generis* succeeded because it reflected the geopolitical reality. Until nations (and colonial governors) forbore commissioning privateers, the idea of the pirate standing opposed to the world was never truthful or viable. Yet once crown and colony were on the same side, they inevitably placed pirates against them. From that moment the swift decline of piracy was not only conceivable but inevitable.

NOTES

1. Cotton Mather, *An Essay upon Remarkables in the Ways of Wicked Men* (New London, Conn.: Timothy Green, 1723), 23.

2. See Sir Edward Coke, *Institutes of the Laws of England; Concerning High Treason, and Other Pleas of the Crown and Criminal Causes* (1628; repr., London: E. and R. Brooke, 1794).

3. 27 Hen. 8, c. 4 (1535), in Danby Pickering, ed., *The Statutes at Large* (Cambridge, England: John Burgess, 1762–1807), 1:348.

4. 28 Hen. 8, c. 15 (1536), in Pickering, ed., *Statutes at Large*, 1:441–43.

5. J. F. Larkin and P. L. Hughes, *Stuart Royal Proclamations* (Oxford: Oxford University Press, 1976), 1:204n.

6. See K. R. Andrews, "The Expansion of English Privateering and Piracy in the Atlantic, c. 1540–1635," in *Cours et Piraterie*, ed. Michel Mollat (Paris: Imprimerie Nationale, 1975); David Hebb, *Piracy and the English Government, 1616–1642* (Aldershot, UK: Scholar Press, 1994).

7. See Joel Baer, "Captain John Avery and the Anatomy of a Mutiny," *Eighteenth Century Life* 18 (1994): 1–26.

8. Joel Baer, "Bold Captain Avery in the Privy Council: Early Variants of a Broadside Ballad from the Pepys Collection," *Folk Music Journal* 7 (1995): 9–15.

9. John Smith, *The Tryals of Joseph Dawson, Edward Forseith, etc. . . . for Several Piracies and Robberies* (London: John Everingham, 1696), 14–15.

10. Ibid.

11. Baer, "Bold Captain Avery," 12.

12. Smith, *Tryals of Joseph Dawson*, 11.

13. Ibid., 11, 6.

14. See Helen Crump, *Colonial Admiralty Jurisdiction in the Seventeenth Century* (London: Longmans, 1931).

15. John Russell Bartlett, ed., *Records of the Colony of Rhode Island and Providence Plantations in New England* (Providence, R.I.: Knowles Anthony, 1858), 3:156.

16. Ibid., 3:321–22.

17. The board's remarks are found in Cecil Headlam, ed., *Calendar of State Papers, Colonial Series, America and the West Indies, Preserved at the Public Records Office* (London: Cassell, 1930), January 7, 1700, n. 14, part viii.

18. Edward Randolph to Board of Trade, May 30, 1698, in Robert Toppan, ed., *Edward Randolph, Including His Letters and Official Papers from the New England, Middle, and Southern Colonies in America . . . 1676–1703* (Boston: Prince Society, 1898–1909), 5:185.

19. Bartlett, *Records,* 3:336–37.

20. Ibid., 3:376–77.

21. Marguerite Appleton, "Rhode Island's First Court of Admiralty," *New England Quarterly* 5 (1932): 138–58.

22. Michael Hall, "The House of Lords, Edward Randolph and the Navigation Act of 1696," *William and Mary Quarterly* 14 (1957): 494.

23. See Marcus Rediker, *Villains of All Nations: Atlantic Pirates in the Golden Age* (Boston: Beacon Press, 2004).

24. Circular letter from Mr. Secretary Craggs to Governors, Dec. 24, 1718, in Headlam, ed., *Calendar of State Papers, Colonial Series,* 1717–1718, n. 803.

25. John Smith, *The Trial of Eight Persons Indicted for Piracy . . . in Boston* (Boston: John Edwards, 1718).

26. Ibid.

27. *An Account of the Pirates . . . Executed at Newport, Rhode Island, July 19, 1723* (Newport, R.I., 1723).

28. Ibid.

Protecting Trade by Suppressing Pirates

BRITISH COLONIAL AND
METROPOLITAN RESPONSES TO
ATLANTIC PIRACY, 1716-1726

David Wilson

The period between 1716 and 1722 witnessed a surge in Atlantic piracy. At first, pirates used the island of New Providence in the Bahamas to launch small-scale attacks on Spanish shipping near Cuba. From here, their operations quickly expanded to preying on all shipping, regardless of nation, throughout the Caribbean, North America, and Africa, with a small number of pirates cruising as far as the Arabian Sea. After 1722, Atlantic piracy declined rapidly to the extent that the historiography has generally declared that the golden age of piracy ended in 1726.[1] While cruising in these regions, pirates impacted several areas of British Atlantic trade, instigating numerous complaints to the British state by British merchants and colonial officials who outlined the necessity to suppress piratical depredations in the Atlantic.

The decline of piracy after 1722 has been previously explained as the result of a state war on maritime crimes. From this perspective, piracy was suppressed through strategies employed by the British state, including delegitimizing peacetime commerce raiding, capturing pirates and meting out justice, and discouraging colonial sponsorship of piracy.[2] As yet, a full evaluation of the eighteenth-century suppression campaigns has not been undertaken. As a result, scholarship has underestimated the role of various actors throughout the Atlantic, including British merchants, colonial representatives, and Royal Navy captains, who shaped and influenced the decline of piracy. The role and motivations of these participants have been underanalyzed in a historiography that absorbs colonial activity within a metropolitan-driven war on piracy. Without a complete consideration of the motivations and activities of actors operating in both domestic and colonial theaters, the effectiveness of British state measures against piracy and, by extension, British state authority over the Atlantic world is overestimated. This chapter argues that there was not a coordinated state war on piracy but rather a series of fragmented and distinctive campaigns, which slowly reduced and isolated the pirate presence in the Atlantic throughout the second and third decades of the eighteenth century.

Suppression in the Metropole

In 1717, after a surge in piratical attacks endangered their ships, British merchants trading to the Caribbean and North America goaded the state into action. Petitions from metropolitan mercantile lobbies requesting naval protection for specific regions precipitated every state measure to suppress piracy in the early eighteenth century. The first petition appeared in May 1717 when the Society of Merchant Venturers of the City of Bristol complained to King George I of piracies committed in the Caribbean. "For several Months past," the merchants wrote, "divers Ships belonging to us as also to others of your Majesties Subjects have been attacked, Rifled and Plundered, and their Crews very Barbarously used by Pirates; upon the open seas in the West Indies, and particularly near the Island of Jamaica."[3]

The merchants requested that the state appoint means for suppressing pirates and protecting the West Indian sugar trade. Shortly afterward, similar requests were received from British merchants concerned in the Chesapeake tobacco trade. The principal concern for these two groups was the effects of piracy on the Jamaican sugar trade and the Virginian tobacco trade.[4] After Atlantic pirates spread to the African coast and the Indian Ocean, slave traders and the East India Company (hereafter EIC) requested state action.[5] In the 1720s, once the failure of state measures in the colonial theater became apparent, there were further complaints by the sugar and tobacco lobbies, which were joined by petitions from the fishing lobby after pirates impacted the Newfoundland fisheries.[6]

Commercial lobbies regularly applied pressure on the king, admiralty, Council for Trade and Plantations (hereafter CTP), and Parliament to protect their trading interests in the Caribbean and North America. The predominance of these mercantile groups in London in the early eighteenth century allowed them to remain in close proximity to and assimilate with the political bodies that influenced their trade.[7] These groups regularly co-operated when their interests overlapped, as was the case with lobbying to suppress piracy. For example, Humphry Morice and Richard Harris, two of Britain's foremost slave traders, spearheaded the campaign to secure the African slave trade against piracy, drawing on their connections with merchants in other trades. In the late seventeenth and early eighteenth centuries, Morice and Harris had helped lead the campaign to remove the Royal African Company's (hereafter RAC) monopoly and open slave trading to independent traders.[8] During their campaign against the RAC, Morice and Harris formed alliances with various Atlantic interests in London, particularly the tobacco lobby, for auxiliary support, and in return transatlantic merchants in the tobacco and sugar trades frequently requested Morice and Harris to represent them before the CTP and admiralty. Both Morice and Harris appear to have been involved in the early efforts urging the state to take action against the growing piratical presence in the Caribbean.[9] Despite their diversity, networks of Atlantic merchants concentrated in London, although they often united with similar merchants in other British cities to advance their collective lobbying interests.[10] While the CTP received numerous accounts from colonial governors, councils, and assemblies concerning the growth of piracy, it was the active soliciting by metropolitan commercial interests that provided the initial impetus for state responses to piracy. Only after the petitions of 1717 were received did the king request the CTP to report on the necessary measures for suppressing piracy in the Caribbean.[11] Consequently, it was the influence of these lobbies considered alongside the metropolitan state's own commercial priorities that dictated measures to curtail piracy.

Between 1716 and 1726, the state's primary reaction to Atlantic piracy was to dispatch naval vessels to specific regions where merchants had suffered losses. In the Americas, station ships were already distributed among the royal colonies.[12] These were usually small warships, either fifth-rates with between thirty and forty guns or sixth-rates with either twenty or twenty-four guns, sent from Britain to act as convoys for merchant ships. There were warships stationed at Jamaica, Barbados, and the Leeward Islands, the primary sugar-producing colonies in the Caribbean, as well as in Virginia, New York, and New England in North America. Jamaica, Barbados, and Virginia tended to receive the more powerful fifth-rate ships due to their perceived commercial importance, by both the British state and metropolitan merchants, as the primary sugar- and tobacco-producing regions.[13] In response to the petitions in 1717, new station ships were fitted out for the Caribbean and North American stations. These were not, however, additional vessels but replacements for the station ships that were returning, or had already returned, to England. Normally, station ships would have been replaced before they had returned to England, but this service had been neglected due to naval campaigns in the Baltic and against the Salé Rovers in the Mediterranean.[14] Therefore, in response to merchant complaints, the state rectified the ongoing neglect of colonial stations. The new station ships were given instructions to maintain constant correspondence with each other and to coordinate if they learned of pirates near their appointed regions.[15] Pressure by metropolitan tobacco and sugar merchants influenced the concentration of station ships to protect Jamaican and Virginian trade rather than to focus on coast-wide efforts to eradicate pirates. Similarly, between 1720 and 1723, two navy ships were dispatched to the previously unpatrolled African coast each year after appeals by slave traders, and a squadron of four ships was sent to the Indian Ocean after pressure from the EIC.[16]

While petitions by mercantile groups preempted the British state's response, naval ships were dispatched to regions that were recognized as key commercial concerns by the state rather than purely out of the need to appease merchants. Tobacco and sugar were the primary colonial cash crops, and the colonies that produced them, particularly Jamaica and Virginia, demanded protection over all other assets due to their contributions to state revenue.[17] Likewise, the slave trade was recognized as one of the key components of the entire plantation system. It needed to be protected from pirates, not just to placate the slave-trading lobby, but also because the state believed its continuance necessary to uphold the entire plantation economy.[18] Piracy significantly threatened these lucrative trades and, as such, they received the focus of naval forces. While each of these trades was backed by influential mercantile lobbies who operated to uphold their own trading interests, each was also significant to state revenue. Therefore, while naval deployment to suppress piracy throughout the Atlantic was influenced by mercantile interests, it was ultimately dictated by the state's own priority to safeguard regions of specific commercial value and, therefore, state revenue from piratical attacks. Consequently, naval vessels were dispatched not to eradicate piracy throughout the Atlantic but rather to prevent pirates from impacting the most profitable zones of British trade. The entire response was influenced by the state's commercial concerns rather than driven solely by mercantile pressure or the need to protect the colonies themselves.

Dispatching naval warships for station duty in specific regions did not suppress piracy, and many factors militated against the effectiveness of naval campaigns. The vast expanse of the Atlantic coastlines and a reliance on largely outdated intelligence meant pursuing pirates was a difficult task: the size of naval ships meant that pirates could escape through shoals and shallow waters. Ship hulls were fouled after long voyages from Britain and rapidly deteriorated due to shipworms, which meant that orders were delayed until ships could be careened. The unavoidable sicknesses that accompanied colonial service meant naval captains had to recruit more sailors on arrival, which was particularly problematic as the Act for the Encouragement of the Trade to America (1708) prohibited the pressing of mariners in America in order to secure commercial shipping crews from naval impressment.[19] A further complication beyond the state of the ships and their crew was the fact that naval captains, particularly those in the colonies, enjoyed relative autonomy. Rather than fall under the authority of colonial governors, naval captains were given the right to dictate their own service while commanding a station ship. They received instructions from the admiralty, but these were often recommendations that were to be followed when the situations allowed rather than strict orders.[20] As such, naval captains could disregard this service in favor of more profitable endeavors as there was little metropolitan oversight and no superior authority in the colonial theater.[21] Expeditions against pirates were often refused due to the incapacity of the ship and crew or because such a voyage was unlikely to be successful and would be a waste of time and supplies.[22] There were frequent protests by colonial officials that captains employed station ships for their own enterprises. This was particularly prevalent in Jamaica, where captains appear to have neglected the protection of Jamaican trade by leaving the station unattended in order to trade on the Spanish American coast.[23] Naval endeavors against piracy relied on the dispositions of captains who acted autonomously, with little supervision from colonial governors or the state, which meant these vessels often failed to execute their mission.

The effectiveness of naval dispatches was also obstructed by the intervention of the same metropolitan commercial lobbies who had demanded state action in the first place. By lobbying to protect the trade of particular colonies, merchant groups obstructed naval attempts to mount a coordinated effort to subdue piracy in regions that were not of substantial commercial concern but were the chief locations where pirates congregated before undertaking further voyages against Atlantic shipping.[24] For example, three additional ships were sent to the Caribbean in 1718 as a task force with a clear directive to suppress piracy.[25] However, a group of prominent London merchants declared to the admiralty that the ships sent to Jamaica in 1717 were not cruising against pirates but were trading on the Spanish coast. They requested further naval protection for Jamaican trade. Orders were dispatched for the three ships to proceed directly to Jamaica in order to protect trade. As a result, the task force did not cruise against pirates but, instead, spent their time convoying merchant vessels from Jamaica. Therefore, although metropolitan interests lobbied for the suppression of piracy, these groups were primarily concerned with the immediate protection of specific regions from pirate attacks and obstructed attempts to subdue pirates operating in other locales.

Between 1716 and 1722, only two station ships successfully cruised against pirates. Francis Hume captured two pirate sloops at Saint Croix in the Virgin Islands in early 1717 as well as a small pirate ship at an island off Venezuela in 1718. Chaloner Ogle defeated Bartholomew Roberts in Africa in 1722. Only Ogle's triumph proved significant, as it resulted in the death of Roberts and the capture of his crew; Hume's success was mitigated by the fact the majority of the pirates managed to escape, fleeing onshore and through the shoals that the naval vessel was unable to navigate.[26] Each of these conquests relied on a number of factors that lay beyond the state's immediate control. For example, Hume's first voyage had required additional support from local political bodies in Barbados and the Leeward Islands. Disease and desertion had greatly reduced his crew, and local politicians supplied the necessary funds to hire enough men to sail the naval ship and provided soldiers from colonial regiments to mount the expedition.[27] Likewise, Ogle required provisions to remain on the African coast long enough to receive intelligence of Roberts's location, and these were supplied by the RAC at Cape Coast Castle.[28] Even with the support of these local bodies, the expeditions had also required fresh intelligence, luck, and the diligence of the naval captains to find and engage the pirates. Like many of their counterparts, these captains could have easily refused to undertake these expeditions due to a lack of resources. Yet, if all naval captains had remained diligent in their duty to suppress pirates, it is difficult to evaluate how much of a difference this would have made. Success also relied on the availability of current intelligence on pirates. Tracking pirates' whereabouts was not always possible, particularly as the majority of naval captains were not instructed to seek out information but were ordered only to react when intelligence was received from local administrators. And typically such reports were outdated by the time they were provided.[29] Furthermore, even with up-to-date news, captains relied on luck to locate pirates among the locales where they had been last sighted. This largely reactive approach meant that naval successes against pirates were not easily achieved. Therefore, between 1716 and 1722, naval vessels remained largely ineffective for stamping out piracy.

Station ships appear to have been more effective in suppressing pirates after 1722, particularly in the Caribbean. Naval commanders, reacting to new antipiracy legislation passed in 1722, engaged in proactive cruising in the Virgin Islands and Bay of Honduras, the two primary haunts of pirates at that time. In these locations, the station ships were quicker in their responses to news of pirates and often met with success, destroying pirate vessels and dispersing or capturing the largely diminished pirate crews. Furthermore, the Jamaican station ships were more actively employed in convoying trading vessels.[30] Increased naval activity in the 1720s, even when restricted to convoying, may have had an indirect impact on the suppression of pirates. Even when naval ships did not encounter pirates, news of a naval presence may have acted as a deterrent. For example, the lack of depredations on Virginian vessels after the station ships were dispatched in 1717 suggests that these were an effective discouragement against pirates operating in the Virginian capes.[31] Thus, although the majority of vessels sent to the colonies do not seem to have cruised against pirates, their very presence created a much more hostile environment for pirates to operate in.

Alongside the continuing dispatch of naval ships, two other measures were used by the state in an attempt to curb piracy: a proclamation of pardon to all pirates in 1717 and new legislation in 1722. The pardon was issued on September 5, 1717, to remain active for one year; it was later extended to July 1719.[32] The initial response of pirates to the amnesty appeared promising but was short lived, as the proclamation proved contentious.[33] Most problematic for pirates, it contained no guarantee they would retain their plunder.[34] Pirates would not return to colonial society only to have their goods seized. In addition, the proclamation did not empower colonial governors to grant pardons but only provided a promise that pirates would be pardoned in the future. The measure was counterproductive, encouraging those intending to surrender to return to piracy while they waited to receive amnesty.[35] In July 1718, the necessary warrant for administering pardons was finally issued, but since it did not address the issue of piratical goods, it remained ineffective.[36] The governors, even when empowered to issue pardons, were largely unable to encourage pirates to surrender if there was a risk they would lose their accumulated plunder.[37]

The state introduced new antipiracy legislation in 1722. The two key provisions of the new law were, first, that accessories to piracy could be tried as pirates themselves and, second, that naval captains would be court-martialed if they received any merchandise on board their ships with intent to trade.[38] The act was passed at a time when Atlantic piracy was already declining, but nevertheless, the law may have provided additional pressure on the illicit markets that sustained it. Due to the nature of these markets, it is hard to evaluate the impact of the act, but it is probable that merchants were discouraged by the additional risk of being tried as pirates. Furthermore, the act is likely one of the reasons that naval vessels, particularly in Jamaica, appeared to be more proactive after 1722. Nevertheless, navy captains still found ways to circumvent the new legislation and continued trading on the coast of Spanish America. In 1723, the governor of Jamaica reported that the navy captains hired sloops, loaded them with merchandise, provided them with men and victuals, and then convoyed these sloops to trade.[39] Another account reported that the station ships charged a fee to convoy trading vessels to the Spanish coast.[40] Thus although Jamaican station ships appear to have been more proactive after 1722, their economic motivations may not have changed. And although the state made efforts through a pardon and legislation to curb Atlantic piracy, it remained unable or unwilling to coordinate a large-scale campaign against Atlantic pirates throughout the period.

The state's failure to initiate a war on piracy is clearly observed in the state's lack of action against the pirates in the Bahamas between 1716 and 1718. The settlements on the Bahamas had been neglected by the turn of the century, leaving only a small population remaining on the islands, without any form of government.[41] Not long after the War of the Spanish Succession, reports were sent to the CTP by the governor of Bermuda that pirates were taking advantage of the desperate and lawless conditions of the Bahamas.[42] In 1717, the CTP recommended that New Providence, in the Bahamas, needed to be settled and secured in order to effectually suppress piracy.[43] However, even with the influx of complaints throughout 1716 and 1717, the state made no preparations for securing the Bahamas.[44]

There are two possible reasons for the state's reluctance to act decisively in the Bahamas. First, the state was faced with a vast amount of debt in the postwar period and could not afford to divert funds to finance the restoration of the Bahamas.[45] Second, the state was simply unwilling to finance such an endeavor. The project would essentially entail funding a new colony, which would not become self-sustaining until it had been sufficiently settled, secured, and developed; none of which could be guaranteed as, even with this investment, the Bahamas did not promise to become a substantial commercial asset.[46] Despite the fact that a number of influential merchants, including Morice and Harris, outlined the need to secure New Providence from pirates, the state did not react.[47] Instead, building up the Bahamas required the intercession and investment of private individuals who sought to profit from restoring the colony. In 1717, a copartnership under the leadership of Woodes Rogers, who had gained fame for his successful privateering voyage to the South Seas between 1708 and 1711, leased the land rights of the Bahamas. Rogers was granted the position of governor after he promised to remove the pirate presence there, only requesting that a garrison be provided for the colony.[48] The scheme was advantageous for the Crown because the pirates would be dislodged with minimal public expenditure.

State measures before 1720 were a resounding failure in tackling Atlantic piracy. Naval dispatches were largely ineffective, pardons proved to be a bureaucratic failure, and there was no state endeavor to dislodge the pirates from the Bahamas. Even after 1720, when naval squadrons proved more effective and new legislation was introduced, piracy continued in the colonial theater. The entire state initiative was driven by metropolitan concerns about the impact of piracy on the chief pillars of colonial trade rather than actual concern for the colonies themselves, and the success of the measures implemented largely relied on the dispositions of autonomous naval captains. Without assessing the actual impact of metropolitan-driven measures in the colonies, it is possible to overestimate their success and, in doing so, inflate the supremacy of state authority in the colonial theater.

Suppression in the Colonies

With state measures having limited effect, colonial governments organized private ships to go in quest of pirates operating on their shores. These were often sloops that were owned by local merchants but that were outfitted by colonial governments using local revenue to pay for supplies and cover wages while in use for public service. Both parties benefitted from this arrangement, as colonial governments did not have sufficient funds to purchase their own vessels, and local merchants wanted the coasts free from pirates but could not do so at their own expense. It was predominantly colonies that did not hold a royal charter, such as Rhode Island and Pennsylvania, that had little choice but to send out vessels on their own. Rhode Island fitted out two sloops in 1717 and two in 1722, and three sloops were fitted out from Philadelphia in 1718.[49] The state could provide only a finite number of warships to the colonial theater, and therefore state focus was predominantly on colonies under direct royal authority rather than those with proprietary or charter status. These colonies could not expect assistance from the Boston and New York station ships either, which had been instructed to concentrate on protecting the shipping of their posts as well as Virginia.[50] These vulnerable colonies had little choice but to furnish their own voyages against pirates operating in their localities. However, even those colonies that received station ships used private ships to deter pirates when naval ships proved ineffectual. In December 1722, despite the presence of at least four station ships, the Jamaican Assembly authorized fitting out a sloop to guard the Jamaican coast.[51] In 1726, a sloop was fitted out at the charge of the Massachusetts government as it was deemed better suited for the service than the naval vessel stationed there.[52] The majority of these private colonial expeditions were unsuccessful because the ships did not encounter the pirates that had been operating nearby. Nonetheless, private ships patrolling may have deterred pirates even without a direct encounter.

When private colonial vessels confronted pirates, the operations often succeeded. For example, two expeditions from South Carolina proved to be the most effective in the period before 1720. Like Rhode Island and Philadelphia, South Carolina was not a royal colony and did not receive a station ship, nor did it receive support from the warships stationed at Virginia despite the close proximity. This was despite the fact that South Carolina appears to have been one of the primary victims of piratical depredations throughout 1717 and 1718.[53] The continuing impact of piracy on local trade encouraged Governor Robert Johnson and the council of South Carolina to organize two separate expeditions, using local vessels and revenue, against pirates operating in their immediate vicinity.[54] The first expedition apprehended Major Stede Bonnet and his crew in the Cape Fear River.[55] The second expedition captured the crew of Captain Richard Worley near the South Carolina coast.[56] Another of the chief successes of the period before 1720 was the elimination of Blackbeard on Ocracoke Island, North Carolina, in 1718, a joint venture undertaken by the Virginian governor Alexander Spotswood and the captains of the Virginian station ships. The organization of the expedition had required partnership because the naval vessels, too large to navigate the small passage of the North Carolina coast where Blackbeard resided, were not suitable for the task. At his own expense, Spotswood hired two sloops and pilots, and the vessels were manned and captained by officers and sailors from the station ships.[57] The operation was not driven by concern for North Carolina trade or its inhabitants but by concern for Virginia and the threat posed by an active pirate presence so close to its shores.[58] More victories followed in 1720 when private colonial vessels successfully engaged three pirate captains: Jack Rackham, Charles Vane, and George Lowther. However, these feats point to a new dimension in local colonial efforts against piracy, as they were carried out by vessels with no support from colonial government bodies.[59] These were fortuitous encounters by individual captains on trading voyages whose overall motivations are unclear. The only surviving evidence that reveals a captain's motivations is that of Walter Moor, the captain of a South Sea Company trading vessel, who engaged Lowther at Blanquilla, an island off the Venezuelan coast. "[I] supposed the sloop to be a Pirate," Moor stated in his deposition, "and did find the sloop just Careened with her sails unbent and her Great Gunns on shore, so took that advantage to attack her before she could gett in a Readiness to attack the said [South Sea Company] sloop Eagle."[60] This was a preemptive assault on a pirate vessel by a trading sloop to ensure that the pirate did not have the opportunity to get into an attacking position.[61] Similarly, it is likely that the other captains sought to safeguard their own trading voyages by seizing the opportunity to suppress a piratical threat and perhaps receive a reward or share of plunder in the process. All of these examples highlight that the colonial suppression of piracy was a fragmented series of campaigns driven by local or, in some cases, individual motivations.

Private colonial expeditions were small-scale and reactionary, often funded by colonial governments and intended to discourage pirates on local coasts. They were not coordinated, proactive attempts to remove the entire pirate presence in the Atlantic. This is not surprising as the colonies did not have the resources to coordinate a large-scale campaign against pirates operating outside their vicinities. The expeditions, necessitated by the failures of metropolitan measures to curb piracy in specific localities, were pragmatic responses by colonial governments, using local resources, to protect the immediate interests of the colony in the face of disruption to trade.

The suppression of piracy required more than a few expeditions against particular targets. The growth and sustenance of piracy from 1716 was partly facilitated through trading links with colonial merchants, particularly at New Providence, in the Bahamas.[62] New Providence developed into an entrepôt for clandestine trade where merchants exchanged provisions for plundered goods, although it is impossible to determine the volume of vessels that were trading with pirates due to the illicit nature of this trade. Still, there are accounts from a number of colonials who had been in the Bahamas during pirate occupation reporting that ships from several colonies, such as Boston, South Carolina, Virginia, and Port Royal, had been trading at New Providence.[63] The suppression of piracy required the removal of this market, but naval captains, colonial governments, and the metropolitan state were unwilling or unable to undertake or fund the necessary expedition. Instead, dislodging pirates from the Bahamas was largely left to the sole endeavors of Woodes Rogers.[64] Throughout his tenure on the Bahamas, Governor Rogers used his own financial resources—including going into debt to purchase provisions and other necessities—in order to sustain the garrison and secure the colony. He repeatedly requested the state and his copartners intercede, but they did not believe they were obligated to help.[65] Nevertheless, Rogers managed to dislodge the pirates from the Bahamas by late 1718. Rogers's arrival on the island divided the Bahamian pirates: some took the pardon and kept their plundered goods; while others who were unwilling to give up their illicit practices voyaged to North America and Africa to prey on shipping there.[66] Furthermore, Rogers successfully used ex-pirates to mount voyages against their former brethren who continued operating in the Bahamas, which again highlights the necessity for colonial officials to hire local shipping to deter pirates and make up for the lack of state-provided maritime defense.[67] Without the determination of one man, the Bahamas would have remained a hub of piratical activity.[68]

Although securing New Providence from pirate occupation was a significant turning point in the suppression of piracy, it did not remove altogether the illicit trade that sustained piracy. Markets for plunder endured, although from 1718 it was largely an opportunistic ship-based trade.[69] For example, both RAC agents and captains of independent slave-trading vessels, who had been attacked by pirates in Sierra Leone, reported that the pirates had found active encouragement among British traders who had established trading outposts along Sierra Leone River.[70] Furthermore, there was recognition by naval captains stationed in the Caribbean, alongside reports by colonial governors, that an illicit trade was carried on with pirates by the inhabitants of the Virgin Islands, who appear to have had little form of colonial governance or oversight. Likewise, Ellis Brand, captain of the *Winchelsea*, stationed at Jamaica, indicated that goods were being sent from Jamaica to the Bay of Honduras when pirates resorted there in the 1720s. The reports suggest that this trade continued despite legislation aimed at discouraging accessories to piracy in 1722.[71] Therefore, while in general there was a widespread decline of colonial sponsorship of piracy due to changing perceptions of commerce raiding in the early eighteenth century, it is important not to overstate this point.[72] There was clear colonial opposition toward piracy when pirates operated off local colonial coasts. However, while open sponsorship of piracy by the colonial elite had ended by the turn of the century, some colonial merchants continued to transact with pirates in a high-risk, opportunistic trade.

Colonial endeavors against piracy proved to be the most effective measure taken before 1720. Colonial officials, particularly Robert Johnson, Alexander Spotswood, and Woodes Rogers, provided the leadership and the financial resources that initiated a turning point in the suppression of piracy by the end of 1718. The successful voyages against Stede Bonnet and Blackbeard alongside the dislodging of pirates from New Providence marked the beginning of the gradual suppression of piracy in the Atlantic for the next eight years. After 1720, independent expeditions continued to be as important as naval activity in sustaining the momentum against piracy. Colonial actors, determined to secure their local boundaries and trade, actively proceeded against pirates operating in their vicinities. This was not a coordinated state war on piracy but rather a series of fragmented and distinctive campaigns that aimed to safeguard immediate localities from pirates. The colonial governments could not have achieved more, since they did not have the resources to mount anything more than pragmatic, short-term, and reactive measures against pirates in nearby waters. Nevertheless, these operations often proved much more effective in suppressing pirates than measures coordinated from the metropole.

Suppression Considered

While metropolitan, naval, and colonial endeavors slowly reduced the pirate presence in the Atlantic, they did not pursue and eliminate all pirates from the colonial theater. In order to evaluate the reasons why piratical attacks dwindled and were no longer as routinely reported after 1722, it is important to understand both the dispersal of pirates in the 1720s and the increased activity of the Spanish *guardacosta*. The campaigns against specific pirate crews and bases by colonial or naval actors between 1717 and 1726 gradually eliminated a large number of Atlantic pirates, while indirect measures, such as increased convoying and active cruising, created a hostile environment that made piracy much more difficult and forced pirates to disband and disperse into colonial populations. Of equal importance, piracy was an opportunistic and economically motivated exploit and, when they could, a number of pirates seized the chance to reenter colonial society.[73] This was especially true after 1720, when pirates took the pardons of European colonial powers. For example, pirates who had remained on Madagascar accepted a pardon that the French East India Company had offered in an attempt to curb the threat to its trade. Similarly, the crew of the *Cassandra*, after taking a rich prize near India, returned to the Caribbean and accepted a pardon offered by the Spanish at Portobello. In both cases, the pirates were reassured they could keep plundered goods.[74] Thus pirates were willing to take pardons as long as they did not face prosecution over their plundered goods. Other pirates seem to have simply left their vessels to conceal themselves among colonial populations. There is not enough evidence to provide an accurate indication of how many pirates accepted French or Spanish pardons or simply dispersed on the fringes of colonial society.[75] However, as early as 1722, there were only a handful of Atlantic pirates still operating, and those who had not been captured or killed had largely disbanded by 1726.[76]

Even though the majority of the New Providence pirates and their off-
shoots had been captured, had been killed, had dispersed, or were inactive,
Atlantic piracy did not end in 1726. Accounts of piracy continued to appear
intermittently in official reports.[77] Nevertheless, these were single occurrences that did not create any significant impact on Atlantic trade. It is likely
that a number of minor piracies on local shipping went unreported in colonial reports and newspapers after 1726. Indeed, this is similar to the situation
from 1722 onward, when only a handful of pirates were still operating, largely
committing depredations on small coastal and fishing vessels, of which there
is little specific information given in colonial reports.[78] This declining impact
is highlighted by the fact that, from 1724, there was no further lobbying by
metropolitan mercantile interests for measures against piracy. One possible
reason behind this may have been the increased availability of marine insurance in the 1720s, which offset the losses sustained by the occasional piratical attack.[79] This is an important point, but metropolitan mercantile lobbies
continued to petition when there were significant numbers of depredations
on colonial shipping by other antagonists. Of much more importance to the
decreasing focus on piracy was that piracy was no longer the chief commercial threat to colonial trade.

In the 1720s, there was a transition from merchants predominantly lobbying for measures against piracy to merchants seeking state intervention
against the depredations by the Spanish *guardacostas*. After peace was declared in 1713, Spanish *guardacostas* were commissioned to guard colonial
coasts and prevent illicit trading with subjects of other nations. The *guardacostas* continually exploited their commissions to capture prizes under any
pretense of trading with the Spanish coast.[80] From 1720, *guardacosta* attacks
on British shipping became even more prevalent throughout the Caribbean
and often stretched as far as the Virginian coast. As the overall impact of
piratical attacks dwindled, *guardacosta* depredations increased so that there
was a clear shift in both colonial correspondence and commercial lobbying
from piracy to the *guardacosta*, so that by 1726 the primary concern of merchants trading to the Americas was the damages sustained from *guardacosta*
attacks.[81] Piracy did not disappear entirely; it simply became less of an issue
than the *guardacosta* in this period. Commercial considerations were the primary factors that linked colonial and metropolitan interests in their endeavors to suppress piracy, and these considerations moved to the *guardacosta* as it
became the greatest threat to colonial commerce in the 1720s.

Conclusion

The suppression of Atlantic piracy in the early eighteenth century was not the result of a coordinated state war on piracy. Instead, it involved a multi-faceted process. A series of fragmented and distinctive campaigns, shaped and influenced in metropolitan and colonial contexts, slowly reduced and isolated Atlantic pirates. These campaigns required the active participation of a number of actors across metropolitan and colonial divides who facili-tated successful expeditions and, more importantly, created the hostile con-ditions that influenced the decline of piracy in the 1720s. While in both con-texts commercial considerations provided the overarching encouragement, it is necessary to appreciate the motivations and activities in each setting to fully understand the suppression of Atlantic piracy. Without considering au-tonomous undertakings in colonial localities, the effectiveness of state mea-sures is greatly overestimated. As such, the suppression of piracy in the early eighteenth century highlights that the administration of the British Atlantic world occurred through a complex ebb and flow of metropolitan policy, the dissemination of that policy in distinctive peripheries, and disconnected en-deavors in the localities. In this way, pirate vessels and the vessels that hunted them provide the lens through which to observe and understand the British Atlantic world in the early eighteenth century.

NOTES

Abbreviations

Adm.	Admiralty
BL	British Library
BOE	Bank of England
CO	Colonial Office
CTP	Council of Trade and Plantations
EIC	East India Company
T	Treasury
TNA	The National Archives of the United Kingdom, Kew

1. See Arne Bialuschewski, "Pirates, Markets, and Imperial Authority: Economic Aspects of Maritime Depredations in the Atlantic World, 1716–1726," *Global Crime* 9 (2008): 52–65; Peter Earle, *The Pirate Wars* (London: Methuen, 2003), 183–208; Mark G. Hanna, *Pirate Nests and the Rise of the British Empire, 1570–1740* (Chapel Hill:

University of North Carolina Press, 2015), 365–415; Marcus Rediker, *Villains of All Nations: Atlantic Pirates in the Golden Age* (London: Verso, 2012), 127–47.

2. Bialuschewski, "Pirates, Markets, and Imperial Authority," 52–65; Hanna, *Pirate Nests*, 222–415; Bryan Mabee, "Pirates, Privateers, and the Political Economy of Private Violence," *Global Change, Peace, and Security* 21, no. 2 (2009): 139–52; Anne Pérotin-Dumon, "The Pirate and the Emperor: Power and the Law of the Seas, 1450–1850," in *Bandits at Sea: A Pirates Reader*, ed. C. R. Pennell (New York: New York University Press, 2001), 25–54; Rediker, *Villains of All Nations*, 127–47; Robert C. Ritchie, "Government Measures against Piracy and Privateering in the Atlantic Area, 1750–1850," in *Pirates and Privateers: New Perspectives on the War on Trade in the Eighteenth and Nineteenth Centuries*, ed. David J. Starkey, E. S. Van Eyck Van Heslinga, and J. A. De Moor (Exeter: Exeter University Press, 1997), 10–28.

3. Petition of merchants of Bristol to the King, May 27, 1717, TNA, CO 323:7, no. 90.

4. Ibid.; instructions to Gordon, June 19, 1717, TNA, Adm. 2:49, 259–61.

5. Entry February 4, 1719, TNA, Adm. 3:31.; entry September 18, 1719, TNA, Adm. 3:32; EIC Petition to the King, BL, IOR/E/1/201, 197.

6. Memorial of Planters and Fisherman at Canteaux, TNA, Adm. 1:2453; *Journals of the House of Commons* (London, 1804), 19:741; Olaf Uwe Janzen, "The Problem of Piracy in the Newfoundland Fishery in the Aftermath of the War of the Spanish Succession," in *Northern Seas: Yearbook 1997, Association for the History of the Northern Seas*, ed. Poul Holm and Olaf Uwe Janzen (Esbjerg, Denmark: Fiskeri- og Søfartsmuseet, 1998), 57–75.

7. Elizabeth Mancke, "Empire and State," in *The British Atlantic World, 1500–1800*, ed. David Armitage and Michael J. Braddick, 2nd ed. (Basingstoke, N.H.: Palgrave Macmillan, 2009), 193–213; Alison Gilbert Olson, *Making Empire Work: London and American Interest Groups, 1690–1790* (Cambridge, Mass.: Harvard University Press, 1992), 94.

8. Entry February 4, 1719, TNA, Adm. 3:31; William A. Pettigrew, *Freedom's Debt: The Royal African Company and the Politics of the Atlantic Slave Trade, 1672–1752* (Chapel Hill: University of North Carolina Press, 2013), 11–44.

9. Entry July 30, 1718, TNA, Adm. 3:31; Pettigrew, *Freedom's Debt*, 81, 157–58; James A. Rawley, *London, Metropolis of the Slave Trade* (Columbia: University of Missouri Press, 2003), 56, 76–81.

10. Pettigrew, *Freedom's Debt*, 81; Rawley, *London, Metropolis*, 42.

11. Addison to CTP, May 27, 1717, TNA, CO 323, no. 89.

12. N. A. M. Rodger, *The Command of the Ocean: A Naval History of Britain, 1649–1815* (London: Allen Lane, 2006), 232.

13. List Book, 1715–1721, TNA, Adm. 8:14; Patrick Crowhurst, *The Defence of British Trade, 1689–1815* (Folkestone, Kent: Dawson, 1977), 180.

14. List Book, 1715–1721, TNA, Adm. 8:14.

15. Instructions to Brand, June 19, 1717, TNA, Adm. 2:49, 262–63.

16. List Book, 1715–1721, TNA, Adm. 8:14.

17. Daniel A. Baugh, "Maritime Strength and Atlantic Commerce: The Uses of 'A Grand Marine Empire,'" in *An Imperial State at War: Britain from 1689 to 1815*, ed. Lawrence Stone (London: Routledge, 1999), 185–223.

18. William A. Pettigrew, "Parliament and the Escalation of the Slave Trade, 1690–1714," *Parliamentary History* 26 (2007): 12.

19. Arne Bialuschewski, "Between Newfoundland and the Malacca Strait: A Survey of the Golden Age of Piracy, 1695–1725," *Mariner's Mirror* 90 (2013): 175; Christian Buchet, "The Royal Navy and the Caribbean, 1689–1763," *Mariner's Mirror* 80 (1994): 31–32; Earle, *Pirate Wars*, 184–87; Rodger, *Command of the Ocean*, 303; Rediker, *Villains of All Nations*, 16–17.

20. See instructions to Brand, Smart, and Pearse, April 11, 1717, TNA, Adm. 2:49, 208–10; instructions to Jacob, June 19, 1717, TNA, Adm. 2:49, 266–69.

21. Entry June 19, 1717, TNA, Adm. 3:31; Lawes to CTP, [August 29, 1717], TNA, CO 138:15, 314–44.

22. Heywood to CTP, December 3, 1716, TNA, CO 137:12, no. 41; Soanes to Hamilton, TNA, CO 152:11, no. 5i.

23. Lawes to the Board, June 21, 1718, TNA, CO 137:13, no. 13; Address of Council and Assembly of Jamaica to the King, August 9, 1718, TNA, CO 137:12, no. 16iii.

24. Entry July 30, 1718, TNA, Adm. 3:31; instructions to Chamberlain, July 30, 1718, TNA, Adm. 2:49, 498–500; Chamberlain to Admiralty, April 29, 1719, TNA, Adm. 1:1597.

25. Instructions to Chamberlain, March 5, 1718, TNA, Adm. 2:49, 384–85.

26. *Boston News-Letter*, August 12, 1717; Hamilton to CTP, March 1, 1717, TNA, CO 152:11, no. 57; Hume to Admiralty, July 3, 1718, TNA, Adm. 1:1879; Ogle to Admiralty, April 14, 1721, TNA, Adm. 1:2242; Ogle to Admiralty, October 6, 1721, TNA, Adm. 1:2242.

27. Entries December 29, 1716, January 5, 1717, and February 25, 1717, TNA, CO 9:3; Lowther to CTP, July 20, 1717, TNA, CO 28:15, no. 24; List Book, 1715–1721, TNA, Adm. 8:14.

28. Hume to Admiralty, July 3, 1718, TNA, Adm. 1:1879; Ogle to Admiralty, April 14, 1721, TNA, Adm. 1:2242; Ogle to Admiralty, October 6, 1721, TNA, Adm. 1:2242.

29. See instructions to Reynolds, Hume, and Rose, March 4, 1717, TNA, Adm. 2:49, 185; instructions to Brand, Smart, and Pearse, April 11, 1717, TNA, Adm. 2:49, 208–10; instructions to Ogle, November 24, 1720, TNA, Adm. 2:50, 290–93.

30. Instructions to Harris, June 6, 1722, TNA, Adm. 2:50, 527; Brand to Admiralty, July 16, 1723, TNA, Adm. 1:1472; Harris to Admiralty, November 16, 1723, TNA, Adm. 1:1880; Harris to Admiralty, April 3, 1725, TNA, Adm. 1:1880; Brand to Admiralty,

December 23, 1725, TNA, Adm. 1:1473; Brand to Admiralty, April 7, 1726, TNA, Adm. 1:1473; Bialuschewski, "Between Newfoundland and the Malacca Strait," 180.

31. Brand to Admiralty, December 4, 1717, TNA, Adm. 1:1472; Brand to Admiralty, March 10, 1718, TNA, Adm. 1:1472.

32. CTP to Addison, May 31, 1717, TNA, CO 324:10, 117–20; *Boston News-Letter*, December 9, 1717; entry December 18, 1718, TNA, Adm. 3:31.

33. CTP to Hamilton, April 4, 1718, TNA, CO 153:13, 278–82.

34. Bialuschewski, "Between Newfoundland and the Malacca Strait," 176.

35. CTP to Craggs, March 27, 1718, TNA, CO 38:7, 338–39; CTP to Craggs, July 1, 1718, TNA, CO 38:7, 343–44.

36. H. M. Warrant to Governors of Plantations, July 11, 1718, TNA, CO 324:33, 170–78.

37. Lawes to CTP, April 28, 1719, TNA, CO 137:13, no. 31; extract of Lawes to Craggs, April 28, 1719, TNA, CO 137:13, no. 31i; Lawes to CTP, December 6, 1719, TNA, CO 137:13, no. 39.

38. 8 Geo., c. 24.

39. Portland to Carteret, July 25, 1723, TNA, CO 137:14, ff. 223–24.

40. Anonymous paper on the sugar trade, [July 22,] 1724, TNA, CO 388:24, no. 155.

41. Michael Craton, *A History of the Bahamas* (London: Collins, 1968), 93; copy of a letter from CTP to Stanhope, March 24, 1716, TNA, CO 23:12, no. 70i.

42. Pulleine to CTP, April 22, 1714, TNA, CO 37:10, no. 4.

43. CTP to Addison, May 31, 1717, TNA, CO 324:10, 117–20.

44. Representation of CTP, December 14, 1715, TNA, CO 23:12, no. 70ii; CTP to Methuen, September 13, 1716, TNA, CO 23:12, no. 72; CTP to Methuen, January 17, 1717, TNA, CO 5:382, no. 18.

45. John Brewer, *The Sinews of Power: War, Money, and the English State, 1688–1783* (New York: Alfred A. Knopf, 1989), 122.

46. William Wood, *A Survey of Trade* (London, 1718), 193.

47. Petition of merchants trading to America to the King, TNA, CO 5:1265, no. 76iv.

48. Rogers to Lords Proprietors of the Bahamas, TNA, CO 5:1265, no. 76ii; Addison to CTP, September 3, 1717, TNA, CO 152:12, no. 34; Rogers's Memorial to the King, TNA, CO 5:1265, no. 76iii; Tim Beattie, "Adventuring Your Estate: The Origins, Costs, and Rewards of Woodes Rogers's Privateering Voyage of 1708–11," *The Mariner's Mirror* 93 (2013): 143–55.

49. *Boston News-Letter*, May 20, 1717, May 27, 1717, June 3, 1717, Oct. 27, 1718; James Logan to [Robert Hunter], October 16, 1718, in Arne Bialuschewski, "Blackbeard off Philadelphia: Documents Pertaining to the Campaign against the Pirates in 1717 and 1718," *Pennsylvania Magazine of History and Biography* 134 (2010): 176.

50. Instructions for Brand, Smart, and Pearse, April 11, 1717, TNA, Adm. 2:49,

208–10; instructions to Brand, June 19, 1717, TNA, Adm. 2:49, 262–63; instructions to Pearse, June 19, 1717, TNA, Adm. 2:49, 263–65; instructions to Smart, June 19, 1717, TNA, Adm. 2:49, 265–66.

51. Lawes to CTP, December 10, 1722, TNA, CO 137:14, ff. 184–87.

52. Memorial to the King, July 8, 1726, TNA, CO 5:10, no. 183.

53. Governor and Council of South Carolina to CTP, October 21, 1718, TNA, CO 5:1265, no. 121.

54. Governor and Council of South Carolina to CTP, October 21, 1718, TNA, CO 5:1265, no. 121; Johnson to CTP, December 27, 1719, TNA, CO 5:1265, no. 143.

55. Governor and Council of South Carolina to CTP, October 21, 1718, TNA, CO 5:1265, no. 121; *Boston News-Letter*, December 29, 1718; *The Tryals of Major Stede Bonnet, and Other Pirates* (London, 1719), iii–vi.

56. Governor and Council of South Carolina to CTP, December 12, 1718, TNA, CO 5:1265, no. 119; *Boston News-Letter*, December 29, 1718.

57. Spotswood to CTP, December 22, 1718, TNA, CO 5:1318, no. 61; Captain's Logs, *Pearl*, July 26, 1715, to December 8, 1719, entry November 17, 1718, TNA, Adm. 51:672; Brand to Admiralty, February 6, 1719, TNA, Adm. 1:1472; *Weekly Journal, Or, British Gazetteer*, April 25, 1719.

58. Although the inhabitants of North Carolina wrote to Spotswood requesting his assistance against Blackbeard, it is clear from the surviving evidence that aiding these inhabitants was not the chief motivation for this voyage. Alexander Spotswood to Mr. Secretary Craggs, October 22, 1718, in *The Official Letters of Alexander Spotswood*, ed. R. A. Brock (Richmond, Va.: The Society, 1882), 1:305; Spotswood to Gordon, November 24, 1718, TNA, Adm. 1:1826; Brand to Admiralty, February 6, 1719, TNA, Adm. 1:1472; Alexander Spotswood to John Carteret, Earl Granville, February 14, 1719, in *The Colonial Records of North Carolina*, ed. William Saunders (Raleigh, N.C.: P. M. Hale, Printer to the State, 1886), 2:324–25.

59. Lawes to CTP, November 13, 1720, TNA, CO 137:13, no. 45; Vernon to Admiralty, April 18, 1721, TNA, Adm. 1:2624; deposition of Walter Moor, March 1724, TNA, CO 152:14, ff. 289–289v.

60. Deposition of Walter Moor, March 1724, TNA, CO 152:14, ff. 289–289v.

61. Ibid.

62. Bialuschewski, "Pirates, Markets, and Imperial Authority," 56.

63. Information of Graves, May 1715, TNA, CO 5:1264, no. 146i; copy of a letter from Carolina, dated in August 1716, TNA, CO 5:382, no. 18i; Musson to CTP, July 5, 1717, TNA, CO 5:1265, no. 73; deposition of Robert Daniell, July 14, 1716, TNA, CO 5:387, no. 5; deposition of John Vickers, TNA, CO 5:1317, no. 45i; Bialuschewski, "Pirates, Markets, and Imperial Authority," 57.

64. Copartners for settling Bahama Islands to CTP, [May 19, 1721], TNA, CO 23:1, no. 31.

65. Rogers to Craggs, January 24, 1719, TNA, CO 23:12, no. 25–27; Governor and Council of the Bahamas to CTP, January 15, 1720, TNA, CO 23:1, no. 22; Rogers to CTP, April 20, 1720, TNA, CO 23:1, no. 23; Governor and Council of the Bahamas to Craggs, November 26, 1720, TNA, CO 23:13, no. 55–80; Rogers to Newcastle, August 26, 1727, TNA, CO 23:12, no. 90ii.

66. Some of those who originally submitted to the pardon changed their minds when it was clear that their previous employment was more rewarding. Governor Woodes Rogers to the Council of Trade and Plantations, October 31, 1718, TNA, CO 23:1, no. 10; Bialuschewski, "Between Newfoundland and the Malacca Strait," 175–76.

67. Governor Rogers to Mr. Secretary Craggs, December 24, 1718, TNA, CO 23:13, no. 20–24; copy of the trial of 10 pirates condemned at Nassau, New Providence, by Governor, Judges, and 7 Commissioners appointed by him, [December 4, 1719], TNA, CO 23:1, nos. 22, 22i.

68. Rogers to CTP, October 31, 1718, TNA, CO 23:1, no. 10.

69. Bialuschewski, "Pirates, Markets, and Imperial Authority," 52–65; Guy Chet, *The Ocean Is a Wilderness* (Amherst: University of Massachusetts Press, 2014), 53.

70. Plunkett to RAC, April 16, 1719, TNA, T 70:6, 97–98; Snelgrave to Morice, April 30, 1719, BOE, 10A61/1.

71. Browne to Admiralty, June 4, 1722, TNA, Adm. 1:1472; letter from Hope, June 25, 1723, TNA, CO 37:26, no. 27; Brand to Admiralty, December 23, 1725, TNA, Adm. 1:1473.

72. See Hanna, *Pirate Nests*, 365–415.

73. Mark G. Hanna, "Well-Behaved Pirates Seldom Make History: A Reevaluation of the Golden Age of English Piracy," in *Governing the Sea in the Early Modern Era*, ed. Peter C. Mancell and Carole Shammas (San Marino, Calif.: Huntington Library Press, 2015), 134.

74. Account of Richard Lasinby, [March] 1722, BL, IOR/E/1/13, no. 98; directors to Lords Justices, August 9, 1723, BL, IOR/E/1/202, 73; Marina Carter, "Pirates and Settlers: Economic Interactions on the Margins of Empire," in *Fringes of Empire: People, Places, and Spaces in Colonial India*, ed. Sameetah Agha and Elizabeth Kolsky (New Delhi: Oxford University Press, 2009), 60.

75. Orme to Admiralty, May 17, 1723, TNA, Adm. 1:2242.

76. Bialuschewski, "Between Newfoundland and the Malacca Strait," 180–81.

77. See Gooch to Newcastle, September 21, 1727, TNA, CO 5:1337, no. 37; deposition of Batting, February 1, 1729, TNA, CO 5:1321, ff. 115–115v; Gooch to CTP, March 29, 1729, TNA, CO 5:1321, ff. 110–17v; Gordon to Newcastle, November 10, 1731, TNA, CO 5:1234, no. 12.

78. Hamilton to Admiralty, September 19, 1723, TNA, Adm. 1:1880; Worsley to Carteret, January 11, 1724, TNA, CO 28:44, no. 65; Bialuschewski, "Between Newfoundland and the Malacca Strait," 180.

79. Chet, *Ocean Is a Wilderness*, 8–26, 51–65.

80. Lord Archibald Hamilton, *An Answer to an Anonymous Libel* (London, 1718), 43–44; A.B., *The State of the Island of Jamaica* (London: Printed for H. Whitridge, 1726), 54, 61.

81. Drysdale to CTP, July 10, 1724, TNA, CO 5:1319, ff. 199–211v; merchants trading to Jamaica to the CTP, May 31, 1724, TNA, CO 388:24, no. 145.; petition of merchants trading to America, TNA, CO 5:4, no. 27.

The Persistence of Piracy in the British Atlantic

Guy Chet

When commenting on Atlantic piracy, many historians identify the 1720s as an end point, when piracy was finally eradicated through an intense campaign of suppression. To these historians, this reflected the growth of British naval command in the Atlantic world, as British officials on land and sea used the courts and the Royal Navy to confront, chase, capture, and execute pirates.[1] In the first decades of the eighteenth century, according to this view, Britain extended its naval policing to the Atlantic and Caribbean, with demonstrable success in suppressing piracy and turning public opinion against pirates and their commercial and political backers.[2] The Royal Navy functioned as an effective police force, which in the course of one generation (from the late 1690s to the 1720s) transformed the Atlantic from a violent frontier into an orderly locus of maritime commerce.

Although this thesis is widely asserted, there is good reason to reject it. First, Atlantic shipping remained at risk from maritime predators well past the 1720s and into the early nineteenth century, in both wartime and peace. This is supported by marine insurance rates, court records, official reports, and a wealth of anecdotal evidence. Second, Britain's naval policing in the Atlantic was intermittent, unenthusiastic, and ineffectual. Moreover, it took place at port and in coastal waters, rather than on the high seas. Historians tend to overstate Britain's command of oceanic trade routes as well as the intensity of its antipiracy campaign. In fact, British officials dealt with piracy not so much as an obstacle to be eliminated but as a normal aspect of maritime trade. Third, the public, too, remained complicit in piratical activity during the eighteenth and early nineteenth centuries, just as it had been in the seventeenth century, during piracy's Golden Age. Coastal communities did not shun or pursue freebooters but continued to regard them as conventional traders—they shielded them from prosecution, traded in pirated goods, and invested in piratical ventures. Thus, the Atlantic in the eighteenth and early nineteenth centuries remained a wild frontier, in which armed commerce was the norm, not the exception. Piracy was eventually ushered out of the Atlantic indirectly and inadvertently, not through forceful confrontation at sea, but in response to the reduced profitability of contraband in the nineteenth century.

Modern historians tend to be overly credulous about British command of both sea and port. A brief survey of statistical and anecdotal data shows that Atlantic commerce remained violent and predatory well into the nineteenth century. Britain's ineffective antipiracy campaign reflected not only the limits of British power at sea but also its weakness on land. The central government's attempts to extend its jurisdiction beyond coastal waters, monopolize violence at sea, direct law enforcement at port, and sanction some forms of maritime commerce while delegitimizing others were consistently resisted and thwarted by large swaths of British society on both sides of the ocean. In actuality, piracy in the Atlantic continued into the mid-nineteenth century, when it finally met a peaceful demise.

Ineffective Suppression in the Eighteenth Century

Historians who date the demise of Atlantic piracy in the 1720s see in court cases, official reports, and antipiracy statutes evidence of decisive and effective crime fighting. They see the enactment of antipiracy laws in England and America and the muscular prosecution of pirates and their collaborators by imperial officials in 1698–1701 as a sharp turning point that led to the eradication of piracy within twenty-five years.

It is evident, however, that piracy did not disappear in the 1720s. Insurance records indicate that risk levels to Atlantic cargoes remained stable in the 1710s, 1720s, and 1730s, and throughout the rest of the century into the 1820s.[3] If piracy had been eliminated in the 1720s, rates would have reflected it, as the main risks to ships, such as storms and poor navigation, remained constant. Anecdotal evidence likewise confirms that maritime predation remained a constant feature of Atlantic commerce well into the nineteenth century: court records, admiralty records, and newspapers chronicle continued piratical attacks from the late 1720s through the 1730s and on throughout the eighteenth century, on both sides of the Atlantic. Thus, a 1730 admiralty memorial to the king in council suggests granting unmotivated naval captains financial incentives to encourage pursuit of pirates, given that "the seas of America and the West Indies [are] infested with piratical ships . . . which commit frequent depredations upon [English] trade."[4] Indeed Massachusetts governor Jonathan Belcher felt compelled in 1731 by "repeated complaints [of much] molestation from piratical vessels" to outline proper procedures for reporting acts of piracy to the British admiralty.[5] The register of the High Court of Admiralty lists numerous commissions issued and transmitted in 1762 and 1772 to colonial capitals from Barbados to Newfoundland, and all colonies in between, for trying pirates in America.[6]

After the Revolutionary War, the persistence of Atlantic piracy was reflected in American public life as well, in the form of antipiracy legislation, congressional reports, petitions to Congress, piracy trials, and accounts in the press regarding piratical attacks on British and American commerce. Piracy represented a significant risk to shipping and an irksome challenge to governments in Europe and America in the late eighteenth century; and it continued to be so in the nineteenth.[7]

In 1817, the American consul in the Danish colony of Saint Thomas recommended to Secretary of State John Quincy Adams that the United States maintain cruisers in the vicinity to protect American shipping from pirate attacks. He pointed out that the Royal Navy kept a few battleships in the area to escort British merchantmen safely into Caribbean harbors. American ships, by contrast, were dissuaded from traveling into some ports for fear of pirates.[8] Although British efforts met with the approval of the American consul, a report to Parliament on persistent seizures of British merchantmen in the West Indies prompted the London *Times* to complain repeatedly that the Royal Navy was not doing enough to suppress pirates in American waters.[9]

The American consul's fears and the *Times*'s criticisms are borne out by American court records. A survey of piracy cases adjudicated in New Orleans Federal Court reveals the persistence of piracy in the early nineteenth century, before, during, and especially in the decade after the War of 1812.[10] During these years (1815–23), more than three thousand acts of Caribbean piracy were recorded in *Niles' Weekly Register*, and numerous piracy cases were adjudicated in the Supreme Court.[11]

Like Britain, the United States attempted to suppress pirates off its southern coasts and in the West Indies.[12] In March 1819, Congress passed an act "to protect the commerce of the United States and punish the crime of piracy," authorizing the president to employ naval force for commerce protection and to instruct naval commanders "to subdue, seize, take and send into port" pirate ships. This act also authorized merchantmen to oppose and capture pirate vessels and to bring captured pirates to face trial, where they would face penalty of death if convicted. Subsequent Congresses kept these provisions in force.[13] Official records from the 1820s reveal these measures' failure to curb the pirate trade and reflect American frustration over this failure.[14]

The persistence of piracy through the eighteenth century reflected objective problems with naval suppression at sea. The sea is a hostile environment for both ships and crews, representing logistical obstacles to continuous presence and effective monitoring. Navies' ability to police maritime trade routes have therefore always been limited compared with governments' capacities on land. Even in coastal waters, eighteenth-century navies could not prevent blockade running or curb the massive scope of wartime smuggling. Against pirates, navies faced an added obstacle in the fact that naval vessels were ill suited to pirate hunting. As Admiral Edward Vernon pointed out, sending a warship to capture a pirate vessel was like sending a cow to capture a hare.[15] Warships were better suited to deterring pirates, as armed escorts for British commercial convoys.[16]

The greatest obstacles to piracy suppression, however, were not at sea but at port, in the commonly held beliefs of Britons about maritime commerce. It was widely accepted that long-distance trade was a violent affair, since the authority of governments and courts did not extend beyond European waters. Both metropolitan and colonial observers in the eighteenth century viewed the Atlantic as a region in which Britons were free to engage in forms of violence that were unacceptable in Europe.[17] In 1700, Governor William Beeston of Jamaica informed the Board of Trade that he could not rely on officers of the Royal Navy to tackle the scourge of piracy, since they themselves engaged in armed commerce and believed themselves not subject to law.[18]

Maritime powers saw Europe as a zone of law and the world beyond as a place of perpetual war. Indeed, Atlantic commerce took place in a war zone—during the "long eighteenth century" (1688–1815), trade was usually conducted against a backdrop of globalized European wars. But even in peacetime, the Atlantic was a place of chronic violence, where no single power could expect others to accept its jurisdiction, its territorial or commercial claims, and its understanding of the law. Late in the eighteenth century, this sense that the Atlantic was legally distinct from Europe started to change in governmental circles in London, but beyond London, in coastal communities and in America, the old view persisted.[19]

In the sixteenth and seventeenth centuries trading firms enjoyed royal monopolies to trade in certain markets or regions, or in certain goods. Thus, any sea captain—foreign or domestic—who acted in violation of such a monopoly knew that he faced the prospect of attack and forced seizure by the chartered trader or trading company. Merchantmen traveled armed, therefore, to defend themselves against attack from the legal trader in a given market. This state of affairs required the legal trader, as well, to travel armed to tackle interlopers. As a result, merchantmen engaged in long-distance trade were equipped for a form of trade that could and did require the use of force.[20]

Early modern Europeans did not share the modern sensibility that war and violence represent a disruption of normal life, politics, and commerce. Mercantilist concepts of the global economy called for and reflected commercial competition between states. In wartime, British predation on French, Spanish, and Dutch commerce was effective in denying enemies the benefit of supplies, while also enriching Britain. But even in times of peace—of which there were precious few for Britain in the long eighteenth century—plunder reinforced national strength in an economic system conceived as a zero-sum game. Maritime predation was, therefore, a feature of peacetime commerce, just as it was of war. It was integral to imperial rivalry; so much so, that long-distance trade was often regarded as a "mild form of war."[21]

English custom regarding maritime trade accommodated violent seizure at sea. Yet English law—statutory law—increasingly sought to regulate and, eventually, abolish it. But the law, as enacted by Parliament and understood by the court, differed from the legal beliefs, as well as the informed legal opinion, of wide segments of British society.[22] In a political culture in which law, authority, and jurisdiction were not codified, common practice and *common law* were the primary guides as to what was constitutional.[23] By contrast, modern histories of piracy often accept eighteenth-century antipiracy statutes, proclamations, and instructions as reliable reflections of reality on board ships, in port towns, and in local government bureaucracies. If a similar approach were adopted to study contemporary society in the twenty-first century, one might conclude that the government has curbed a host of social ills that, in actuality, it has been impotent to control, such as drug abuse and underage drinking. Antipiracy statutes and prize court procedures are similarly misleading. In fact, the supremacy of local custom and common law over parliamentary statutes and royal decrees from London was particularly evident in matters relating to piracy and contraband trade.[24]

This divergence explains how privateering, for example, was understood in governmental circles in London, on the one hand, and in British ports elsewhere in Britain and the empire, on the other. Critically, this also explains why historians have so readily accepted the dating of piracy's demise in the 1720s. Scholars who argue that piracy was suppressed in the early eighteenth century, and supplanted for over a century by state-sanctioned and state-regulated privateering, accept the legal distinction national governments drew between pirates and privateers. Yet virtually every modern account of piracy that highlights the distinction between piracy and privateering includes a disclaimer that this legal boundary was, in *practical* terms, a vague and moving target.[25] Most modern scholars acknowledge that it was impossible to keep privateers within legal bounds and prevent them from broadening their operations into piracy, often mixing privateering and piracy in the same voyage. This recognition should call into question the legalistic distinction articulated by eighteenth-century governments, turning it to a purely academic one. Yet many modern scholars accept this as a meaningful and real distinction.[26]

As inhabitants of premodern states, however, contemporaries in the seventeenth, eighteenth, and early nineteenth centuries intuitively accepted as a practical and ethical reality the murkiness and irrelevance of the legal categories handed down by central governments.[27] Whereas state authorization for commerce raiding matters a great deal to modern scholars, it was a relatively hollow concept in a society that did not recognize that the state had the jurisdiction, the legal authority, the moral legitimacy, and the practical ability to allow or disallow armed commerce. While eighteenth-century statutes and edicts articulated the criminality and heinousness of piracy, wrecking, and smuggling, English communities continued to practice all these trades and did not consider them illegal, unpatriotic, or even disreputable.

This was reflected in everyday practice and, therefore, also in everyday language. The term *privateer* was a semantic novelty in the early seventeenth century. In time, and for some, it came to signify something distinct from piracy, but in common usage and in most quarters *privateer* simply signified a private ship of war, without suggestion of a government commission to commit seizures at sea. Terms such as *pirate, privateer, filibuster, buccaneer,* and *freebooter* were used interchangeably and synonymously by English, Dutch, and French mariners, in both war and peace.[28] This lack of clarity was not a symptom of laymen's ignorance of the subtleties of law; eminent legal scholars, too, were prone to denying or disregarding the alleged contrast between piracy and privateering.[29] Occasionally, even imperial authorities used these terms inconsistently when referring to commerce raiders.[30]

Since the eighteenth and early nineteenth centuries are widely regarded as a golden age of privateering, historians who argue that piracy had ended in the 1720s accept as credible the legal pretense that privateers were a different species of maritime predator. This contradicts eighteenth-century beliefs, practice, and language. The fact that modern scholars have readily accepted only the legalistic definition of privateering—the parliamentary and court definition—suggests that historians have been overexposed to one side of a robust legal, ideological, and cultural contest over the regulation of maritime trade; the side that eventually, in the mid- and late *nineteenth* century, won.

Modern scholars' own experience of the state—that is, their experience of powerful, effective, and credible state bureaucracies in their daily lives—might explain their willingness to accept as credible certain kinds of evidence, such as statutory law, prize court procedure, privateering commissions and instructions, and parliamentary and court discourse. This, in turn, leads some to an unwarranted credulity regarding premodern state authority, jurisdiction, power, and competence.

These historians see a swift and revolutionary transformation in public attitudes against piracy and toward state authorities between the 1690s and 1720s, thanks to an effective legal, naval, law-enforcement, and public-relations campaign by the British government against pirates and their political and commercial associates. But scholars in other fields of imperial administration have demonstrated the limits of central governments' ability to enforce laws at a distance, in peripheral localities. Although the state's monopoly on violence was articulated in law, it was not accepted as legitimate nor as a practical reality in coastal communities, even as they accepted state sovereignty in other matters. Rather than a meaningful change in the commercial ethics and practices of merchants, consumers, and local officials in

the early eighteenth century, one can see a persistence of old habits and attitudes regarding piracy and illegal trade. This is not surprising, given that this
era was characterized by weak central bureaucracies with limited reach, limited resources, limited manpower, and limited legitimacy in local communities. The result was that the ocean persisted as a zone of violence and armed
commerce, rather than becoming a trading zone regulated by the British
state and policed by its navy.

Conclusion

Oceans, as Henry David Thoreau pointed out, are wild frontiers "reaching
round the globe," only minimally pacified, regulated, and civilized by governments on land: "Serpents, bears, hyenas, tigers rapidly vanish as civilization
advances, but the most populous and civilized city cannot scare a shark far
from its wharves."[31] Similarly, the activities—and the actors—of maritime
predation in the early modern era were, for the most part, beyond the practical reach of central governments, and according to many in Britain and
North America, beyond their legal jurisdiction as well.

Despite efforts by state authorities to eradicate piracy, armed commerce
at sea continued throughout the long eighteenth century, long past its alleged demise in the 1720s. Freebooting was seen as an honest, legitimate,
and conventional trade; indeed, it was understood to be a normal feature
of maritime trade in the long eighteenth century. By contrast, the notion
that landed governments had the jurisdiction to regulate, delegitimize, or
disallow certain commercial practices at sea was seen as novel and specious.
Legalistic distinctions between privateering and piracy were not discernible
in practice, nor widely accepted as legally binding or morally meaningful in
seafaring communities and by local authorities. Since privateers functioned
as pirates, contemporaries in the Atlantic world—both proponents and op-
ponents of freebooting—saw in the eighteenth century not a transition to an
age of privateering (as often claimed by modern scholars) but simply a con-
tinuation of the golden age of piracy.

Piracy was eventually, in the 1830s and 1840s, ushered out of the Atlantic
indirectly and inadvertently, not through forceful confrontation at sea but in
response to the reduced profitability of commerce raiding and smuggling.
First, long-term shifts in the maritime economy made commerce raiding

less profitable in the Atlantic. As Atlantic cargoes declined in value in the eighteenth century—with sugar, fish, and other consumer goods increasingly replacing the gold and silver cargoes of the sixteenth and seventeenth centuries—Euro-American freebooters expanded their operations to newly established trade routes in the Pacific and Indian Oceans, which offered richer prizes. Moreover, in the late eighteenth century, commerce raiding in the Atlantic grew less profitable in comparison with peaceful trade. The opening of new markets in Central and South America, the growing volume of trade, more effective convoy protection, and cheap insurance combined to increase profits from peaceful trade. Merchantmen maximized profits by increasing in size, while avoiding the risks and costs that freebooting entailed—from cannons and munitions to expenses associated with smuggling, such as bribes and fees paid to officials, scouts, guards, and fences. Thus, the long eighteenth century saw a decline in the relative size of Britain's privateering fleet, from 41 percent of all British merchant vessels during the War of the Spanish Succession (1701–14) to just 18 and 9 percent, respectively, during the French Revolutionary Wars (1792–1802) and the Napoleonic Wars (1803–15). While these percentages should be understood in the context of a rapidly growing merchant fleet, the trend points to changing economic incentives against freebooting. This decline took place notwithstanding strong encouragement for privateering from the British government and despite weak anti-privateering efforts by French, Spanish, and American navies.[32]

These long-term forces undermining Atlantic commerce raiding were reinforced by military events and economic policies in the first half of the nineteenth century. Centuries of near constant war had created economic conditions that allowed pirates and illegal traders to prosper and multiply in the sixteenth, seventeenth, and eighteenth centuries. Wartime scarcities, increased demand, disruptions in supply, embargoes, high tariffs, and high taxes produced an expansive and flourishing black market in pirated and contraband goods, which boosted local economies and generated high profits for illegal traders. By contrast, the long peace that followed the Napoleonic Wars created conditions that deflated profits in this black market. Moreover, the following decades saw British tariffs reduced—first gradually, then drastically—and in most cases eliminated altogether.[33] Designed to combat smuggling, British free-trade policies deflated the profitability of piracy as well. Thus, the scope of piracy in the Atlantic diminished peacefully in the decades following the Napoleonic Wars, rather than through a violent campaign of confrontation and suppression by state authorities. By the midcentury mark, piracy in the Atlantic was a thing of the past, even as it persisted in the South Sea and beyond the horn of Africa.

NOTES

I am grateful to the University of Massachusetts Press for allowing me to draw portions of this chapter from my monograph *The Ocean Is a Wilderness: Atlantic Piracy and the Limits of State Authority, 1688–1856* (Amherst: University of Massachusetts Press, 2014).

1. Marcus Rediker, *Between the Devil and the Deep Blue Sea: Merchant Seamen, Pirates, and the Anglo-American Maritime World, 1700–1750* (New York: Cambridge University Press, 1987), 256, 281–85; Marcus Rediker, *Villains of All Nations: Atlantic Pirates in the Golden Age* (Boston: Beacon Press, 2004), 127, 144; Robert Ritchie, *Captain Kidd and the War against the Pirates* (Cambridge, Mass.: Harvard University Press, 1986), vi, 235–36; Robert Ritchie, "Government Measures against Piracy and Privateering in the Atlantic Area, 1750–1850," in *Pirates and Privateers: New Perspectives on the War on Trade in the Eighteenth and Nineteenth Centuries*, ed. David Starkey, E. S. van Eyck van Heslinga, and Jaap de Moor (Exeter, UK: University of Exeter Press, 1997), 10–12, 16; N. A. M. Rodger, *The Command of the Ocean: A Naval History of Britain, 1649–1815* (New York: W. W. Norton, 2005), 232; Daniel Baugh, ed., *Naval Administration 1715–1750* (London: Printed for the Navy Records Society, 1977), xiii; David Starkey, *British Privateering Enterprise in the Eighteenth Century* (Exeter, UK: University of Exeter Press, 1990), 19; James Lydon, *Pirates, Privateers, and Profits* (Upper Saddle River, N.J.: Gregg Press, 1970), 30–33, 36–59, 260; Janice Thomson, *Mercenaries, Pirates, and Sovereigns: State-Building and Extraterritorial Violence in Early Modern Europe* (Princeton: Princeton University Press, 1994), 51–53; Peter Galvin, *Patterns of Pillage: A Geography of Caribbean-Based Piracy in Spanish America, 1536–1718* (New York: Peter Lang, 1999), 1; Kris E. Lane, *Pillaging the Empire: Piracy in the Americas, 1500–1750* (Armonk, N.Y.: M. E. Sharpe, 1998), 165, 191; Mark Hanna, "The Pirate Nest: The Impact of Piracy on Newport, Rhode Island, and Charles Town, South Carolina, 1670–1730" (PhD diss., Harvard University, 2006), 9; Joel Baer, "General Introduction," *British Piracy in the Golden Age: History and Interpretation, 1660–1730* (London: Pickering and Chatto, 2007), 1:xiv, xvii; Benerson Little, *The Sea Rover's Practice: Pirate Tactics and Techniques, 1630–1730* (Washington, D.C.: Potomac Books, 2005), 15–16; Shirley Hughson, *The Carolina Pirates and Colonial Commerce, 1640–1740* (Baltimore: Johns Hopkins University Press, 1894), 128; C. H. Haring, *The Buccaneers in the West Indies in the Seventeenth Century* (London: E.

P. Dutton, 1910), 272; Jennifer Marx, *Pirates and Privateers of the Caribbean* (Malabar, Fla.: Krieger, 1992), 8–9.

2. Ritchie, "Government Measures against Piracy and Privateering," 11–12, 16; Rediker, *Between the Devil and the Deep Blue Sea*, 282–85; Lane, *Pillaging the Empire*, 165, 191.

3. See Guy Chet, *The Ocean Is a Wilderness* (Amherst: University of Massachusetts Press, 2014), 10–14.

4. Baugh, *Naval Administration*, 62.

5. *By His Excellency Jonathan Belcher, Esq; A Proclamation. Whereas His Majesty Hath Received Repeated Complaints, That the Trade of His Subjects in the West-Indies, and Else-Where, Suffers Much Damage and Molestation from Piratical Vessels* (Boston: B. Green, 1731); *The Tryals of Sixteen Persons for Piracy, &c. . . . on Monday the Fourth Day of July, Anno Dom. 1726* (Boston: Printed for and sold by Joseph Edwards, 1726); John Cockburn, *A Faithful Account of the Distresses and Adventures of John Cockburn* (London, 1740); *Boston News-Letter*, October 31–November 8, 1734, 1; *Boston News-Letter*, June 26–July 3, 1735, 2; *Weekly Rehearsal*, April 14, 1735, 2.

6. John Jameson, ed., *Privateering and Piracy in the Colonial Period* (1923; repr., New York: A.M. Kelley, 1970), 579–80; *The Following Circumstances Relating to the Famous Ansell Nickerson* (Boston, 1773). See also T 1/380/37, Treasury Board Papers and In-Letters, UK National Archives, Kew; Henry Atton and Henry Holland, *The King's Customs* (New York: A. M. Kelley, 1967), 1:337, 469.

7. Edward White, "The Marshall Court and International Law: The Piracy Cases," *American Journal of International Law* 83 (1989): 730; Gardner Allen, *Our Navy and the West Indian Pirates* (Salem, Mass.: Essex Institute, 1929), 3, 11; U.S. Congressional Serial Set (USCSS), H.R. Doc. No. 25-129.

8. Caspar Goodrich, *Our Navy and the West Indian Pirates: A Documentary History* (Annapolis, Md.: U.S. Naval Institute, 1916–17), 1480; Allen, *Our Navy*, 11–12.

9. *Times* (London), July 24, 1822, 3c; August 1, 1822, 3a–b; August 8, 1822, 2d; and November 18, 1822, 2d–e. See also Matthew McCarthy, *Privateering, Piracy, and British Policy in Spanish America, 1810–1830* (Woodbridge, U.K.: Boydell, 2013), 149–51.

10. Data collected from a database of the U.S. National Archives Southwest Region indicates that 8 cases were adjudicated there in the three years prior to the War of 1812, 40 cases during the war, and 124 cases in the twelve years following the war's end.

11. Kenneth Scott, "Bonaparte Toscan and the Cuban Pirates," *American Neptune: A Quarterly Journal of Maritime History* 6 (1946): 93; White, "The Marshall Court," 727, 733. *Niles' Weekly Register* was an American weekly news magazine.

12. Great Britain, Admiralty Office, "Pirate Vessels" (June 30, 1823), Peabody Essex Museum collections, 517; Goodrich, *Our Navy*, 314–17, 492–94, 1456–75, 1470–71,

1473–80, 1932–33, 1939; Allen, *Our Navy*, 2–4, 6–25; Richard Lowe, "American Seizure of Amelia Island," *Florida Historical Quarterly* 45 (1966): 22–23, 24n28, 27; Edwin Dickinson, "Is the Crime of Piracy Obsolete?," *Harvard Law Review* 38 (1925): 348–49; Francis Bradlee, *Piracy in the West Indies and Its Suppression* (1923; repr., Glorieta, N.Mex.: Rio Grande Press, 1990), 23, 29–30, 33–37; W. H. Beehler, "The United States Navy and West India Piracy 1821–25," *Frank Leslie's Popular Monthly* 29 (1890): 2–3, 4–16.

13. Allen, *Our Navy*, 17, 97–98.

14. uscss, S. Doc. No. 16-100; H.R. Doc. No. 16-38; H.R. Rep. No. 17-53; H.R. Doc. No. 17-8; S. Doc. No. 17-4; H.R. Rep. No. 18-124; H.R. Doc. No. 18-6; H.R. Doc. No. 18-14; H.R. Rep. No. 81-22; H.R. Rep. No. 18-47; Goodrich, *Our Navy*, 314–15, 1932–34; Allen, *Our Navy*, 15–16, 19–21; *A Correct Report of the Trial of Josef Perez for Piracy* (New York: J. W. Bell, 1823); a member of the bar, *A Brief Sketch of the Occurrences on Board the Brig Crawford on Her Voyage from Matanzas to New York* (Richmond: Samuel Shephard, 1827); *Piracy and Murder: Particulars of the Horrid and Atrocious Murders Committed on Board of the Brig Crawford* (New York: E. M. Murden and A. Ming Jr., 1827); *The Trial of Peter Heamen and Francois Gautiez before the High Court of Admiralty at Edinburgh . . . for Piracy and Murder* (Leith: Printed at the Commercial List Office for William Reid, 1821); Ferdinand Bayer, trans., *Dying Declaration of Nicholas Fernandez, Who with Nine Others Were Executed in Front of Cadiz Harbour, December 29, 1829. For Piracy and Murder on the High Seas* (New York, 1830); *The Confession of Chas. Gibbs Alias James Jeffreys, Who Has Been Sentenced to Be Executed at N. York, on the 22d April 1831 for Piracy and Murder on Board the Brig Vineyard* (Boston, 1831); congressional stenographer, *A Report of the Trial of Pedro Gibert, Bernardo de Soto . . . on an Indictment Charging Them with the Commission of an Act of Piracy, on Board the Brig Mexican, of Salem* (Boston: Russell, Odiorne, and Metcalf, 1834); 1/1/4, 1/2/4, Central Criminal Court: Depositions, uk National Archives, Kew.

15. Parke Rouse, "Early Shipping between England and Chesapeake Bay," *The American Neptune: A Quarterly Journal of Maritime History* 30 (1970): 133–35; Allen, *Our Navy*, 3; Galvin, *Patterns of Pillage*, 37; Rediker, *Villains of All Nations*, 29.

16. See Patrick Crowhurst, *The Defence of British Trade, 1689–1815* (Folkestone, uk: Dawson, 1977), 43–80.

17. Eliga Gould, "Zones of Law, Zones of Violence: The Legal Geography of the British Atlantic, circa 1772," *William and Mary Quarterly* 60 (2003): 474; Anne Pérotin-Dumon, "The Pirate and the Emperor: Power and the Law on the Seas, 1450–1850," in *Bandits of the Sea: A Pirate Reader*, ed. C. R. Pennell (New York: New York University Press, 2001), 29–30; Alejandro Colas and Bryan Mabee, "The Flow and Ebb of Private Seaborne Violence in Global Politics: Lessons from the Atlantic World, 1689–1815," in *Mercenaries, Pirates, Bandits, and Empires: Private Violence in Historical Context*, ed. Alejandro Colas and Bryan Mabee (New York: Columbia

University Press, 2010), 87; Jan Glete, *Navies and Nations: Warships, Navies, and State Building in Europe and America, 1500–1860* (Stockholm: Almqvist and Wiksell International 1993), 2:478; Hanna, "The Pirate Nest," 174. From the perspective of treaty law, the idea that law and order—and treaties—did not extend beyond "the line" (west of the prime meridian, south of the Tropic of Cancer) originated in the 1559 Treaty of Cateau-Cambresis between France and Spain. However, this legal doctrine merely codified, or reflected, the state of perpetual violence and war in the Atlantic. Since European courts and enforcement agencies did not extend "beyond the line," one could not expect legal protection or remedy in those waters.

18. Hanna, "The Pirate Nest," 129–30.

19. Gould, "Zones of Law," 479–81, 507–9.

20. Pérotin-Dumon, "The Pirate and the Emperor," 29–30.

21. Bryan Mabee, "Pirates, Privateers, and the Political Economy of Private Violence," *Global Change, Peace, and Security* 21 (2009): 140, 145 (quoting maritime historian J. H. Parry), 151; Richard Pares, *War and Trade in the West Indies, 1739–1763* (Oxford: Clarendon Press, 1936), 410; John McNeill, *Atlantic Empires of France and Spain: Louisbourg and Havana, 1700–1763* (Chapel Hill: University of North Carolina Press, 1985), 241n72; Colas and Mabee, "Flow and Ebb of Private Seaborne Violence," 87; Timothy Sullivan, "The Devil's Brethren: Origins and Nature of Pirate Counterculture, 1600–1730" (PhD diss., University of Texas at Arlington, 2003), 287; Glete, *Navies and Nations*, 1:117.

22. See Christopher Hill, *Liberty against the Law: Some Seventeenth-Century Controversies* (New York: Penguin Books, 1996); Georg Friedrich de Martens, *An Essay on Privateers, Captures and Particularly on Recaptures, According to the Law, Treaties and Usages of the Maritime Powers of Europe*, trans. Thomas Hartwell Horne (London: Printed for E. and R. Brooks et al., 1801), 2–3, 29; Johan Friderich Schlegel, *Neutral Rights, or, An Impartial Examination of the Right of Search of Neutral Vessels under Convoy: and of a Judgment Pronounced by the English Court of Admiralty the 11th June, 1799, in the Case of the Swedish Convoy* (Philadelphia: Printed at the Aurora Office, 1801), 46–47, 85–86; Virginia Lunsford, *Piracy and Privateering in the Golden Age Netherlands* (New York: Palgrave Macmillan, 2005), 3, 6.

23. Jack Greene, "The Glorious Revolution and the British Empire, 1688–1783," in *The Revolution of 1688–1689*, ed. Lois Schwoerer (Cambridge: Cambridge University Press, 1992), 263–66; Jack Greene, *Peripheries and Center: Constitutional Development in the Extended Polities of the British Empire and the United States, 1607–1788* (Athens: University of Georgia Press, 1986), 62–65, 75, 235n18; James Henretta, *"Salutary Neglect": Colonial Administration under the Duke of Newcastle* (Princeton: Princeton University Press, 1972), 319; Linda Colley, *Britons: Forging the Nation, 1707–1837* (New Haven, Conn.: Yale University Press, 2009), xiv–xv, 378–81.

24. Statutory law is not necessarily made up exclusively of statutes passed by legis-

latures. Rather, it is a legal system in which the source of what is the law is a written code (a combination of statutes, regulations, proclamations, and even judicial decisions), which supersedes communal customs and legal beliefs. In the early modern era, the vast majority of Germans, Englishmen, and Americans adhered instead to a system of common law, in which judicial judgments are based on the legal norms and beliefs of the community.

25. Ritchie, "Government Measures against Piracy and Privateering," 10–12, 16–19. See also Faye Kert, *Trimming Yankee Sails: Pirates and Privateers of New Brunswick* (Fredericton, Neb.: Goose Lane Edition, 2005), 13; Carl Swanson, *Predators and Prizes: American Privateering and Imperial Warfare, 1739–1748* (Columbia, S.C.: University of South Carolina Press, 1991), 5–6; Roger Marsters, *Bold Privateers: Terror, Plunder, and Profit on Canada's Atlantic Coast* (Halifax, N.S.: Formac, 2004), 6; Galvin, *Patterns of Pillage*, 4–5; Hughson, *Carolina Pirates*, 14–15; Rodger, *Command of the Ocean*, 162; Sullivan, "The Devil's Brethren," 283–84, 286–87; Starkey, *British Privateering Enterprise*, 31, 245; Jameson, *Privateering and Piracy*, ix; Lunsford, *Piracy and Privateering*, 1–3, 31–33, 41–43, 47–49; John Bromley, *Corsairs and Navies, 1660–1760* (London: Hambledon Press, 1987), 407–8; Haring, *Buccaneers in the West Indies*, 240; Peter Earle, *The Pirate Wars* (New York: Thomas Dunne, 2005), 195; Little, *Sea Rover's Practice*, 19–20; Luke Pike, *A History of Crime in England* (Montclair, N.J.: Patterson Smith, 1968), 2:371; Jerome Garitee, *The Republic's Private Navy: The American Privateering Business as Practiced by Baltimore during the War of 1812* (Middletown, Conn.: Published for Mystic Seaport by Wesleyan University Press, 1977), 4–5, 7–8, 153, 226; James Cable, *The Political Influence of Naval Force in History* (New York: St. Martin's Press, 1998), 26.

26. See, for example, Starkey, *Pirates and Privateers*, 3–4; Ritchie, "Government Measures against Piracy and Privateering," 18–19.

27. See, for example, Martens, *Essay on Privateers*, 2–3, 29; Schlegel, *Neutral Rights*, 46–47, 85–86; Lunsford, *Piracy and Privateering*, 3, 6.

28. *Sun* 545 (June 27, 1794); *Morning Post* 15595 (March 10, 1821); *An Appeal to the Government and Congress of the United States against the Depredations Committed by American Privateers on the Commerce of Nations at Peace with Us* (New York, 1819), 53–55; *Boston News-Letter* 1637 (June 26–July 3, 1735): 2; John Esquemeling, *The Buccaneers of America* (1678; repr., London: George Allen and Unwin, 1951), ix; Woodes Rogers, *Life Aboard a British Privateer in the Time of Queen Anne: Being the Journal of Captain Woodes Rogers, Master Mariner* (1889; repr., London: Conway Maritime Press, 1970), 87; Lunsford, *Piracy and Privateering*, 3, 178, 207; Donald Shomette, *Pirates on the Chesapeake: Being a True History of Pirates, Picaroons, and Raiders on Chesapeake Bay* (Centreville, Md.: Tidewater Publishers, 1985), 230–32, 239; Hanna, "The Pirate Nest," 36; Bromley, *Corsairs and Navies*, 5–6; W. Frank Craven, "The Earl of Warwick, a Speculator in Piracy," *Hispanic American Historical Review* 10 (1930): 459;

Richard Pares, *Colonial Blockade and Neutral Rights, 1739–1763* (Oxford: Oxford University Press, 1938), 22; Gomer Williams, *History of the Liverpool Privateers and Letters of Marque, with an Account of the Liverpool Slave Trade* (London: W. Heinemann, 1897), 300.

29. Martens, *Essay on Privateers*, 3n; Schlegel, *Neutral Rights*, 46–47, 85–86.

30. Britain, Public Record Office, *Calendar of State Papers, Colonial Series*, 40 vols. (London, 1860–1939), 14:634; Robert Beatson, *Naval and Military Memoirs of Great Britain, from 1727 to 1783*, 6 vols. (London: Printed for Longman, Hurst, Rees and Orme, 1804), 5:27, 6:146, 244; James Brown Scott, ed., *The Armed Neutralities of 1780 and 1800: A Collection of Official Documents* (New York: Oxford University Press, 1918), 331–32. Other instances can be found in 42/25/209, Home Office, UK National Archives, Kew; Britain, Public Record Office, *Calendar of State Papers, Colonial Series*, 14:639–40, 16:326.

31. Henry David Thoreau, *Cape Cod* (Boston: Ticknor and Fields, 1866), 174–75.

32. Henning Hillmann and Christina Gathmann, "Overseas Trade and the Decline of Privateering," *Journal of Economic History* 71 (2011): 731–33, 740–49; David Starkey, "A Restless Spirit: British Privateering Enterprise, 1739–1815," in *Pirates and Privateers: New Perspectives on the War on Trade in the Eighteenth and Nineteenth Centuries*, ed. David Starkey, E. S. van Eyck van Heslinga, and Jaap de Moor (Exeter, UK: University of Exeter Press, 1997), 137–39; Kenneth Porter, ed., *The Jacksons and the Lees: Two Generations of Massachusetts Merchants, 1765–1844*, 2 vols. (Cambridge, Mass.: Harvard University Press 1937), 1:21–22.

33. For the dramatic effects of Britain's free-trade policies on smuggling, see W. D. Chester, *Chronicles of the Customs Department* (London: R. Clay, Sons and Taylor, 1885), 51; Neville Williams, *Contraband Cargoes: Seven Centuries of Smuggling* (Hamden, Conn.: Shoestring Press, 1961), 204, 221; John Banks, *Reminiscences of Smugglers and Smuggling* (1871; repr., Newcastle, UK: F. Graham, 1966), 5; Charles Harper, *The Smugglers: Picturesque Chapters in the Story of an Ancient Craft* (Newcastle, UK: Frank Cass, 1966), 12–14; W. A. Cole, "Trends in Eighteenth-Century Smuggling," *Economic History Review* 10 (1958): 395; Frank Bowen, *Ships for All* (London: Ward Lock, 1952), 216; Kenneth Clark, *Many a Bloody Affray: The Story of Smuggling in the Port of Rye and District* (Rye, UK: Rye Museum, 1968), 28; Jeremy Black, *The British Seaborne Empire* (New Haven, Conn.: Yale University Press, 2004), 193; Cal Winslow, "Sussex Smugglers," in *Albion's Fatal Tree: Crime and Society in Eighteenth-Century England*, ed. Douglas Hay et al. (New York: Pantheon, 1975), 144, 147; G. D. Ramsay, *English Overseas Trade during the Centuries of Emergence* (London: Macmillan, 1957), 166–67, 173, 175.

Modeling Piracy

A Model of Piracy

THE BUCCANEERS OF THE SEVENTEENTH-CENTURY CARIBBEAN

Virginia W. Lunsford

The spate of attacks by pirates in recent years has taken the world by surprise.[1] In the early years of the twenty-first century, piracy erupted in the Strait of Malacca, a key channel bordered by Indonesia, Singapore, and Malaysia through which 40 percent of maritime trade must transit. Simultaneously, pirates from the East African nation Somalia began to capture vessels in the Gulf of Aden, the Red Sea, and the Indian Ocean, and over time, their activities and range steadily increased, coming to a head in 2011. That piracy exists today—and exists in powerful enough form to result in hundreds of attacks and captures—surprises many. Indeed, this is not the mythical and romanticized piracy of Hollywood, with rugged tall ships flying the Jolly Roger while swashbuckling captains search for buried treasure. No, modern piracy—like all true piracy—is frightening, disturbing, and costly.

It has also been challenging to eradicate. For instance, in East African waters, in the Gulf of Aden and off Somalia's coast, various naval assets, including a multinational naval task force with U.S. Navy participation (called Combined Task Force 151), have been conducting counterpiracy operations since 2009, and while there has been a striking decrease in piratical activity, the problem remains.[2] "While the effectiveness of naval disruption operations has increased and more pirates have been arrested and prosecuted, this has not stopped piracy," cautioned United Nations Secretary-General Ban Ki-moon in 2011. "The trend of the increased levels of violence employed by the pirates as well as their expanding reach is disconcerting."[3] Despite the recent decline in Somali piracy, for example, experts warn that it could again intensify, as the causes for piracy remain intact and have even spread geographically.[4] In other words, piracy has been stifled but not eliminated. It is worrisome that in November 2016, for the first time in two and a half years, Somali pirates attacked a merchant ship, a Korean tanker. Only time will tell if this is an isolated incident or the resumption of the earlier trend.[5] Meanwhile, piracy has erupted off the coast of West Africa, especially around Nigeria, and presents a growing problem.[6] Moreover, piracy is again on the rise in Southeast Asia, this time in the waters near the Philippines and Indonesia and perpetrated by the Philippine insurgent group Abu Sayyaf.[7]

Ban Ki-moon's frustrations have long been felt by those charged with suppressing piracy, for as history reveals, the problem of entrenched and flourishing piracy has never been solved by high seas naval action alone. The so-called golden age of piracy, from approximately 1530 to around 1730, was the time when seagoing robbery was most extensive, prevalent, threatening, and profitable. Throughout the era and around the globe, a variety of piratical groups practiced their trade. Their depredations challenged the authority of the expanding European empires and the nascent world economy. "Pirates created an imperial crisis with their relentless and successful attacks upon merchants' property and international commerce," writes Marcus Rediker about piracy vis-à-vis the eighteenth-century British. "Their numbers," he continues, "were extraordinary, and their plunderings were exceptional in both volume and value."[8] His comment could be equally applied to the Dutch, the French, the Portuguese, and the party who probably was victimized most severely, the Spanish.

Those authorities who endeavor to combat contemporary piracy would be wise to learn from the golden age of piracy of the sixteenth, seventeenth, and eighteenth centuries. These early modern episodes provide instructive case studies that reveal how piracy blooms and flourishes over time. In turn, they offer us ways to analyze the pirates of the contemporary world—including those now operating off the coasts of Nigeria and the Philippines—so that we can ascertain these modern raiders' viability and gain insight in how to suppress them. Although the means, ends, locations, and character of the various historical pirate groups often differed noticeably from one another, pirate communities that achieved a lengthy and remunerative existence shared several key qualities. In sum, long-term, intractable, thriving piracy is a complex activity that relies on the following six integral factors: (1) an available population of potential recruits; (2) access to goods (via vulnerable trade routes or places where wealth is stockpiled); (3) at least one secure base of operations; (4) a sophisticated organization; (5) some degree of outside support; and (6) cultural bonds engendering vibrant group solidarity. Actions that interfere with the smooth workings of any of these factors, especially more than one, weaken piracy's sustainability.

The Buccaneers' Background

The rise and fall of the Caribbean buccaneers provide an important case study.[9] Who were the buccaneers? The term is often but erroneously used to refer to pirates in general. In actuality, the buccaneers were a specific group of marauders: a motley yet ferocious brotherhood based in the seventeenth-century Caribbean. While various Europeans suffered from their depredations at one time or another, the buccaneers' central operational goals were to assault Spain's American colonies, prey on Spain's lucrative trade in the Americas, and raid Spanish ships bound for Europe. This they did with great brutality and ferocity. The movement expanded over time, ultimately boasting invasion forces numbering hundreds and even thousands of men. The buccaneers captured various Spanish ships, and even more striking, conquered established and sizeable Spanish settlements in the Caribbean, despite the colonies' not insignificant defensive measures. The wealth the marauders plundered was staggering in its value; the number of settlements they attacked and people they savagely tortured and slayed was stunning.

The buccaneers' piratical endeavors were serious, sensational, and sustained over a long period. Their achievements can be attributed, in large part, to the fact that these Caribbean marauders met the six conditions for successful and long-term piracy. They had a steady supply of available (and talented) recruits. Spanish trade in the Caribbean as well as to Spanish colonial settlements, both on the coast and inland, was accessible. They operated from several secure bases of operation. They possessed a sophisticated organization. Several European states offered financial and political support. Finally, intense cultural bonds engendered tight group solidarity. The result was a community of fierce, brutal, and seemingly invincible marauders who voraciously raided and terrorized the Caribbean for decades, with their period of greatest activity ranging from around 1650 through 1700.

Golden Age pirates can be notoriously challenging to research, as extant sources are somewhat scarce. In general, men in the early modern maritime trades were typically itinerant and illiterate, and they experienced high mortality rates, and thus left fewer traces of their existence. Moreover, those involved in allegedly criminal activity (like piracy) did not wish to incriminate themselves by leaving any sort of evidence of their actions.[10] However, a remarkable primary source, Alexandre Exquemelin's *Bucaniers of America*, provides some of our best knowledge about buccaneer exploits and practices.[11] Exquemelin's memoir is that exceptional treasure: a firsthand account written by someone from within a pirate community (Exquemelin served as a "surgeon" [medical officer] during the era of Henry Morgan). Exquemelin's work was first published in Amsterdam in 1678 as *De Americaensche Zee-Roovers* and thereafter translated into various foreign languages and reprinted a myriad of times. It represents a window into the history of this long-lost and elusive brotherhood. In his vivid and densely detailed text, Exquemelin recounted his knowledge about the seventeenth-century West Indies, describing its climate and weather, its flora and fauna, the region's natural resources, the customs of its native American inhabitants, the food and occupations of the colonists, and the colorful lifestyles of local inhabitants. He was no less attentive in presenting information about the buccaneer community. Furthermore, what makes Exquemelin's account even more valuable is that it is generally reliable; modern historians judge it to be largely accurate in its descriptions.[12]

Exquemelin's descriptions include revealing accounts of buccaneer mores, missions, tactics, and means of attack, and thus give us greater insight as to how this force of outsiders could have been so effective in their challenges against the organized state power of Spain. The buccaneers appear to have come into existence organically, evolving from a concentration of dispossessed hunters and liberated indentured servants resident on the islands of Hispaniola and Tortuga. Originally French in origin and always retaining a heavy French contingent, the *boucanier* community, over time, came to include men of a variety of European ethnic backgrounds, most significantly the English and the Dutch.

Exquemelin reported that the buccaneers initiated their first forays around 1602. While that start date may not be accurate (Exquemelin did not arrive on the scene until later), his description of their evolution appears logical. Beginning as bands of boar and cattle hunters on Hispaniola, they expanded and metamorphosed over the years into a marauding brotherhood that targeted colonists, especially the Spanish, ruthlessly. Even more striking, buccaneer warfare escalated and transformed over the course of the century, progressing from mere ship-on-ship attacks waged by buccaneer crews of twenty-five to thirty, to sophisticated amphibious landings that involved hundreds, and ultimately to invasion forces counting thousands of men who raided substantial settlements—sometimes far inland—which after victory, they occupied for weeks or even months. One cautious estimate avers that just between 1655 and 1671 alone, the buccaneers sacked eighteen cities, four towns, and thirty-five villages.[13] The monetary results of these raids were impressive; while earlier practitioners such as the crews of Pierre François of Dunkirk and Bartolomeu Português managed to capture prizes of 100,000 and 70,000 pieces of eight respectively, later missions resulted in heists valued conservatively at 250,000 to 260,000 pieces of eight (and these estimates do not even include ancillary prize proceeds such as slaves, munitions, grain, herds of cattle, and textiles).[14] The buccaneers sought to capture ships, lucrative property, goods, and people (who could be ransomed quickly), for their intent was simply to amass as much wealth as possible.

Although the Spaniards—and later, other European powers who established colonies in the Caribbean—tried to combat the marauders' assaults by sending more soldiers, amassing greater numbers of arms, and erecting stronger fortifications,[15] colonial settlements often remained quite defenseless.[16] Consequently, beyond the loss of goods and capital, the buccaneers left death, despoliation, and destruction in their wake. Part and parcel of the buccaneer style was the constant and often creative use of brutal violence to achieve the desired ends. Exquemelin dispassionately reports, in his wording, "the usual manner" of tortures the buccaneers used to achieve their goal of conquest and plundering.[17] For example, they routinely put their prisoners on the rack, disjointing their arms; in a torture known as "woolding," they twisted cords around their victims' foreheads and wrung so hard that their "eyes bulged out, big as eggs"; they hanged prisoners, whipped and bludgeoned them, sliced off noses and ears, singed faces with burning straws, and finally stabbed them to death.[18] Prisoners were subjected to a torture called "strappado," in which the victim's hands were fastened behind his or her back while he or she was hung by a rope attached to the wrists; this torture caused intense pain and usually dislocated the shoulders. Exquemelin describes captives being wrenched in this fashion "so violently that . . . [their] arms were pulled right out of joint."[19] Captives' hair was set on fire, and they were crushed by rocks and stones until their bodies were bloody and broken.[20] Women were kidnapped, abused, raped, and held for ransom.[21] Children were starved, forced to march long distances, and allowed to perish. Men were hung by their genitals "till the weight of their bodies tore them loose," after which the buccaneers "would give the wretches three or four stabs through the body with a cutlass." The buccaneers were not done. Some prisoners, bound and feet smeared with grease, were roasted. "Others," Exquemelin reports, "they crucified, with burning fuses between their fingers and toes."[22]

Certainly, the barbarous François l'Olonnais stands out for his sheer inventiveness in the infliction of sadistic brutality. On one occasion, according to Exquemelin, "the Buccaneers . . . took a number of prisoners, whom they treated most cruelly, inflicting on these poor folk every torment imaginable." He appears to have been driven by a veritable thirst for blood. "When l'Olonnais had a victim on the rack," Exquemelin writes, "if the wretch did not instantly answer his questions he would hack the man to pieces with his cutlass and lick the blood from the blade with his tongue." At another time, l'Olonnais grew furious when two local men's guidance led the buccaneers into trouble, and his savagery escalated: "Then l'Olonnais being possessed of a devils' fury, ripped open one of the prisoners with his cutlass, tore the living heart out of his body, gnawed at it, and then hurled it in the face of one of the others, saying, 'Show me another way, or I will do the same to you.'"[23]

No less repugnant were the practices of the so-called "maniac" Dutchman, Rock Bresiliaan (also known as Rock the Brazilian). He "perpetrated the greatest atrocities possible against the Spaniards," according to Exquemelin.[24] "Some of them he tied or spitted on wooden stakes and roasted them alive between two fires, like killing a pig."[25] Other sources relate the gruesome tale of a woman captive who, according to Spanish reports, was "set bare upon a baking stove and roasted, because she did not confess of money."[26] Equally grisly was the buccaneer Montbars of Languedoc. He sliced open the stomachs of his prisoners, removed one end of the intestines, and nailed it to a post. He then beat the victim on the buttocks with a burning log, forcing him to dance to death.[27]

In addition to the extreme human suffering, the buccaneers' carnage wrought great damage on Spanish colonial trade because they assaulted the lynchpin of Spain's colonies and indeed the basis of the empire's economy: American bullion, primarily Peruvian silver. Spain's colonies were organized into a system predicated on the fundamental need to ensure the successful mining, transport, and delivery of precious gold and silver. Settlement patterns, military defense, naval operations, and political administration all supported the absolute necessity to safeguard the transit of the annual treasure fleets, with the year's cargo of precious metals, sailing from the West Indies to Seville, Spain. The buccaneers, however, regularly attacked key nodes in this system, pinpointing treasure ports such as Vera Cruz, Cartagena, Porto Bello, and Panama for raids, and causing Spain to spend more money and resources to protect the system's vulnerabilities. Naturally, buccaneer assaults on traffic within the Spanish West Indies dampened local trade as well. As Exquemelin relates, "the Spaniards were compelled to equip . . . frigates to protect their shipping and cruise against the Buccaneers . . . [and] were driven to reduce the number of their [merchant] voyages—but this did them no good."[28]

The Spanish military apparatus guarding Spain's Caribbean colonial system was not inconsequential. On the contrary, it was quite effective against assaults in general. It is easy to focus only on the penetrations of this system, the victories obtained by attackers, and conclude that Spain mounted a flimsy defense against outside challengers. However, the Spanish system was difficult to breach and required both military ingenuity and a concentration of resources on the part of the attackers if they hoped to achieve their goal.[29] While imperfect and sometimes erratic in its implementation, the defense system consisted of a formidable network of designated nodes, including the treasure ports as well as smaller ancillary cities, protected by extensive and often well-armed fortifications, several dedicated naval fleets, local naval patrols, garrisons of Spanish soldiers, and local colonial militias. The Spanish also made it a priority to collect and use relevant intelligence and transported the most valuable cargoes under secrecy and accompanied by heavily armed naval escorts. Havana, the jewel in the Caribbean colonial crown and the most important of the treasure ports, was so heavily protected that attackers never did it any real damage, and indeed, were usually hesitant to attack it at all.[30] As proof that the defensive system largely worked over several centuries, the all-important annual treasure fleet was captured only once, in 1628, despite many attempts to take it.[31]

So how were the buccaneers able to succeed against this formidable Spanish system? What were the keys to the terrifying buccaneer effectiveness? There were many buccaneer advantages, including their striking tactical creativity and flexibility. Paramount, however, was their possession of the six qualities integral to resilient piracy.

The Six Factors of Piracy Applied

First, the buccaneers had access to a vast pool of potential recruits. Their population was comprised of alienated, indigent, and dispossessed sailors, soldiers, hunters, and indentured servants who represented the flotsam and jetsam of the harsh colonial systems of France, England, and the Netherlands. Indeed, the buccaneering movement had its very origin in a coterie of French boar and bull hunters based on French Hispaniola and Tortuga, and these hunters continued to support and join the buccaneers as the movement evolved and expanded over time.[32] Sailors and soldiers drifted into the group as well.[33]

According to Exquemelin, however, indentured servants from the French Tortuga and Hispaniola and from Jamaica, after it fell to the English in 1655, became an especially significant source of men. Their rough lives, typically characterized by "atrocious cruelties" and deprivation, noted Exquemelin, toughened and hardened them, both physically and psychologically.[34] If servants could survive their term of indenture, they were free, but they typically lacked means to support themselves. Thus, they naturally gravitated toward buccaneering, Exquemelin related. He claimed to have been an indentured servant for the French West India Company on Tortuga, drawing from personal experience in his observations. When Exquemelin finished his period of servitude, which he characterized as very cruel and exploitative because he fell "into the hands of the wickedest rogue in the whole island," he was penniless and devoid of other opportunities.[35] Thus, he told his readers, he had no choice but to join the buccaneers.[36] Likewise, even celebrated buccaneer captains such as François l'Olonnais and even Henry Morgan initially arrived in the Caribbean as indentured servants, Exquemelin reported. (Morgan himself disputed this claim and affirmed that he was never an indentured servant.)[37]

Second, the buccaneers enjoyed the protection of secure and permanent bases of operation, namely, the two islands of Tortuga and Jamaica. The existence of a refuge was hardwired into the movement, in fact, for the brotherhood was born in Tortuga and French Hispaniola in the early years of the seventeenth century and based in Tortuga thereafter. From 1629 to 1639, Spain tried several times to invade and capture Tortuga in order to quell the movement and eradicate the growing French presence there, but the island's mountainous geography ultimately made this effort fruitless.[38] After

1655, when the English invaded and captured Jamaica, buccaneering quickly spread there as well. By the mid-seventeenth century, then, the movement was firmly entrenched in two key locations, Port Royal, in Jamaica, and Tortuga, with buccaneers from each location freely communicating, supporting, and joining forces with one another.[39] As a result, the movement quickly intensified, expanding in numbers and evolving in scope and mission.[40] Moreover, in addition to these two permanent bases, the buccaneers used an informal network of isolated islands and coastal locations as temporary staging bases and rendezvous points. Spots such as Cabo Gracias a Dios, Isla de la Vaca, Bayamo and other islets off the southern coast of Cuba, Bleeckveldt Bay, Cabo Tiburón, and El Golfo Triste functioned as temporary havens where the buccaneers could acquire provisions, careen and repair ships, and rendezvous with one another.[41]

Fortunately for the buccaneers, the strategic location of Tortuga and Jamaica within the Caribbean gave the marauders a third key advantage: easy access to Spain's colonial settlements and local and transatlantic shipping routes. The buccaneers were in close proximity to the lively intercoastal traffic between Spanish Hispaniola, Cuba, and the Spanish Main. The treasure ports of Cartagena and Porto Bello were nearby (and Havana too, for that matter, although the buccaneers never attacked this supremely fortified location).[42] Vulnerable and remunerative settlements abounded. Indeed, no target was more than a couple of weeks' sail away.[43] Occasional impediments such as challenging weather or currents, Spanish naval assets on patrol, hostile and/or recalcitrant native peoples, and/or a lack of provisions could sometimes present problems.[44] In general, however, Tortuga and Jamaica offered superb, centrally located bases of operation and sanctuaries.

Moreover, these bases were made available by a fourth buccaneer advantage: the support of the outside parties, such as France, England, and the Netherlands, who envied Spanish predominance in the region and aimed to strengthen their own hands at Spain's expense. Per the Treaty of Tordesillas (1494), Spain considered the Caribbean region to be theirs alone; thus any other Europeans were, in Spanish eyes, invaders and interlopers. Naturally, the French, English, and Dutch were eager to break the Spanish monopoly. All three states aided the buccaneers by providing sporadic legal protection, such as occasional letters of reprisal, donations of materiel, trade opportunities, and injections of capital.[45] Even more important, the French and English eagerly welcomed the quasi-military support that the buccaneers provided for Tortuga and Jamaica. After all, even if the French and English authorities could not directly control the marauders, hosting them in Tortuga and Jamaica delivered formidable advantages. True, the buccaneers followed no outside party's orders per se, but in one fell swoop, they represented both a savage attack force that did great damage to the Spanish colonial system and a body of fearless defenders who protected Tortuga and Port Royal. Additionally, they were the source of periodic economic stimulus when they returned from an operation with their plunder and spent it in an orgy of debauchery.[46]

Spain, obviously aware of this French and English complicity, repeatedly endeavored to use diplomatic entreaties and pressure at the highest levels to force the Franco-English support to stop. However, enjoying the benefit of plausible deniability that hosting the buccaneers conferred, the French and English monarchs ignored the Spanish protests. Both monarchs claimed they had no knowledge of buccaneer activities and zero control over the marauders. "The [Spanish] ambassadors were informed that these men were not subjects of the French and English kings," Exquemelin explained. "The King of France excused himself by saying he had no fortifications on Hispaniola [or Tortuga], and received no tribute from the island," he continued. Meanwhile, the king of England was no more forthcoming, declaring "he had never commissioned those on Jamaica to conduct hostilities against His Catholic Majesty [of Spain], and to satisfy the Spanish court he recalled the governor of Jamaica and installed another in his place." The conclusion was predictable. "Meanwhile," Exquemelin noted, "the rovers continued their marauding."[47]

Two other factors were central to buccaneer success, and they were no less instrumental: effective organization and intense group solidarity. These qualities, inextricably intertwined in the buccaneers' case, derived from one of the most distinguishing and core qualities of the buccaneers, their radical and homegrown form of direct democracy. Indeed, democracy was the fundamental quality around which their entire society was arranged, and the virtue that anchored their special community. The fluid and egalitarian system resulting from their democratic practices and culture produced a potent force of highly organized, keenly motivated, passionately committed, cohesive, and flexible warriors who were extremely successful in their military exploits.

According to Exquemelin, when men joined the buccaneers, they were entering into a separate culture, a vibrant and rich "manner of living" and "way of life," a society marked by, in the words of pioneering sociologist Émile Durkheim, a distinctive "collective consciousness," which enabled them to establish deep bonds of solidarity despite their copious numbers, tradition of rugged self-reliance, geographical dislocation between two separate islands (French Tortuga and English Jamaica), and diverse ethnic backgrounds.[48] By "collective consciousness," Durkheim meant "the totality of beliefs and sentiments common to the average members of a society," in other words, the universally shared beliefs, ideas, values, and attitudes within a particular social group. This "collective consciousness" is the bedrock foundation of that society and provides the basis for members' solidarity and identity.[49]

Participation in the buccaneer brotherhood was entirely voluntary; the only requirement was that each member bring "what he needs in the way of weapons, powder and shot."[50] According to Exquemelin, there was no formal hierarchy within the society nor any enduring system of operational ranks or chains of command. All buccaneers were equal in status. Together, they resolved "by common vote where they shall cruise" and to that end, collectively drew up a sort of labor agreement that, revealing their hunter origins, they called the *chasse partie*, literally, the "division of the hunt." Each *chasse partie* specified the terms for that specific mission and the distribution of the profits. Profit distribution followed a customary formula: typical *chasse parties* called for equal wages among the men, after the needs of the ship, the carpenters, the provisioners, and the wounded had been met.[51] "Everything taken—money, jewels, precious stones and goods—must be shared among them all," Exquemelin explains, "without any man enjoying a penny more than his fair share."[52]

As equals participating in a direct democracy, the brotherhood relied on honor, trust, and integrity in order to function. The buccaneers were, as Exquemelin notes, "extremely loyal and ready to help one another." They also were "generous to their comrades: if a man has nothing, the others will come to his help."[53] Pledging their commitment to the other buccaneers and promising conduct that would conform to group dictates, the buccaneers swore solemn oaths (on the Bible, ironically) to the brotherhood and the group code. Before embarking on a military operation, they also shook hands and swore oaths "to stand by each other till death."[54] The oath, then, played a vital role in the functioning of the society. In recognition of this truth, the brotherhood declared that "should any man be found to have made a false oath, he would be banished from the rovers, and never more be allowed in their company."[55] The buccaneers had a justice system—"the duel is their way of settling disputes"—but again, dishonorable conduct when participating in a duel brought the severest punishment: execution.[56] During missions—especially those that were large in scope, involving thousands of men—they established a modicum of more traditional military order and rank, but this stratification was temporary and existed only because the men complied with it. This adaptation was especially evident after the 1655 English capture of Jamaica and the consequent influence wielded by English soldiers on buccaneer culture. In other words, there was no durable command structure backed up by a formal, punitive, disciplinary system, as in the case of traditional, professional, European militaries; no buccaneer would be subject to punishment or a court martial if he did not comply. The system of rank was not hierarchical in the classic sense but rather existed for the sake of immediate military efficiency and the sensible division of labor. And always, all major decisions were determined by common vote.[57]

A captain led the mission, but he was chosen by the other buccaneers, usually because of his reputed courage, experience, access to a ship, and/or military ingenuity. Thus, he led only because his men permitted him to do so.[58] Even in cases where one man possessed his own ship and thus considered himself to be a "captain," the other buccaneers had the choice as to whether or not they wished to work under his command.[59] If the men became dissatisfied with a captain's leadership, they reserved the right to leave.[60] Additionally, while a captain apparently retained the luster of his fame and the influence that renown conferred, once an operation was over, his formal leadership power evaporated. The captain's status, then, was mission specific and temporary; he was only the greatest among equals, so to speak, and his rank was bestowed on him by his brother buccaneers, making him the creature of his men. While he had the right and responsibility to provide *military* leadership during a mission, his underlying equality in *social* status was manifested in buccaneer mores. Exquemelin explained, for example, that "the captain is allowed no better fare than the meanest on board. If they notice he has better food, the men bring the dish from their own mess and exchange it for the captain's." Likewise, "when a ship has been captured, the men decide whether the captain should keep it or not."[61] And the captain's portion of the profits, which were typically a bit greater in compensation for his leadership, had to be authorized and voted on by the men.[62]

Buccaneer captains inspired fervent loyalty from the men. These captains, seemingly imbued with special qualities such as unusual bravery and insight, appear to have enjoyed the distinctive allure of what Max Weber termed "charismatic domination."[63] As a result, the captain was recognized as "singular" and was duly honored by his peers' election of him to the supreme position of power within buccaneer society. Because of the brotherhood's democratic process, however, each man had a say in the leadership and thus followed because he *wanted* to follow. As Weber said about those who hold charismatic authority, "the leader is personally recognized as the innerly 'called' leader of men. Men do not obey him by virtue of tradition or statute, but because they believe in him."[64]

At the same time, the buccaneers' elastic and democratic military culture resulted in a force of deeply self-reliant and independent warriors who could operate without the constant guidance of a senior officer. When the tenure of one captain ended (for whatever reason), buccaneer society had a ready pool of experienced men from which to draw; the brotherhood did not dissolve simply because certain captains ceased to lead. Like the mythical hydra, cutting off the head of the brotherhood (the captain) simply resulted in more heads sprouting in its stead. No matter the captain, buccaneers preyed on the Spanish consistently both for material and ideological reasons. Certainly, the buccaneer cycle of wild marauding and equally wild debauching necessitated that they embark on missions regularly and zealously, and Spanish settlements and ships offered rich prey. However, the choice to target the Spanish was also based on a buccaneer antipathy— and sometimes even profound odium—for Spain and its people, based both on Spain's role as defender of the Catholic Church (many buccaneers were apparently Protestant, and fiercely Protestant at that), and Spain's domineering attitude in the Americas.[65] Motivated by these intense feelings, the buccaneers' voluntary and participatory character and democratic culture resulted in a militarized brotherhood distinguished by its ruthless bravery, flexibility, unity, and ingenuity. And given the shifting, decentralized command structure, the buccaneers could adapt their military approach quickly to whatever the circumstances presented, and in keeping with whichever brother had the best idea.

Pity the Spanish, then. The buccaneers were unyielding in their courage, preferring to perish while fighting, and fighting together as brothers, rather than surrender, even when the situation appeared dire.[66] Using small arms almost exclusively—muskets, pistols, and cutlasses—they employed innovative guerilla infantry tactics and operations that flummoxed their enemy and defied the rules of conventional European military practice, although the buccaneers were, it turns out, very adept at conventional warfare too. The realization and implementation of these creative tactics did not come solely from above, in the form of the captain's decree, but also emanated from the rank-and-file "soldier," in keeping with the democratic nature of their order. For instance, Exquemelin relates the contagion of instant tactical adaptability that occurred when one buccaneer—not a captain—figured out how to solve a particularly thorny tactical challenge. Attempting to breach a Spanish fortress, the buccaneers were beset by withering fire. "The rovers suffered heavy damage," Exquemelin wrote. "They were in great anxiety, not knowing how best to set about the attack." Just then, one buccaneer "pierced through the shoulder by an arrow" turned injury to inspiration. "In a fury he wrenched it out, took a wad of cotton from his pouch, tied it to the arrowhead and set fire to it," Exquemelin reported. The crafty buccaneer then inserted the arrow into his musket and "shot it into the palm-leaf thatch of some houses within the fortress walls." His fellows buccaneers, "seeing his idea, began to do the same," and the battle turned to their favor. "By daybreak, the fire had burnt through the palisades almost completely," according to Exquemelin. "The earth rampart ... started to collapse, and ... the guns ... pitched down into the moat." Thanks to quick-thinking confreres, the buccaneers' triumph was complete. "Finally, most of the defenders succumbed, either from the fire or from the rovers' deadly bullets."[67]

Buccaneering's democratic ethos and the practices that flowed from it contrasted strikingly with the rigid, hierarchical structure of regular European societies and professional militaries. During the seventeenth century, western military culture was in the midst of the profound changes wrought by the early modern Military Revolution, the series of radical transformations that resulted in the creation of the modern, professional military force. Armies and navies were growing in size and complexity, with the tactical role of the infantry and the technological capabilities of artillery taking center stage. As the state amassed greater power, political organization, and financial strength, it established large, standing, professional military forces, rather than disbanding troops at the end of a conflict. (Spain was the first state to go through this process and thus was the first to become a "fiscal military state.")[68] These standing troops, in turn, were inculcated both with a sense of unity and national identification, as manifested in such new developments as the use of uniforms, and with a deep sense of discipline instilled through incessant drill and the strict, incontestable, and hierarchical leadership of a multitude of junior officers belonging to the new entity of the professional officers corps.[69] Training was routinized, responsibilities were tied to rank, and as William McNeill averred, "Soldiers became replaceable parts in a sort of human machine, and so did their officers."[70] Even England's New Model Army, the militarized arm of Cromwell's radical Puritan forces in the English Civil War, retained a conventional, hierarchical structure and character, despite the leveling rhetoric of Puritan ideology.[71]

The buccaneer brotherhood—as a society composed of equal individuals, each with his own voice and power and beholden to no one—possessed an entirely different organizational character. What is striking, however, is the remarkable degree to which the same—or better—military result occurred. Buccaneers were incredibly well trained and ferociously disciplined. Their pastime was training, as it were, since their "main exercises are target-shooting and keeping their guns clean,"[72] and they were willing to endure terrible deprivation to achieve their military objective.[73] They were absolutely single-minded in the pursuit of their missions, and their remarkable discipline and training enabled them to achieve their objectives time and again. They need not be hierarchical, highly structured, or part of a larger network in order to be effective. They need not to look outside themselves for leadership, inspiration, or organizational guidance. On the contrary, although the buccaneer movement was autonomous, self-generating, militarily irregular, structurally egalitarian, and fluid in its membership and leadership, it was still highly organized and effectual. What might appear to be weaknesses, imparting incoherence and military incompetence, instead were great strengths.

It is easy to see, then, how the comparatively liberating and democratic culture of the buccaneers would be alluring to poor, luckless young men, especially since their options elsewhere were bleak. Indeed, despite all of the violence and dangers that the buccaneering life inevitably entailed, its participants remained devoted to their special brotherhood. As Exquemelin affirmed, "for they are so accustomed to the buccaneering life that it is impossible for them to give it up."[74]

After decades of unbridled success, how did the buccaneer phenomenon
come to an end? Spanish naval intervention and tough defensive measures,
while sometimes effective in mitigating the effects of buccaneering (and
sometimes not[75]), ultimately were not enough to eradicate them. Rather,
the demise of buccaneering was primarily due to the weakening of several
of the six factors of piracy, as outlined above. Specifically, the buccaneers
lost the help of outside parties, they were cut off from permanent bases
of operations, and to a certain extent, their sources of personnel dwindled.
Consequently, their culture unraveled as well.

The withdrawal of support from rival European states at the close of the
seventeenth century had manifold consequences on the buccaneering movement and undercut the buccaneers' might. Eventually, France and England
did not provide the same level of financial and legal aid, since they were ad-
vancing their interests in the Caribbean in other ways and thus would not
need to rely on the maverick, loose-cannon buccaneers. The Dutch, represented in the Caribbean by the Dutch West India Company, in due course
discouraged trade with the marauders as well.[76] Moreover, starting in 1670,
when Spain conceded the legality of England's claim of Jamaica, England
gradually outlawed the use of Jamaica as a buccaneer safe haven. At the same
time, European states—especially England—were able to co-opt buccaneers
into their official imperial systems by conferring pardons, granting political and military positions, delivering pecuniary rewards, and granting pres-
tigious titles. A prime exemplar of this phenomenon was Henry Morgan.
Despite his buccaneer transgressions, he was elevated to the rank of knight
in 1674, becoming Sir Henry Morgan, and proclaimed the lieutenant governor of Jamaica in 1675. Later, Captain Holford, "an old Buccaneer" who became a servant of the English state, delivered pirate captain Charles Vane to
Jamaican authorities in 1719.[77] Meanwhile, in 1692, a devastating earthquake
in Jamaica destroyed much of the infrastructure and personnel the buccaneers used to mount their campaigns and sustain their overall way of life.
Ten years later, in 1702, when the War of the Spanish Succession erupted,
Englishmen in Jamaica were freely given letters of marque to maraud as legal English privateers.[78] Not only did this action serve to bring these surviving buccaneers under English state control, it also reinforced their English
national identity and pitted them against their erstwhile buccaneer brothers,
the French, England's primary adversary in the war. In combination, then, all
of these factors eliminated the buccaneers' safe havens, curtailed the popu-

lation of possible recruits, lessened buccaneer supplies and materiel, and interfered with the unique buccaneer organization and culture, diluting their beliefs and weakening their bonds of solidarity.

Conclusion

As we consider how to address the problematic phenomenon of modern piracy, it would behoove us to think beyond only purely naval solutions on the high seas and also take into account the six factors underlying the long and productive careers of the Caribbean buccaneers. Without a doubt, the key to eradicating contemporary piracy lies in disrupting the larger, complex systems that support the activities. Yes, it is essential to protect maritime commerce in the region and intercept the pirates in action on the high seas through the use of naval and/or coast guard assets. However, it is unreasonable to expect that the navy alone, working in isolation without support and charged with escort duties and patrolling a vast expanse of open sea, can eliminate piracy. Indeed, the longer the system supporting the piracy is permitted to stay in place and grow, the more intractable the piracy problem will become. Above all, we must not underestimate contemporary piracy's potential severity simply because we assume that pirates in small, unsophisticated craft (such as those used in the Strait of Malacca and near Somalia and Nigeria) pose no real problem. The Spanish of the seventeenth-century Caribbean made that grave mistake vis-à-vis the buccaneers; such a misfit group with makeshift means, they thought, was no threat to the power of the Spanish empire and its mighty military.[79] How very wrong they were. Indeed, this is one of the vital lessons that the history of the golden age of piracy imparts: do not underestimate pirates. Along with our understanding of the six fundamental factors underlying the success of the buccaneer enterprise, we would be most wise to remember it.

NOTES

1. For the most current statistics regarding piracy off the Horn of Africa, see the International Maritime Bureau's Piracy Reporting Centre at the International Chamber of Commerce's Commercial Crime Services website: https://www.icc-ccs .org.

2. Tom Shanker, "U.S. Reports That Piracy off Africa Has Plunged," *New York Times*, August 29, 2012.

3. Congressional Research Service, "Piracy off the Horn of Africa," April 27, 2011, 1, https://fas.org/sgp/crs/row/R40528.pdf.

4. Gus Lubin, "Piracy Could Surge off of the Infamous Somali Coast, Experts Warn," *Business Insider*, October 21, 2016, http://www.businessinsider.com /piracy-somalia-could-come-back-2016-10.

5. Eoghan Macguire, "'Resurrection' of Somali Pirate Attacks Feared after Tanker Shootout," NBC News, November 20, 2016, http://www.nbcnews.com/news/world /resurrection-somali-pirate-attacks-feared-after-tanker-shootout-n685731.

6. "The Ungoverned Seas," *Economist* (U.S.), November 29, 2014.

7. Joe Cochran, "Southeast Asia Replaces Horn of Africa as the World's Hotbed of Piracy," *New York Times*, September 17, 2016.

8. Marcus Rediker, *Between the Devil and the Deep Blue Sea: Merchant Seamen, Pirates, and the Anglo-American Maritime World, 1700–1750* (Cambridge, UK: Cambridge University Press, 1987), 254–55.

9. Elsewhere, I have analyzed the example of the North African corsairs, whose marauding activities lasted for some three hundred years. See Virginia Lunsford, "What Makes Piracy Work?," *Proceedings: The Independent Forum on National Defense*, December 2008, 28–33.

10. Virginia Lunsford, *Piracy and Privateering in the Golden Age Netherlands* (New York: Palgrave McMillan, 2005), 6.

11. A. O. Exquemelin, *De Americaensche Zee-Roovers* (Amsterdam: Jan ten Hoorn, 1678). An incredibly popular text, *Bucaniers of America* went through any number of reprintings and translations during the early modern period. For its publication history, see Carolyn Eastman's essay in this collection. References are to the most accurate modern edition in English, which provides an exact translation from the seventeenth-century Dutch: Alexandre O. Exquemelin, *The Buccaneers of America*, trans. Alexis Brown (Mineola, N.Y.: Dover Publications, 2000).

12. See, for example, David Cordingly, who writes of Exquemelin: "Careful comparison of his stories with the events described in Spanish documents of the period has shown that he gets most of the facts right but is often mistaken about place-names and dates. Some of his wilder stories appear to be secondhand accounts which he probably heard in taverns, but it is clear that he took part in a number of buccaneer expeditions. . . . Exquemelin's book . . . has provided the basis for all serious histories of the buccaneers and, in spite of some inaccuracies, remains the standard work on the subject." David Cordingly, *Under the Black Flag: The Romance and the Reality of Life among the Pirates* (New York: Random House, 1995), 40. For another balanced appraisal of Exquemelin, see Peter Earle, *The Sack of Panama* (London: Jill Norman and Hobhouse, 1981), 265–66.

13. Jack Beeching, introduction to Exquemelin, *Buccaneers of America*, 13.

14. Exquemelin, *Buccaneers of America*, 75–80, 93–118, 141–63.

15. See, for example, the report in *Ordinaire Leydse Courant*, "Nederlanden," August 29, 1686, which relates that the French had just sent four frigates to America "to suppress the pirates there."

16. For more on beleaguered Spanish outposts and the Crown's attempts made to protect them, see the following documents in the General Archive of the Indies, Seville, Spain: Panama 30, N. 68: *Cartas y Expedientes de Cabildos Seculares: Panamá*, 1616; Mexico 28, N. 28; Panama 95: *Entrada de Piratas en Portobelo, Darien y Mar del Sur*, 1679–1681; Panama 96: *Entrada de Piratas en Portobelo, Darien y Mar del Sur*, 1682–1687; Indiferente 2578: *Piratas en las Costas de Barlovento*, 1681–1684; Santo Domingo 856: *Invasión de Piratas en la Florida*, 1684–1702; Guatemala 42, N. 77: *Caratas de Cabildos Seculares*, March 18, 1671; Panama 81: *Empréstito de 1000,000 Pesos para Rescutar Portobelo*, 1678; and Panama 99: *Resguardo del Darién y Tierra Firme contra la Pirateria*, 1683–1694.

17. Exquemelin, *Buccaneers of America*, 147, 169, 226.

18. Ibid., 200.

19. Ibid., 150. In this torture, sometimes, weights were added to the victim's body to intensify the pain and physical damage.

20. Ibid., 147–50, 200.

21. Ibid., see esp. 201.

22. Ibid., 151.

23. Ibid., 106–7, 117. It seems fitting that, according to Exquemelin, l'Olonnais met his own horrible end, imprisoned by native American peoples, by whose hands he "was hacked to pieces and roasted limb by limb."

24. Ibid., 80.

25. Ibid.

26. Ibid.

27. Cordingly, *Under the Black Flag*, 127, 129, 131–32.

28. Exquemelin, *Buccaneers of America*, 69, 83.

29. Paul Hoffman, *The Spanish Crown and the Defense of the Caribbean, 1535–1585: Precedent, Patrimonialism, and Royal Parsimony* (Baton Rouge, La.: LSU Press, 1999), 224.

30. Exquemelin, *Buccaneers of America*, 128–29.

31. In 1628, a Dutch West India Company fleet, led by Piet Heyn, captured the treasure fleet in Cuba.

32. Exquemelin, *Buccaneers of America*, 54–59, 68, 167–68.

33. For example, see ibid., 80, 93. Moreover, the English settlement of Jamaica in 1655 was the result of a failed Cromwellian military invasion of Santo Domingo. Thus, there were a plethora of soldiers among the colonial Jamaican population. For

more about the character of the English military at this time, see Mark Kishlansky, "The Case of the Army Truly Stated: The Creation of the New Model Army," *Past and Present* 81 (1978): 51–74.

34. Exquemelin, *Buccaneers of America*, 55–57, 64–66.

35. Ibid., 34.

36. Ibid.

37. Ibid., 89, 119.

38. Ibid., 31–33.

39. Ibid., 119–21, 128, 141, 167–68.

40. Ibid., 83–85.

41. Ibid., 72, 79, 80, 168, 171, 215, 219, 224.

42. Ibid., 128–29.

43. Ibid., 69.

44. See, for example, ibid., 113–17, 209–18.

45. Ibid., 63, 89, 171; J. J. Baud, *Proeve eener Geschiedenis der Strafwetgeving tegen de Zeerooverij* (Utrecht: D. Post Uiterweer, 1854), 106; Dionisius van der Sterre, *Zeer aenmerkelijke reysen gedaan door Jan Erasmus Reyning* (Amsterdam, Jan ten Hoorn, 1691), 67–69; and the following documents in the Dutch West India Company Archive in the Netherlands National Archive (Algemeen Rijksarchief), the Hague, the Netherlands: WIC no. 617: "Artijckelen aen Nicolaas van Liebergen," March 2, 1683, *Secrete Brieven en Papieren van Curaçao, 1680–1689*, fol. 324; WIC no. 617: "Interrogatorien van Jan Elkis," February 27, 1683, *Secrete Brieven en Papieren van Curaçao, 1680–1689*, fol. 245–47; WIC no. 617: "Interrogatorien van Gerritt Slocker," 1683, *Secrete Brieven en Papieren van Curaçao, 1680–1689*, fol. 249–50; WIC no. 617: Article 13, "Pointen ende Articulen bij de Heeren Bewinthebberen vande WIC ter Vergaderinge Vande Thienen," c. 1683, *Secrete Brieven en Papieren van Curaçao, 1680–1689*, fol. 349; WIC no. 617: Article 1, "Artijckelen van beschuldinge ten laste van de geweesene Director Nicolaes van Liebergen," c. 1683, *Secrete Brieven en Papieren van Curaçao, 1680–1689*, fol. 448; and WIC no. 468: "Brief aan Willem Kerckrink, Directeur van Curaçao," July 2, 1688, *Kopieboeken van Brieven naar Amerika, 1684–1689*, fol. 155vs–56. See also the following document in the General Archive of the Indies in Seville, Spain: Escribania 597A: *Comisiones Gobernacion de Cartagena*, 1684.

46. Exquemelin, *Buccaneers of America*, 81–82.

47. Ibid., 67.

48. Ibid., 70, 119, 156; and Émile Durkheim, *The Division of Labor in Society*, trans. W. D. Halls (1984; repr., New York: The Free Press, 2014).

49. Durkheim, *Division of Labor*, 63.

50. Exquemelin, *Buccaneers of America*, 70. He goes on to explain that the buccaneers "use good weapons, such as muskets and pistols. . . . They use cartridges, and

have a cartouche containing thirty, which they carry with them always, so they are never unprepared" (75). They also carried cutlasses and knives and made use of rudimentary grenades.

51. For a typical *chasse partie*, see ibid., 71.

52. Ibid., 71–72.

53. Ibid., 72, 82.

54. Ibid., 100.

55. Ibid., 72.

56. Ibid., 72, 133.

57. Ibid., 100, 171–73.

58. For references to the election of the captain, see ibid., 80, 84, 119.

59. See the case of François l'Olonnais, in ibid., 89, 93, 105.

60. See, for example, ibid., 133, 207–8.

61. Ibid., 70–71.

62. Ibid., 172.

63. Weber defines this form of authority in the following manner: "There is the authority of the extraordinary and personal *gift of grace* (charisma), the absolutely personal devotion and personal confidence in revelation, heroism, or other qualities of individual leadership." See Max Weber, "Politics as a Vocation," in *From Max Weber: Essays in Sociology*, ed. and trans. H. H. Gerth and C. Wright Mills (New York: Oxford University Press, 1946), 79.

64. Ibid.

65. Beeching, introduction, 9. See also Exquemelin's anti-Spanish asides, such as on Rock the Brazilian, *Buccaneers of America*, 80.

66. Exquemelin, *Buccaneers of America*, 81, 100.

67. Ibid., 181–82.

68. Jan Glete, *War and the State in Early Modern Europe* (New York: Routledge, 2002), 69–91.

69. See Michael Roberts, "The Military Revolution, 1560–1660," in *The Military Revolution Debate: Readings on the Military Transformation of Early Modern Europe*, ed. Clifford J. Rogers (Oxford: Westview Press, 1995), 13–35; Geoffrey Parker, *The Military Revolution: Military Innovation and the Rise of the West* (New York: Cambridge University Press, 1988); and William McNeill, *The Pursuit of Power: Technology, Armed Force, and Society since A.D. 1000* (Chicago: University of Chicago Press, 1982).

70. William McNeill, *The Age of the Gunpowder Empires, 1450–1800* (Washington, D.C.: American Historical Association, 1989), 23.

71. Mark Kishlansky, "The Case of the Army Truly Stated: The Creation of the New Model Army," *Past and Present* 81 (1978): 51–74.

72. Exquemelin, *Buccaneers of America*, 75.

73. See, for example, the ferocious starvation experienced by Henry Morgan and his men during their mission to raid Panama. See ibid., 185–96.

74. Ibid., 226.

75. For example, see how the buccaneers, under Henry Morgan's command, destroyed and captured three Spanish naval ships in the wake of the buccaneers' Maracaibo raid. Ibid., 156–57.

76. See the following document in the Dutch West India Company Archive, located in the Netherlands National Archive (Algemeen Rijksarchief) in the Hague: WIC no. 468: "Brief aan Willem Kerckrink, Directeur van Curaçao," July 2, 1688, *Kopieboeken van Brieven naar Amerika, 1684–1689*, fol. 155vs–56.

77. *A General History of the Pyrates*, ed. Manuel Schonhorn (Mineola, N.Y.: Dover, 1972), 140–41. This text was originally published under the pseudonym Captain Charles Johnson as *A General History of the Robberies and Murders of the Most Notorious Pyrates* (London: Printed for and sold by T. Warner, 1724).

78. *A General History of the Pyrates*, 71.

79. Exquemelin, *Buccaneers of America*, 68, 155–63.

The Economic Way of Thinking about Pirates

Peter T. Leeson

To most people, economics is the study of particular subjects—money, markets, international trade. To economists, however, it's something else: a particular way of thinking about human behavior. That behavior might be the buying and selling of traders on the floor of the New York Stock Exchange. Or it might be the ritual divination practices of an ancient African tribe; litigation by landholders in Anglo-Norman England; voting by politicians in the U.S. Senate. Any goal-oriented human behavior can be analyzed using the economic way of thinking, and virtually every kind has been.[1]

The power of the economic way of thinking, its ability to bring such a wide variety of human activity under its lens, stems from its uniquely encompassing and simple assumptions: resources are scarce, and people are rational.

Scarcity is the assumption that people must make choices—you can't have it all. Rationality is an assumption about how people make choices—as best you can given your goals and the constraints you face imposed by scarcity.

Scarcity implies incentives: benefits and costs. The benefit of a choice you make is the value you expect to get from it. The cost is the value you expect to give up because you didn't make a different one. Rationality implies a certain response to incentives: when the cost of a choice rises relative to the benefit, you're less likely to make it, and vice versa.

The economic way of thinking about pirates uses this approach to analyze the behavior of sea bandits. It treats pirates as people who faced constraints and responded rationally to incentives in making choices to achieve their goals. In other words, the economic way of thinking about pirates treats them as people who are like everyone else.

The economic way of thinking about pirates typically considers the pirate crew or ship as its unit of analysis because piracy required the collaboration of multiple criminals; a one-man crew wouldn't have made it far. Much as one might view Ford Motor Company as a collection of workers and owners rationally pursuing profit—a firm—specialized in the production of automobiles, one might also view a pirate crew as a firm, albeit specialized in the production of something quite different: maritime plunder. Which is how the economic way of thinking about pirates sees their crews. In this view, the often very different choices made by eighteenth-century pirate crews and Ford Motor Company—or, for that matter, pirate crews and eighteenth-century merchant crews—reflect not differences in their underlying goals or rationality but rather differences in their incentives.

This chapter uses the economic way of thinking about pirates to analyze the infamous practices of pirates of the golden age: the democratic organization of their ships; use of a unique pirate flag, the Jolly Roger; and reliance on heinous torture. I develop the logic behind how pirates used these practices to influence their incentives and those of their victims to maximize profit from plunder.[2]

Caveat lector: At the risk of losing your attention before we've begun, I should point out that I'm an economist, not a historian. I'm not even an economic historian, though I'm an economist who enjoys history and often writes about it. I note this so that you know what you're in for—an economic analysis of well-known aspects of golden age pirates. And, what you're not— new historical material relating to golden age pirates. The economic way of thinking about pirates isn't the only way of analyzing them, of course. But it's a useful one, revealing underappreciated aspects of the behaviors for which they're best known.

The Economic Way of Thinking about Pirate Democracy

Early eighteenth-century pirates were criminals. They could no more rely on public institutions of law and order to facilitate cooperation with one another than can the members of drug-peddling street gangs today. This posed a problem, since piracy was jointly produced: successful maritime marauding required groups of pirates to live and work together at sea, often for long periods. If pirates couldn't produce internal order, their crews would be torn apart—quite literally—by intracrew theft and violence, precluding their ability to profit.

Pirates solved this problem by developing the famed "pirate code," articles of agreement governing their ships, or as I prefer to call them, "constitutions." The constitution governing the *Royal Fortune* circa 1720, as given in *A General History of the Pyrates*:

I.   Every Man has a Vote in the Affairs of Moment; has equal Title to the fresh Provisions, or strong Liquors, at any Time seized, and may use them at Pleasure, unless a Scarcity make it necessary, for the Good of all, to vote a Retrenchment.

II. Every Man to be called fairly in Turn, by List, on board of Prizes, because, (over and above their proper Share) they were on these Occasions allowed a Shift of Cloaths: But if they defrauded the Company to the Value of a Dollar, in Plate, Jewels, or Money, Marooning was their Punishment. If the Robbery was only betwixt one another, they contented themselves with slitting the Ears and Nose of him that was Guilty, and set him on Shore, not in an uninhabited Place, but somewhere, where he was sure to encounter Hardships.

III. No person to Game at Cards or Dice for Money.

IV. The Lights and Candles to be put out at eight a-Clock at Night: If any of the Crew, after that Hour, still remained enclined for Drinking, they were to do it on the open Deck.

V.   To keep their Piece, Pistols, and Cutlash clean, and fit for Service.

VI. No Boy or Woman to be allowed amongst them. If any Man were found seducing any of the latter Sex, and carry'd her to Sea, disguised, he was to suffer Death.

VII. To Desert the Ship, or their Quarters in Battle, was punished with Death or Marooning.

VIII. No striking one another on board, but every Man's Quarrels to be ended on Shore, at Sword and Pistol.

IX. No Man to talk of breaking up their Way of Living, till each shared a 1000 l. If in order to this, any Man should lose a Limb, or become a Cripple in their Service, he was to have 800 Dollars, out of the publick Stock, and for lesser Hurts, proportionately.

X.   The Captain and Quarter-Master to receive two Shares of a Prize; the Master, Boatswain, and Gunner, one Share and a half, and other Officers one and a Quarter.

XI. The Musicians to have Rest on the Sabbath Day, but the other six Days and Nights, none without special Favour.[3]

Simple, surely; but effective nonetheless. Pirate constitutions proscribed intracrew theft and violence; stipulated the terms of piratical compensation, including employment insurance; regulated activities, such as drinking and smoking, which, if left unregulated, threatened the operation of the collective crew; and provided punishments for breaking these rules. Equally important, pirate constitutions established democracy as the mechanism for making important crew decisions. Chief among them, the selection of officers.

Two officers were especially important on a pirate ship: the captain and the quartermaster. When pirates were "in chase"—engaging a prospective prize—snap decision making was indispensable, hence, so was having a crew-member with unilateral authority. That was the captain. When not in chase, pirates needed a crewmember with the authority to carry out "everyday" ad-ministrative duties, such as punishing rule violations: the quartermaster.

The offices of captain and quartermaster were no less critical to profitable piracy than rules governing theft and violence. But their very indispensabil-ity created another problem: how to prevent officers from abusing their au-thority for private gain at the expense of ordinary crewmembers.

Pirates, in other words, confronted the "paradox of power" that would later be articulated by James Madison in Federalist No. 51.[4] Officers strong enough to do what crewmembers wanted and needed were also strong enough to do what crewmembers didn't want or need and, left uncontrolled, surely would. This concern wasn't hypothetical. Many pirates were former merchant sailors and had suffered abuse by dictatorial officers aboard mer-chantmen, which were organized autocratically.

Pirates' remedy was the same one Madison proposed—more than half a century before he proposed it: democratic checks and balances, divided power.

Pirates popularly elected and deposed captains and quartermasters. The threat of removal incentivized officers to hew closely to the activities for which their offices were created—and no more. Competition for office in-centivized behavior that appealed to the interest of the crew. The division of authorities between captain and quartermaster—and ordinary crew—lim-ited the scope for abuse further still, as did pirate constitutions themselves, which facilitated common knowledge among crewmembers about legitimate and illegitimate uses of officer power. If a crew's articles entitled the quarter-master to a one and one-quarter share of prizes and he distributed to himself any more, everyone would know he was self-dealing, subjecting him to a

coordinated crewmember response—such as being sent on a permanent va-
cation to the nearest desert island. By minimizing officers' corruption, pirates
maximized profit.

Which presents a puzzle: If democracy was profit maximizing for early
eighteenth-century pirates, why was autocracy used aboard early eighteenth-
century merchantmen, whose owners were no less profit driven? Or to put
the same puzzle differently: If autocratic organization maximized profit for
merchant ships, how could its opposite have done so for pirates?

Very easily, it turns out. Merchant ships confronted what economists call
a "principal-agent problem." Principals are owners of assets, for example the
stockholders of Ford Motor Company. Agents are people that principals
hire to use their assets when it's not profitable for them to do so themselves:
Ford's employees. A principal-agent problem emerges when the interests of
these parties diverge, leading the agents to behave in ways that harm the
principals. To avoid this, and make cooperation between principals and
agents profitable, their interests must somehow be aligned.

Eighteenth-century merchant vessels and their cargoes were owned by
external financiers—wealthy landlubbers who funded commercial voyages.
Since owners usually didn't sail on the vessels in which they invested, their
ships and cargo were beyond their eyes or reach when away at sea. This situation invited sailor opportunism, such as the theft of cargo, shirking in
work activities, even absconding with vessels. To prevent such behavior,
merchant-ship owners appointed a "manager": a captain to whom they gave
a small share in their ship and whom they endowed with autocratic authority to monitor, and to financially and physically "discipline," their sailors.

Merchant-ship autocracy prevented sailors from taking advantage of
owners. But it enabled captains to take advantage of sailors—skimming their
wages, skimping on their victuals, even skinning their hides—as more than
a few sailors complained. Captain self-dealing was costly not only to sailors
but also to owners, for given the prospect of abuse, owners needed to offer at
least some sailors higher wages to attract them to merchant shipping. Nevertheless, this cost to owners was more than offset by the still larger savings
of preventing sailor opportunism. On net, autocratic captains yielded them
higher profit, the reason for merchantmen's autocratic organization.

And what of the principal-agent problem for pirates? They didn't have
one. The reason: pirates stole their ships. They were both owners and employees of their vessels—the principals and the agents. Pirate crews still

needed officers, but not autocratic ones. They could use democratic officers instead, limiting officer self-dealing, which accrued to their bottom line.

Eighteenth-century pirate and merchant ships, therefore, faced different incentives. Different organizational forms maximized their profit. So, pirate and merchant ships were organized differently.

The Economic Way of Thinking about the Jolly Roger

On the face of it, thieves that alert victims to their presence with an unmistakable ensign must be idiots—or at least irrational; definitely not profit maximizing. Yet this is exactly what early eighteenth-century pirates routinely did with their infamous flag, the Jolly Roger.

To understand how the Jolly Roger could have been precisely what it seems it was not—a rational profit-maximizing choice—consider a concept economists call "signaling." A signal is an activity that one party engages in to communicate to another party an otherwise unobservable trait he possesses. Ever wonder why some job applicants bother to print their applications on fancy paper? It's not as though employers have a special fondness for watermarks; most applications end up in the garbage, not a frame on the wall. Signaling provides a clue.

Suppose there are two types of job applicants, the detail-oriented type, and the not-so-detail-oriented type. An employer whose firm requires detail-oriented tasks wants to hire the former, not the latter. But there's a problem: the employer can't tell simply by looking at job applicants which type an applicant is. Even the contents of their applications might not help. So, the employer guesses. As a result, some detail-oriented job applicants don't get hired even though they want to work for the employer and the employer wants them to work for him.

In such a situation, these applicants might use a signal to communicate their detail-oriented identity to the employer. What kind of activity could accomplish that? The kind that detail-oriented applicants would engage in but not-so-detail-oriented ones probably wouldn't. Simply writing on your application "I'm the detail-oriented type," then, wouldn't work: this is as easy for a not-so-detail-oriented applicant to do as it is for a detail-oriented one; both types do it, undermining the signal's ability to communicate.

Submitting your application on fancy paper, on the other hand, might work. The reason: it takes less effort, and thus is less costly, for detail-oriented applicants to think of this detail and carry it out than it is for not-so-detail-oriented ones. If the latter's cost is high enough, they won't submit on fancy paper. In which case the employer can reliably infer that applications received on fancy paper are from detail-oriented applicants, enabling him to hire them—to his benefit and theirs.

What does signaling the kind of employee you are with fancy paper have to do with the Jolly Roger? A lot.

An important cost of producing maritime plunder was the damage that pirate crewmembers and their ship would likely sustain if they had to battle with prizes. Maximizing profit required minimizing this cost, leading early eighteenth-century pirates to adopt a simple policy: "No Quarter should be given to any Captain that offered to defend his Ship."[5] To those who submitted peacefully, pirates promised mercy; to those who didn't, death.

Pirate ships were typically much stronger than the merchantmen they attacked. They had more men and guns. Moreover, nothing prevented pirates who overwhelmed a resistant prize from carrying out their deadly promise; if captured, pirates would get the hangman's noose whether their victims lived or died. So, their threat was credible. Edward Low, for instance, "had [a victim's] Ears cut off close to his Head, for only proposing to resist . . . [his] black Flag."[6] This had a predictable effect on merchantmen's incentives: most found it in their interest to surrender to pirate attackers without much ado.

There was just one snag. For this strategy to work, pirates' victims needed to know when they were under attack by a pirate crew as opposed to some other, less ominous attacker, whose advances they might be more willing to resist. Pirates weren't the only belligerents who prowled the trading lanes traveled by eighteenth-century merchantmen. In certain areas, a merchantman might also encounter a "coast guard" vessel, a ship commissioned by a government, such as Spain's, to protect its colonial trade monopoly against smuggling by foreign interlopers.

As government-commissioned vessels, at least in principle, coast guards were more limited than pirates in how they could respond to resistant merchantmen. Killing them in cold blood was frowned upon. As a result, merchantmen were more willing to resist coast guards than pirates. When Captain William Wyer, for instance, asked his crewmembers "if they would stand by him and defend the ship" against an approaching, unknown belligerent, "they answered, if they were Spaniards they would stand by him as they had Life, but if they were Pirates they would not Fight."[7]

Coast guard and pirate ships weren't easily distinguishable, especially at a distance. They looked more or less the same, which posed a problem for pirates: uncertain whether its attacker was a pirate or coast guard crew, a merchantman might hazard resistance, foiling the effectiveness of pirates' "surrender-or-die" policy.

Pirates' solution to this problem was to use a signal. Their "fancy paper," an unmistakable flag: the Jolly Roger. The distinctiveness of this ensign, a "large black Flag, with a Death's Head and Bones a-cross," or variants thereupon, left little question about the identity its flyer was claiming: pirate.[8] But this feature of the Jolly Roger alone wasn't enough to make it an effective signal—just as simply writing "I'm the detail-oriented type" on your job application isn't.

The reason, the same: just as anyone can claim to be detail oriented, anyone can claim to be a pirate. Recall that for a signal to accurately reveal the sender's unobservable trait to its receiver, it needs to be cheap for one type to send, but too costly for the other. Only then will the signal be used exclusively by one type, allowing the receiver to reliably infer from it the sender's "true identity."

In the context of early eighteenth-century pirates, this meant that flying the Jolly Roger needed to be cheap for pirates but prohibitively expensive for coast guards. If not, coast guards would fly it too, imitating the real outlaws in an attempt to exploit merchantmen's unwillingness to resist them. And that would destroy the Jolly Roger's ability to reliably communicate "pirate," upon which the profit-enhancing capacity of pirates' surrender-or-die strategy relied.

The cost difference required for the Jolly Roger to be an effective signal came from the law. The Jolly Roger was an internationally recognized emblem of piracy. A pirate flag discovered aboard a captured vessel was considered prima facie evidence that its crew was engaged in piracy, a capital offense. As the court declared at the trial of Bartholomew Roberts's crew, for instance, the defendants had acted "under a Black Flag, flagrantly by that, denoting your selves common Robbers, Opposers and Violators of all Laws, Human and Divine."[9]

Since pirates were already outlaws facing execution if captured, the additional cost of carrying a Jolly Roger was nil. For coast guards, however, which at least officially weren't outlaws and enjoyed government sanction, carrying a Jolly Roger was taking a serious risk. Without it, a Spanish coast guard crew captured by the English under suspicion of illegitimately harassing its merchantmen might escape punishment. At least they would escape with their lives. With the flag, the coast guard crew was likely to be condemned as having "turned pirate" and punished accordingly.

Thus, while pirates used the Jolly Roger, coast guards typically did not. Merchantmen therefore knew when they saw the pirate flag that their attackers were probably genuine pirates, leading them to submit peacefully, which enhanced pirates' profit.[10]

The Economic Way of Thinking about Pirate Torture

It's a curious thing: if a child's parents dressed her for Halloween as Charles Manson, most people would think seriously about calling protective services; yet every year when droves of parents dress their children as pirates for Halloween, most everyone thinks it's adorable. It's curious because pirates inflicted cruelties on more victims than Manson—and cruelties far more gruesome.

Some pirates showed a fondness for cutting off victims' body parts—ears and noses—which they occasionally fed to the mutilated. The buccaneers of the seventeenth century preferred "woolding," crushing the victim's skull under the pressure of rope until his eyes popped out. Another option was the "sweat," "the Manner of" which, one eyewitness explained, "is thus: Between the Decks they stick Candles round the Mizen-Mast, and about twenty five Men surround it with Points of Swords, Penknives, Compasses, Forks, &c. in each of their Hands: *Culprit* enters the Circle; the Violin plays a merry Jig, and he must run for about ten Minutes, while each Man runs his Instrument into his Posteriors."[11]

You would be forgiven, then, for thinking that pirates must have been mad sadists—or rather supersadists, the likes to which contemporary crazed killers, such as Manson, could only aspire. But your conclusion would be wrong, or at least too hasty. Pirate torture, like their other infamous practices, can also be explained, perhaps better, as rational profit-maximizing behavior—albeit the grisly kind.

Overwhelming a merchantman without a fight was only half the battle for piratical profit maximization. The other half was dealing with recalcitrant crewmembers whose vessels had been successfully overtaken. In this, too, pirates faced an important potential cost of producing maritime plunder.

The central problem was simple: pirates' captives, quite naturally, were reluctant to hand over their goods to their captors. Some stashed their valuables in hiding spots aboard their ships. The cook aboard a prize taken by Bartholomew Roberts's crew, for instance, hid his "Rings and Buckles" so the pirates wouldn't take them.[12] More desperate captives went a step further. They destroyed their valuables. One of Edward Low's victims, for example, "hung eleven thousand moydores of gold in a bag out of the cabbin window, and as soon as he was taken by the said Lowe, cutt the rope and lett them drop into the sea."[13] There was no way for such captives to retrieve their goods; but there was no way for pirates to either, which seems to have been the point.

The effect on pirates' profit was clear. Valuables that were hidden and unrecovered, or destroyed, was revenue lost. Time spent hunting for stashed goods like Easter eggs was time not spent hunting for new prizes, revenue lost again.

The captive resistance problem that pirates faced *after* overtaking a prize was simply an extension of the prize resistance problem they faced *before* overtaking it. Pirates' solution to the former therefore extended their solution to the latter: once a merchantman had submitted, "surrender or die" became "give up all your goods or die."

There was, however, a difficulty. How could pirates know if captives had hidden or destroyed booty and thus should be punished? "Surrender or die" worked because pirates could easily tell if a prize resisted; it's hard to miss incoming cannon fire. Captive resistance, on the other hand, could be much more subtle, surreptitious; there was often a good chance for victims to stash or destroy valuables without being seen.

Killing captives indiscriminately was no solution. That would only make things worse. If your odds of being slaughtered are the same no matter what you do, why not hide or destroy your valuables?[14] Pirates needed to restrict punishment as much as possible to captives who were uncooperative. But, since such behavior was often hard to detect, the expected cost of hiding or destroying booty—the probability of being caught times the punishment—might often be too low to deter it.

In this respect, the situation that pirates faced was not unlike the one faced by contemporary highway patrolmen. Only a small fraction of traffic violators are likely to be observed in action. Patrolmen's solution: offset the low probability of detection with especially stiff penalties for those who are caught. The odds of being pulled over going ninety miles per hour on a highway where the limit is fifty-five miles per hour may be only one in one hundred. But the penalty suffered in that event—an enormous fine and possibly the revocation of your license—is draconian. So, most of the time you keep it reasonably close to fifty-five miles per hour despite the unlikelihood of being caught if you don't.

Pirates' approach was similar. They offset the low probability of detecting captives hiding or destroying valuables with outrageously brutal punishment for those who were detected. What's worse than being killed? Being heinously tortured, then killed. This explains why pirates went to the trouble of "*making their Hellish Inventions for unheard of Barbarities*," as one court remarked.[15] "Give up your goods or die" was in fact "give up your goods or have your body parts removed piece by piece and fed to you."

But there was a hitch. Torturing captives was itself costly for pirates. The more elaborately brutal, hence effective, the torture, the more time pirates spent torturing instead of searching for the next prize. More brutal torture might also invite a more vigorous response from the captive, potentially leading to an injured pirate. In the case of hidden valuables, pirates' cost of torture might be more than balanced by the valuables retrieved. But in the case of destroyed goods in particular, it couldn't be. The most heinous torture in the world can't raise sunken booty from the depths of the ocean floor.

In confronting this dilemma, pirates confronted what economists call a "credible-commitment problem." To discourage captives from destroying cargo, pirates wanted to promise brutal torture. But the cost of following through if a captive actually destroyed cargo exceeded the benefit, so their promise wasn't credible. Pirates' problem was the same one that highway patrolmen would face if their cost of writing you up for speeding exceeded the sum they could collect from you in fines. In that case, you wouldn't expect to be written up, so the threat of being fined wouldn't stop you from speeding.

On the other hand, if patrolmen could somehow commit themselves to always write up people they caught speeding—even when the cost exceeded the benefit—the threat of the fine would become credible, and you would drive closer to the limit. The trick is in finding an effective commitment device.

The commitment device that pirates found was establishing a reputation as people willing to cut off their nose—or rather a recalcitrant captive's nose—to spite their face. If captives believed that pirates were willing to punish uncooperative behavior no matter the cost, they would expect to be heinously tortured if they were caught engaging in such behavior even when the immediate effect on pirates' bottom line was negative. So, they would cooperate. And what better way for pirates to make captives believe this than to actually follow through on torture when captives destroyed goods?

Pirates could use the very behavior that posed their credible-commitment problem to overcome that problem because they had not one but multiple victims, whom they encountered over time, which allowed pirates to develop a reputation. Following through today on torture that was more trouble than it was worth was like making an investment in not having to use torture at all tomorrow. The value of that investment would evaporate if pirates' reputation was undone by failing to follow through on torture when it was promised, which committed pirates to keeping their word.[16] Hence Lowe's response to the fellow who tossed his gold overboard: he "cutt off the said Masters lipps and broyl'd them before his face."[17] Costly in the short run, but profit maximizing in the long run.

Conclusion

Thinking about pirates economically allows one to understand their infamous practices in a consistent manner—a significant benefit, since, on the surface, pirate practices present a bundle of contradictions. Were early eighteenth-century pirates armed robbers, or were they pioneers of constitutional democracy? Trying to hide from the law, or trying to make their criminal identity crystal clear? Cruel torturers, or merciful to their victims? The answer to each of these questions is "yes" not because pirates were bipolar but rather because they responded rationally to the incentives they faced in pursuit of their goal: profit.

Seen this way, pirates' seemingly schizophrenic behavior was perfectly consistent. To make money from armed robbery, pirates needed to incentivize teamwork with one another—the reason they developed constitutional democracy. To minimize the cost of engaging in armed robbery, pirates needed to incentive prizes to acquiescence without a fight—the reason they identified themselves with an unmistakable flag, the Jolly Roger, despite their eagerness to avoid government capture. And to maximize revenue from armed robbery, pirates needed to incentivize victim cooperation—the reason they were cruel toward the recalcitrant and merciful toward the compliant. *Homo economicus* inhabited the eighteenth century, just as he inhabits the twenty-first. At sea he sometimes just went by a more ominous name: pirate.

NOTES

1. See, for instance, Gary S. Becker, *The Economic Approach to Human Behavior* (Chicago: University of Chicago Press, 1976); Gordon Tullock, *The Selected Works of Gordon Tullock*, 10 vols., ed. Charles K. Rowley (Indianapolis: Liberty Fund, 2006); and Peter T. Leeson, *WTF?! An Economic Tour of the Weird* (Stanford: Stanford University Press, 2017).

2. My discussion is based on my previously published work on this topic. See, for instance, Peter T. Leeson, "An-*arrgh*-chy: The Law and Economics of Pirate Organization," *Journal of Political Economy* 115 (2007): 1049–94; *The Invisible Hook: The Hidden Economics of Pirates* (Princeton: Princeton University Press, 2009); "Pirational Choice: The Economics of Infamous Pirate Practices," *Journal of Economic Behavior and Organization* 76 (2010): 497–510.

3. *A General History of the Pyrates, from Their First Rise and Settlement in the Island of Providence, to the Present Time*, ed. Manuel Schonhorn (1726–1728; repr., Mineola, N.Y.: Dover, 1999), 211–12.

4. Clinton Rossiter, ed., *The Federalist Papers* (1788; repr., New York: Mentor-Penguin, 1961).

5. William Snelgrave, *A New Account of Some Parts of Guinea, and the Slave Trade* (1734; repr., London: F. Cass, 1971), 206.

6. *General History of the Pyrates*, 335.

7. *Boston News-Letter*, June 9–16, 1718.

8. *The Trials of Eight Persons Indicted for Piracy &c* (Boston: John Edwards, 1718), 24.

9. *A Full and Exact Account, of the Tryal of All the Pyrates, Lately Taken by Captain Ogle* (London: J. Roberts, 1723), 5.

10. The Jolly Roger was an "imperfectly discriminating" signal, however. It didn't work 100 percent of the time. Some coast guards found the temptation to cash in on pirates' fearsome identity too hard to resist; they flew a Jolly Roger despite the risk. Still, most did not, keeping the flag's effectiveness as a signal for pirates intact.

11. *British Journal* (London), August 8, 1724.

12. *Full and Exact Account*, 14.

13. Karen Kupperman Ordahl, John C. Appleby, and Mandy Banton, eds., *Calendar of State Papers, Colonial Series, America and West Indies, 1574–1739* (London: Routledge, 2000), CD-ROM, March 25, 1724, Item 102, vol. 34 (1724–1725), 71–73.

14. Killing captives indiscriminately would also undermine pirates' "surrender or die" policy. If word got out that pirates were reneging on their promise of mercy for compliant victims, victims would become more willing to resist them.

15. *Tryals of Sixteen Persons for Piracy &c* (Boston: Joseph Edwards, 1726), 14.

16. There was another side to the reputation that pirates invested in creating: kindness, even generosity, toward fully cooperative captives. Hence to the stick, pirates added the carrot. For details, see Leeson, "P*irational* Choice."

17. Ordahl et al., *Calendar of State Papers*, 71–73.

SECTION 4

Images of Pirates in Their Own Time and Beyond

Henry Every and the Creation of the Pirate Myth in Early Modern Britain

Margarette Lincoln

In 1694, a new ballad hit the London streets inviting people to sing along to a story of the notorious deeds of the pirate Henry Every. Called "A Copy of Verses, Composed by Captain Henry Every, Lately Gone to Sea to Seek His Fortune," it purported to be the true words of an Englishman turned pirate to ravage the Indian Ocean. It began "Come all ye brave Boys, whose Courage is bold / Will you venture with me, I'll glut you with Gold?" The pirate boasted that at sea he and his men would take on all comers—notably England's traditional, Catholic enemies and heathens—but show mercy to those who surrendered. He appealed for followers, men who, like himself, felt that they had somehow been wronged by their country, then concluded his verses with a flourish, "The Sword shall maintain me as long as I live."

The activities of notorious pirates such as Every had been recorded in popular verse earlier in the century, but in the 1690s pirates became powerful figures in ballad literature, a genre with its own printed form and thematic conventions.[1] Ballads were printed as broadsides on one side of a large sheet of paper, sometimes accompanied by a woodcut illustration. No music was printed with the words. Instead, the lyrics were usually written for a popular tune that was named on the sheet. If not already known, the tune was easy to pick up because ballad mongers would sing new works on street corners to attract customers. These ballads had immediate appeal. The content was emotional, the language colorful but simple, and although the stories were often sensational, they routinely paid lip service to conventional morality: villains got their just deserts in the end. Consequently, ballads such as the verses attributed to Every appealed to many classes, including the illiterate and semiliterate.

The known facts about Every's life are sparse. He was baptized on August 23, 1659, in Devon, a county in the West of England that produced many seafarers. He used several aliases (Henry Avery, Benjamin Bridgeman, and others), as seamen often did if they wished to make a fresh start in different ships. He briefly served in the Royal Navy from 1689 to 1690 and was afterward employed as sailing master on one of four vessels taking part in a venture in the Spanish Americas. A group of London investors had put together a complicated deal. The group had obtained a trading and salvage license from Charles II of Spain under the terms of the Treaty of Madrid (1670), whereby England and Spain recognized each other's possessions in the Caribbean. The aim was to recover treasure from Spanish wrecks and to get more money by capturing French privateers who were harassing Spanish possessions. Unfortunately, the expedition was delayed for a long time at Corunna when the House of Trade (Casa de Contratación), which operated Seville's commercial monopoly in the West Indies, blocked its departure. The London investors tried to get the correct passes so that the expedition could go ahead. Meanwhile they stopped the seamen's wages and kept them on short rations to save money. After months of stalemate, some crew members managed to get news home to their wives that they were being mistreated and had received no pay. The women, already finding it hard to feed their families, petitioned the Crown on their husbands' behalf, the accepted method of addressing authorities in order to obtain redress from injury. Yet by the time the Privy Council had set up an official inquiry, Every had persuaded some of his crew to seize their ship and turn pirate. Some claimed marauding was his intention all along.

After his successful mutiny, Every directed his ship toward the Indian Ocean, signaling his change of allegiance by changing its name from *Charles II* (after the Spanish king), to *Fancy*, a word that then had connotations of invention and originality as well as caprice. By September 1695 he was at the mouth of the Red Sea, where he teamed up with other pirate captains waiting to attack the Indian fleet transporting Muslims on the annual pilgrimage to Mecca. In the fierce battle that followed, Every was lucky enough to secure a valuable prize. His ship captured the *Ganj-i-Sawai* belonging to Aurangzeb (1618–1707), the Mogul emperor who had ruled most of India for nearly half a century. The ship contained an enormous amount of treasure and, reportedly, the emperor's daughter or granddaughter, who was traveling to Mecca with her retinue and with an elderly concubine of the emperor as guardian. In a stroke, Every possessed a fortune. He was never brought to justice and was to become one of the greatest pirates the world has ever known. From the first, his story was embroiled in claim and counterclaim, exaggeration, confusion, and myth.

Once news of a pirate's exploits reached London, such outlaws immediately became popular heroes. For one thing, pirate atrocities were mostly directed against the shipping of other nations, often long-term trade rivals or enemies, such as the Spanish. For another, the victims of English piracy were often of a different faith. England was predominantly Protestant; the victims of its pirates were invariably Catholic or non-Christians. Therefore, the populace felt liberated to celebrate pirate deeds. In an age when communications were poor and when people did not necessarily want to be told the truth about their popular heroes, the history of piracy was always going to be bound up with legend. Critics have pointed out that early modern readers did not expect published texts to be either wholly factual or absolutely fiction.[2] Every is a prime example of this trend at work.

Every's escapades, reworked, colored, exaggerated, and obfuscated, helped to create a burgeoning pirate literature.[3] In turn, this literature now provides us with insights into preoccupations and debates of the time. Given the limitations of contemporary records, rather than look for hard data about Every, it is more rewarding to see how his story inspired different representations of piracy and to explore what this tells us about audiences of the time.

Early Stories of Every

Swashbuckling narratives came into being partly because great swathes of the public wanted to believe in daring piracies. They themselves led downtrodden lives, usually at the mercy of the powerful. Pirates symbolized the hopes and fantasies of those who heartily wished that they, too, were free to roam the world, fight for treasure, and live in a social environment where they could make up the rules. Moreover, events of the seventeenth century had tarnished the reputation of the elite in England. In recent memory, many self-serving people had switched political and even religious allegiances, often several times, in the hope of advancement. They may have changed sides with the ups and downs of the civil wars (1642–51), during the Interregnum under Oliver Cromwell (1649–60), with the restoration of the monarchy (1660), or at the so-called Glorious Revolution (1688), which saw the Catholic James II ousted from the throne and replaced by Protestant William III and Mary II. Great men who achieved success by these means were not greatly respected. Admiration for pirates, therefore, was not simply a case of ordinary people taking a gleeful interest in those who appeared to rob the wealthy. As we shall see, Every's case indicates that the lower orders in society felt a burning sense of social injustice and, given an opportunity, were prepared to challenge the system. When some of Every's crew were tried in London, the jury proved unwilling to apply the laws of the land to their case.

Every's escapade immediately caused English trade with India to falter. The Mogul was incandescent with rage and imprisoned East India Company officials, leaving the English government desperate to bring Every and his crew to justice. The merchants who had organized the expedition badly needed to defend themselves against any accusation that they had mismanaged the affair and taken too hard a line with the seamen. They also needed to strengthen their insurance claim so that at least they made something out of the fiasco. They produced the ballad "Composed by Captain Henry Every" as part of their defense. The piece seemed to prove beyond doubt that Every had always intended to turn pirate.[4] In fact, it was a clever attempt to use the very medium that helped to make pirates into popular heroes to condemn Every as an outlaw.

A moment's reflection would have counteracted any notion that Every chose to celebrate his piracy in ballad form and send a copy of his verses back to England. In fact, the eminent merchant Sir James Houblon had submitted a manuscript of the ballad as evidence to the Privy Council in 1694, then holding an inquiry into Every and the commercial venture that had employed him. Houblon was in the firing line because he had led the group of investors who had put the deal together. In the end, the authorities gave the merchants a sympathetic hearing. Britain was at war with France, the economy was doing badly, and government was disposed to do all it could to protect the country's trading interests.

Meanwhile, Every and his crew had scattered. Some settled in North America, some in the Caribbean.[5] Others returned to the British Isles. Several were discovered in England and Ireland when their unexplained wealth caused suspicion. One man turned king's evidence to avoid being hanged, so in 1696 six of Every's crew were tried at the Old Bailey. Amazingly, the jury failed to convict. Here was certain proof that ordinary people sympathized with freebooters. But the government desperately needed a conviction to help restore relations with the Mogul. There was a swift retrial on a different set of charges. This time the judge harangued members of the jury in advance, emphasizing that it was their duty to impose harsh justice. "No man can believe just as he lists [wishes]," the judge told them. The law had to be obeyed. Failure to convict would bring shame on the nation, which would then be regarded as "a nest of pirates."[6] James Houblon's merchant brother, John, being one of the lords of the admiralty, helped to officiate at the trial and bring about the verdict merchants needed.

Although the process would be considered legally dubious today, all six members of Every's crew were found guilty at the retrial and hanged at Execution Dock on November 26, 1696.[7] Extracts from the trial report were printed to publicize the Crown's case against them. Furthermore, the execution of these six crew members was described in another ballad that encourages audiences to take a critical view of piracy. "Villany Rewarded; or the Pirates' Last Farewel to the World" is illustrated with horrific woodcuts showing two pirates on the scaffold. Its verses make clear that pirates are to be regarded as freeloaders who take the bread of others: one of the condemned men bemoans his wicked past, confessing that he seized merchant ships at random, killed those who would not submit, and lived "upon others' good."[8]

There is no indication in the published account of the trial that the accused pirates had anything to say about Every's fate. Wild rumors about him circulated from the 1680s, but he had simply vanished. Later reports said he had returned to the West of England. *A General History of the Robberies and Murders of the Most Notorious Pyrates* (1724) claimed that Every was cheated out of his money there by merchants who had discovered his identity and that he died impoverished in Bideford. Yet he may have been one of the very few pirates to get clean away with his booty. He may never have returned to England. One hustler, Captain John Breholt, hoping to profit from a scheme to repatriate the English pirates on Madagascar in 1707, paraded a woman at various London venues who claimed to be Every's abandoned wife.[9] She elicited much sympathy for her plight but the scheme came to nothing.

Marriage and Madagascar

No account of Every's life was printed until November 1708, when the *Monthly Miscellany* explained that he had settled a colony on Madagascar and imported a cargo of women to please his crew. At this point, Every's story became fused with the emerging myth of Madagascar as a pirate lair awash with loot. He was now represented as someone who, through his own efforts, had raised his status from lowly subject to powerful king of an island larger than Britain, and likely to establish a new line of rulers in his exotic realm. The tale paralleled and mocked the nation's colonial ambitions.

Around 1709, an anonymous author writing under the false name Adrian van Broeck brought out *The Life and Adventures of Capt. John Every, the Famous* English *Pirate, (Rais'd from a Cabbin-Boy, to a King) Now in Possession of Madagascar.* The tale has a strong monarchist bent. Supposedly, this popular narrative was taken from the journal of someone who had escaped from Madagascar with firsthand knowledge of events, but it is heavily based on the version published the previous year in the *Monthly Miscellany.* Its author claims that Every had married the Indian princess from the *Ganj-i-Sawai* and set up home with her on Madagascar. He insists that Every paid the princess all the respect that was due to her noble birth and "plunder'd her of something more pleasing than the Jewels" only after they had been properly married by one of her priests. Afterward, Every's men drew lots for her attendant women but each, before enjoying their prize, followed their captain's chaste example and was married by the same priest.[10] But what seems to have happened on board the captured ship was mass rape over several days, with some of the women committing suicide rather than submit to violation. The pirates took all the Mogul treasure onto their own ship. Afterward, they allowed the male captives to sail home but kept the surviving women.

Every's supposed marriage to an Indian princess attracted publicity because, in this period, the status of women in marriage was a matter of lively debate. Notorious pirate liaisons, distant from Britain, could be safely used to explore male and female perspectives on the institution of marriage. In 1710, the writer and social commentator Ned Ward included a dialogue "Between King Every, the Pirate, and His Indian Princess at Madagascar" in his *Nuptial Dialogues and Debates.* This was an ambitious project that Ward had begun two years earlier, consisting of a series of dialogues on the married state. He chose the version of Every's story that depicted him as honorable in matters of love, insisting that the pirate waited for the princess to consent to marriage and took her as his "lawful Wife," though it was easily in his power to make her a victim to his lust. The couple's imagined state of easy domesticity on Madagascar allows Ward to touch on negative views of the position of women in marriage. The princess is presented as deeply unhappy on two accounts: she feels like a captive and she is exiled from her homeland.

> What tho', by your Consent, I share a Throne,
> I'm still a Prisoner in a Land unknown?
> Fetter'd amidst the Pomps and Joys of Life,
> And but a Slave, although a lawful Wife.[11]

Many married women of the time compared their situation to that of slaves; Ward opportunely contributes to the discussion while also exploiting popular interest in pirate lifestyles. Later in this work, the princess challenges Every to admit that he, too, is homesick. The pirate seems to confess that it is so but resolutely follows his head, not his heart. If he were to be discovered in England he would be tried, hanged, and gibbeted, so he counsels resignation: they should make the best of their situation and never think of their homes. Ward depicts the male pirate as the more realistic of the two. In this imagined dialogue, Every sets out the wider context and quells his wife's emotional outburst with rational argument. She may be unhappy but should submit to his superior intellect.

Charles Shadwell's popular play *The Fair Quaker of Deal* also alludes to Every's piracies within the wider contemporary context of gender relations in marriage. It was first performed at the Theatre Royal in Drury Lane in 1710 and encompasses in its frame of reference the plight of London's prostitutes. Cribidge, a naval lieutenant, contemplates a mercenary marriage to a rich woman. A fellow lieutenant, the unscrupulous Sir Charles Pleasant, imagines that, once married, Cribidge would put his wife aside and find pleasure elsewhere: "mutiny, as Every did; turn your Captain [wife] ashore, then set up for a Pirate." Here piracy is explicitly compared to whoring. Later in the play, Mizen, a "finical Sea-Fop," tries to steal another man's betrothed, an act which is also likened to piracy.[12] The self-serving life of a pirate plainly serves as a metaphor for the mercenary nature of the contemporary marriage market and the sex trade. Yet within the comic framework of this popular play, any criticism is light touch.

Male behavior toward women is also a central theme in Charles Johnson's play *The Successful Pyrate*, though it has also been deemed "a meditation on responsible imperialism and just monarchy."[13] The play, first performed in 1712, is clearly inspired by Every's adventures. (Johnson is not the same author as Captain Johnson, reputed author of *A General History*.) The playwright aimed for a box office hit and focused on the love interest in his adaptation of the pirate's story. His treatment of that theme is constrained by the conventions of the popular theater and he did not produce a great work, though it sold better in print form and reached a third edition by 1713. The audience is told that the hero, Arviragus (based on Every), turned pirate and declared war on mankind when he returned from a voyage to find that a friend had deceived him. In his absence, this false friend had stolen his lands and his mistress. Arviragus, "perfect Master of Gallantry as well as Courage," allegedly forgave his former mistress. Yet his behavior toward women in the play falls far short of gallantry. After taking the Great Mogul's ship, Arviragus tries to woo the Indian princess on board "and by most constant Service gain her Love," but the princess insists that she loves another man. Arviragus is sure that "Women are changeable" and that she will soon fall for his charms. He forces his unwanted attentions on her. Johnson is not as subtle as Ward in his presentation of the female point of view, yet the play vividly betrays male fears of loss of freedom in marriage. In a feeble gesture toward the pirate custom of dividing all loot into shares, Arviragus proposes that his crew draw lots for the remaining women on board. The plan backfires: his men wish to remain unfettered, with no "Arbitrary Wives" to control their actions, and turn against him.[14]

The pirate's determination to have his own way with the princess also undermines any representation of him as a gallant hero. The play concludes with an implausible denouement when Arviragus discovers that the princess's true love is in fact his own son. At this point he ceases his unwelcome suit. Meanwhile, his crew reject all endeavors to marry them off to the women they have captured, most of whom turn out to be the same whores and jades that they had deserted in London and hoped never to see again. The audience, unless it has managed to suspend all disbelief, is left with an impression of Arviragus as an aging tyrant and his pirate crew as a feckless rabble eager to escape domestic responsibility. At the end of the play, the princess is reunited with her true love. The improbable presentation of the young lovers' romantic relationship fails to engage. Worse still, a complaint was soon made to Charles Killigrew (Master of Revels and partly responsible for stage censorship) that the play glamorized villainy.

King of Pirates

By the 1720s, a more critical attitude was being taken toward Every's piracies, but the theme of piracy itself was still a manifestly commercial one that could attract a large readership. Daniel Defoe's book *The Life, Adventures, and Pyracies, of the Famous Captain Singleton: Containing an Account of His Being Set on Shore in the Island of Madagascar* (1720) capitalizes on the exotic connotations of that island, although the author only briefly mentions the pirate rendezvous in the actual text. He does, though, use Madagascar to consider how pirates might be rehabilitated in society. He relates how Singleton joins up with Every on Madagascar, their combined forces totaling about twelve hundred men. Singleton devises a scheme whereby pirates who wish to give up "the trade of pirating" can buy land from the inhabitants and set up plantations. He claims that about fifty pirates did just this. Every, on the other hand, is irredeemable. He prefers to build fortifications near the coast as a base for pirate attacks. In the novel, Defoe conveniently leaves Every's fate open ended, although Every is clearly used as a foil to indicate Singleton's better qualities.

The opportunist Singleton does manage to get safely back to England with his money, helped by his Quaker friend William, suggesting that pirates are most successful when eschewing women altogether.[15] All the same, both are forced to live in constant disguise as Armenian merchants, fearing to speak English in public, and Singleton makes a token marriage with William's widowed sister. Popular literature of the time highlights the recurrent affinity between pirates and merchants.[16] Accounts of the pirate Every also underline the comity between merchants and outlaws. Stories of his alleged retreat to Madagascar describe how he made a trading agreement with the local king, as chartered companies often did. Later, again like trading companies, Every was said to have built a fort there in an effort to establish his authority.[17]

In 1720, the industrious Defoe published an account that directly focuses on Every's exploits. It takes the form of two letters, ostensibly from Every himself. In his preface, Defoe claims that he wishes to correct the "ridiculous and extravagant accounts that have been put upon the world" regarding the pirate's career. Undoubtedly, in the years since Every's daring act of plunder, more details about his actual treatment of the women on the *Ganj-i-Sawai* had emerged. Yet Defoe has the pirate insisting that all reports of violence against the women on the ship were untrue. He never ravished the Great Mogul's daughter, murdered her, or raped the women in her retinue. On the contrary, Every insists, the princess and her women were treated with more decency and humanity than ever women were treated by pirates before. His explanation remains unconvincing. Every writes, "I have heard that it has been reported in *England* that I ravish'd this Lady, and then used her most barbarously; but they wrong me, for I never offer'd any Thing of that Kind to her, I assure you; nay, I was so far from being inclin'd to it, that I did not like her; and there was one of her Ladies who I found much more agreeable to me, and who I was afterwards something free with, but not even with her either by Force, or by Way of Ravishing."[18] The pirate claims that he had even put an armed guard on the great cabin where the princess took refuge to ensure his crew did not molest her or her noble attendants. Being more civilized than his crew, Defoe's Every insists that he dined in the cabin with the princess most amicably, though he did not understand a word of her language.

The lower-class women in the Mogul's ship fared less well. "As for the Ship where the women of inferior Rank were, and who were in Number almost two hundred, I cannot answer for what might happen in the first Heat," Defoe has Every write, "but even there, after the first Heat of our Men was over, what was done, was done quietly, for I have heard some of the Men say, that there was not a Woman among them but what was lain with four or five Times over, that is to say, by so many several Men, for as the Women made no Opposition, so the Men even took those that were next them, without Ceremony, when and where Opportunity offer'd."[19] After a day or two, Every and his trusted crew members decide that the men would be ruined for work by having sex with so many women, so all the prisoners are put into one ship and allowed to sail home. As with so many narratives of the period, it is difficult to determine if the work is intended to be ironical. Is the pirate damned by his own tongue? Or are his words meant to be the honest testimony of a popular hero?

The way in which the pirate describes the different treatment given to the high- and low-ranking women suggests that the abuse of lower-class women was an affair of less concern. In an age when men regarded young female servants and shop assistants as fair game, this may in fact have been the case.[20] A traditional sea song about Every, "The Ballad of Long Ben," dismissed the princess's retinue as "whores" and showed no disapproval that Every's men "made free with the girls."[21] Yet on this point, too, it is hard to tell whether Defoe's account is factual and influenced by contemporary lived experience, or ironical and intended to prompt criticism of the pirates' actions. The ambiguity ensures that different readers could take away different interpretations.

As writers adopted a more nuanced attitude toward piracy, some commentators saw that there was an uncomfortable parallel between the avid empire building of nation states, which usually meant seizing distant lands inhabited by other peoples, and certain types of pirate activity. The satirical writer Ned Ward teases out this argument in his *Nuptial Dialogues* when reflecting on the pirate Every's career. Ostensibly, Ward is discussing relations between the sexes in an imagined dialogue between Every and his Indian princess on Madagascar. Yet the princess's complaints touch on political as well as personal issues. Her unhappy marriage and her loneliness on the island are compounded by the guilt she feels, knowing that Every has seized power by force. His majesty is nothing but a charade:

> Debar'd of Friends, and from my Native Soil
> Chain'd for my life, within a barb'rous Isle.
> How then can I subsist without remorse,
> Since all my Joys are the effects of Force?
> Or how, without gross Flattery, applaud
> A doubtful Stage that's founded upon Fraud.[22]

Every boldly retorts that the right of kings depends on the power of the sword and that conquerors are everywhere accepted as rightful rulers. He goes on to claim that man is truer to his essential nature, which is noble, when he rejects a servile life suited to beasts and aspires instead to rule:

> Who then would to their native Soil be ty'd,
> Where they must bend and cringe to others Pride,
> Like a Mill-Horse, within one Circle move,
> And on their Country fix a slavish Love.[23]

Instead the couple will create a lasting dynasty on the island:

> But make ourselves as happy and secure,
> As distant Tyrants that despise our Pow'r,

> Be proud to think we may with Conduct be
> The builders of a lasting Monarchy,
> And that a Royal Issue of our own,
> May long succeed in our Establish'd Throne.[24]

The kind of society Every visualizes in Madagascar is in the same mold as that found at home in England. Some readers might have been left with the impression that both are tyrannical and unjust.

A few pirates were indeed absorbed into Malagasy society and came to wield considerable power. Reports of these developments may have helped to create the short-lived myth of Captain Every as a powerful ruler on Madagascar. For those familiar with the history of European contact with that island, Every's alleged success was also a criticism of the English nobility. A generation earlier, members of the elite had made no headway in their ambition to colonize it. In 1637 advisors in the court of Charles I considered that the king's seventeen-year-old nephew, Prince Rupert, might conquer the island to show his martial promise, but his mother soon put a stop to that far-fetched idea.[25] The pirate Every, a common seaman, was now credited with achieving what Prince Rupert and other courtiers had been unable to do.

By the mid-1720s, the British government had taken an even harsher line with pirates and, with colonial support, was doing a better job suppressing them.[26] Writers of popular works were also adopting an ever more critical perspective on Every's piracies. *The History and Lives of All the Most Notorious Pirates, and Their Crews* (1725), attributed to Daniel Defoe, claims that Every "Ravish'd the young Princess, and used other beastly Actions to the Ladies of her Retinue."[27] There is no mention of marriage. Allegedly, Every forced the princess back to Madagascar, where she bore him a child, who did not live beyond infancy. Soon afterward, the princess died of a broken heart. The author considers politics as well as relations between the sexes. He implies that Every not only disrupted the trade of the East India Company by antagonizing the Great Mogul but also damaged Britain's imperial ambition by setting a negative example of how a conquering power should behave toward indigenous peoples. The negative effects of imperialism was a subject of contemporary debate and Every's alleged behavior on Madagascar therefore became a matter of concern among the educated classes.[28] The book also claims Every became so powerful that tribal leaders sued for his protection in their own quarrels and he was able to exact from these leaders an annual tribute, "which was commonly their Daughters and young Virgins to be given unto his Subjects."[29] Whether or not this was true, the British government would have wished to disassociate itself from rumors of such practices. The author of the work claims to be offering it as a caution to seamen tempted by a freebooting lifestyle. He prefaces it with a useful summary of the laws against piracy and insists that Every got his just deserts in the end.

John Gay's satirical opera *Polly* (1728), sequel to his popular hit *The Beggar's Opera*, is similarly indebted to elements of Every's story but makes more of the colonial context and the social inequalities that spur people to crime. *Polly* is set in the West Indies, and Gay explores colonization as well as piracy and marriage. The hero, Macheath, disguises himself as a black man, turns pirate, and gives himself the name Morano. While living on the wrong side of the law, he exhibits nostalgia for his native land and fantasizes about returning to London. Yet his ambition is only to spend his treasure on his wife. Gay criticized the mercenary view of marriage held by most of the elite. Morano has made a love match to a transported criminal, which will hardly advance him in colonial society, whereas ambitious British planters generally marry for "treasure." Gay exploits the contemporary fascination with pirates to show the interconnectedness of many contemporary issues relating to power and wealth. He specifically draws attention to the plight of the poor who enjoy neither.[30]

Yet Every's exploits in the Indian Ocean also inspired works that were unreservedly intended as entertainment. Romances targeted at female readers and promoting sexual fantasies about abduction and rape situations had become popular. Penelope Aubin (c. 1679–1731), who specialized in sensational, short narratives, responded to this readership. Her stories routinely involved innocent English women captured by pirates or infidels and placed in immediate danger of being ravished. In 1722, for example, she wrote about two English ladies who had been shipwrecked and captured. The essential drama of the plot is summed up in a short exchange between the Muslim captor and one of his victims, Emelia: "Come, come, trifle not with me; I resolved to possess you and will not be deny'd." The heroine replies, "Villain, I fear you not, I'll sacrifice you to preserve my virtue; die infidel," and stabs him with his own dagger.[31] Aubin's later romance *The Life of Charlotta Du Pont* (1723) is in the same mode but features a heroine captured by pirates. The pirate captain found himself so aroused by the heroine's beauty, "he resolv'd to gratify his Flame by enjoying *Charlotta* at Midnight by force." As he proceeded to freedoms that affronted her modesty she, "taking a sharp Bodkin out of her Hair, stab'd him in the Belly so dangerously, that he fell senseless on the Bed."[32] At this point, a Spanish warship fortuitously caught up with the pirate ship and Charlotta was freed.

Conclusion

Piracy, as a cultural theme, was just as marketable in the early modern period as it is today. Scandalous piracies that netted fabulous sums of money and discomfited the authorities generated a range of highly saleable printed products. Every's exploits above all others helped to cement pirate literature as one of the features of the age. Different accounts of his piracies, published over decades, show how his story persisted and could be packaged in different genres, selling at different prices, to attract all levels of society. The truth of such accounts was not vitally important to readers. Even the author of *A General History of the Robberies and Murders of the Most Notorious Pyrates* embellished the available data to produce an exciting and dramatic narrative. Yet if pirate exploits lent themselves to myth, pirate narratives were also a versatile means of rehearsing the problems and issues of the age while, at the same time, creating other forms of engagement.

NOTES

1. Claire Jowitt, *The Culture of Piracy: English Literature and Seaborne Crime 1580–1630* (Farnham, UK: Ashgate, 2010), 2, 25–30; C. H. Firth, ed., *Naval Songs and Ballads* (London: Publications of the Navy Records Society, 1908), xlix.

2. See Lennard Davis, *Factual Fictions: The Origins of the English Novel* (New York: Columbia University Press, 1983), 24; Margarette Lincoln, "Tales of Wonder 1650–1750," *Journal for Eighteenth Century Studies* 27 (2004): 219–32.

3. See Frederick Burwick and Manushag N. Powell, *British Pirates in Print and Performance* (New York: Palgrave Macmillan, 2015), 28–32.

4. Joel H. Baer, "Bold Captain Every in the Privy Council: Early Variants of a Broadside Ballad from the Pepys Collection," *Folk Music Journal* 7 (1995): 8.

5. Rebecca A. Simon, "The Problem and Potential of Piracy: Legal Changes and Emerging Ideas of Colonial Autonomy in the Early Modern British Atlantic, 1670–1730," *Journal for Maritime Research* 18 (2016): 127.

6. *The Tryals of Joseph Dawson, Edward Forseith, William May, William Bishop,*

James Lewis, and John Sparkes for Several Piracies and Robberies by Them Committed (London: John Everingham, 1696), 7–8.

7. For the execution ritual, see Margarette Lincoln, *British Pirates and Society, 1680–1730* (Farnham, UK: Ashgate, 2014), 33–39.

8. Firth, *Naval Songs and Ballads*, 133–34.

9. Arne Bialuschewski, "Greed, Fraud, and Popular Culture: John Breholt's Madagascar Schemes of the Early Eighteenth Century," in *Money Power and Print: Interdisciplinary Studies on the Financial Revolution in the British Isles*, ed. Charles Ivar McGrath and Christopher Fauske (Newark: University of Delaware Press, 2008), 110.

10. Adrian van Broeck, *The Life and Adventures of Capt. John Every, the Famous English Pirate, (Rais'd from a Cabbin-Boy, to a King) Now in Possession of Madagascar* (London: J. Baker, 1709), 31.

11. Edward Ward, *Nuptial Dialogues and Debates* (London: H. Moore and A. Bettesworth, 1710), 2:133.

12. Charles Shadwell, *The Fair Quaker of Deal: or, the Humours of the Navy. A Comedy* (London, 1710), 18, 59.

13. Burwick and Powell, *British Pirates*, 29.

14. Charles Johnson, *The Successful Pyrate* (1712; 2nd ed., London: Bernard Lintott, 1713), 37.

15. Burwick and Powell, *British Pirates*, 109.

16. Mercantilism also helped create the conditions for piracy. See Shannon Lee Dawdy and Joe Bonni, "Towards a General Theory of Piracy," *Anthropological Quarterly* 85 (2012): 681.

17. "Epistle to the Reader," Plymouth and West Devon Record Office 373/1 p. 17 (December 14, 1716).

18. Daniel Defoe, *The King of Pirates: Being an Account of the Famous Enterprises of Captain Every, the Mock King of Madagascar. In Two Letters from Himself* (1719; repr., London: A. Bettesworth et al., 1720), 58.

19. Ibid., 59.

20. Dan Cruickshank, *The Secret History of Georgian London: How the Wages of Sin Shaped the Capital* (London: Random House, 2009), 38.

21. See "The Ballad of Long Ben," Wikisource, last modified March 21, 2016, accessed September 1, 2016, http://en.wikisource.org/wiki/The_Ballad_of_Long_Ben.

22. Ward, *Nuptial Dialogues and Debates*, 2:133.

23. Ibid, 2:141.

24. Ibid, 2:148.

25. Marlin E. Blaine, "Epic, Romance, and History in Davenant's 'Madagascar,'" *Studies in Philology* 95 (1998): 297.

26. See Mark G. Hanna, *Pirate Nests and the Rise of the British Empire, 1570–1740* (Chapel Hill: University of North Carolina Press, 2015), 369–72.

27. Daniel Defoe, *The History and Lives of All the Most Notorious Pirates, and Their Crews* (London: Edward Midwinter, 1725), 11.

28. See Richard Hingley, *The Recovery of Roman Britain 1586–1906* (New York: Oxford University Press, 2008), 170–74.

29. Defoe, *History and Lives*, 15.

30. See Robert G. Dryden, "John Gay's *Polly*: Unmasking Pirates and Fortune Hunters in the West Indies," *Eighteenth-Century Studies* 34 (2001): 539–57.

31. Penelope Aubin, *The Noble Slaves: or, the Lives and Adventures of Two Lords and Two Ladies, Who Were Shipwreck'd* (London: E. Bell et al., 1722), 48.

32. Penelope Aubin, *The Life of Charlotta Du Pont, an English Lady; Taken from Her Own Memoirs* (London: A. Bettesworth, 1723), 47.

"Blood and Lust"

MASCULINITY AND SEXUALITY IN
ILLUSTRATED PRINT PORTRAYALS OF
EARLY PIRATES OF THE CARIBBEAN

Carolyn Eastman

"Why is it that the pirate has, and always has had, a certain lurid glamour of the heroical enveloping him round about?" asked *Howard Pyle's Book of Pirates*, a large-scale, richly illustrated book for children published in 1921. "Would not every boy . . . rather be a pirate captain than a Member of Parliament?" To answer his own question, Pyle waxed lyrical: "What a life of adventure is his, to be sure! A life of constant alertness, constant danger, constant escape! . . . What a setting of blood and lust and flames and rapine for such a hero!"[1]

Pyle avoided detailed discussions of "lust" and "rapine" for his young readers, but the fact that he invoked them at all is both telling and representative of pirate tales over the centuries. Gender and sexuality play leading roles in portrayals of piracy and seafaring in such wide-ranging performances as Johnny Depp's gender-bending Jack Sparrow, the courtship antics of *The Pirates of Penzance*, Errol Flynn's rendering of Captain Blood as a "devil-may-care philanderer," and John Belushi's 1979 *Saturday Night Live* skit about "manly" life aboard the *Raging Queen*.[2]

Neither are these emphases unique to the modern era. Ubiquitous as they are now, conventions for depicting pirates as dangerous, lusty, gendered heroes have a long history, one that is rooted as much in the book trade as in the so-called "man's life at sea." These representations were born during the golden age of piracy (from roughly 1670 to 1730) and were reworked and codified in numerous illustrated books published in Europe and circulated throughout the Atlantic world. The volumes developed, reiterated, and augmented stereotypes about pirates to attract and titillate European and American readers who could afford illustrated books and whose lives adhered to far more conventional standards of behavior than the ones exhibited by the fictional pirates.

Early modern readers encountered pirates as a series of literary and pictorial conventions that emerged in the late seventeenth century. The pirates' drawn swords, eccentric clothing, and scowls glaring at the viewer amplified the books' emphases on masculinity and sexuality. Books like *Bucaniers of America* by Alexandre Exquemelin (1678) and *A General History of the Pyrates* (1724), by an author who called himself Captain Charles Johnson, earned their immense popularity at least in part by combining mesmerizing narration with vivid, full-page illustrations of pirates.

Examining these texts and images in tandem—particularly for the innovations developed from one edition or engraver to the next—allows us to see the vital intersections between manliness and sexuality, the transnational history of book publishing, and the role of images in the imaginative construction of bourgeois European identity.[3] The creation of what became stereotypical images of pirates—images that would continue to inform artists like Howard Pyle and filmmakers in the twentieth century and beyond—was sealed early on with a complex interplay between text and image in early print culture. Looking closely at the recurrence and reiteration of gendered representations of pirates, specifically as texts and images were copied and enhanced over many decades, allows us to see how writers and engravers played with sexualized masculinities to make their books increasingly appealing to readers. Gender and sexuality were at the heart of these portrayals, granting pirates an outsider masculinity all the more striking for the ways it permitted middling and elite readers to imagine a social world in which men did not need to exercise self-control, a world of manliness without constraint.

Imagining the Hypermasculine Pirate:
Bucaniers of America

In the late seventeenth and early eighteenth centuries, the pirates who disrupted trade in the Caribbean, West Africa, North America, and all points in between seemed to exemplify the dynamism and extranational energy made possible by maritime movement across the Atlantic Ocean. These men (and, famously, some women) formed international crews so fearsome that they proved to be major impediments to reliable European economic exchange. Just as European powers sought to create orderly means of drawing goods from the New World to enrich the Old, pirates became more numerous and audacious in their attacks, looting 2,500 merchant vessels in the ten years between 1716 and 1726 alone.[4] One eighteenth-century commentator estimated that England lost as much to pirates as it did to Spain and France during the catastrophic War of the Spanish Succession (1701–14). By the 1720s Parliament had enacted harsh new laws against piracy and conducted well-publicized criminal trials and hangings to punish pirates for their misdeeds. The display of juridical force aimed to discourage what had clearly become a highly lucrative line of work.

As important as piracy was to European and American political, economic, and maritime development, it also proved significant to the history of the book. Early modern print media developed modes of describing and representing pirates to titillate readers' imaginations about manly action and adventure. The most significant early text to do so was Alexandre Exquemelin's *De Americaensche Zee-Roovers* (translated shortly thereafter as *Bucaniers of America*). A quarto volume with full-page illustrations, it emerged from Jan ten Hoorn's Amsterdam press in 1678 to become an unexpectedly long-lasting success. Exquemelin had worked as a buccaneer himself in the Caribbean, giving him an insider's knowledge that made his breathless narrative all the more authoritative. His first-person experience with some of the most terrifying pirate leaders and his description of their lair on the tiny island of Tortuga did not merely provide European readers with new information, nor did it tell the tale from the perspective of an educated, elite European, as did so many travel volumes of the era. Rather, *Bucaniers* offered something more: a narrative with an insider's view of dramatic sieges, torture of Spanish leaders, and freewheeling pirate life. Its action took place in the Caribbean, figuring the New World as a site of drama, individual agency, and a decided lack of hierarchy—all contrasting markedly with European society. Together, the book's voice, location, and subjects seemed to indicate that new forms of masculine freedoms were available in piracy.

Sales of the initial edition were so strong that the book appeared shortly thereafter in German (Nuremberg, 1679), Spanish (Cologne, 1681 and 1682), English (at least eight London editions between 1684 and 1704), and French (at least six Paris and Brussels editions between 1686 and 1713), as well as a second Dutch edition in 1700. It would be revived in the 1740s for continued publishing success through the end of the eighteenth century and into the nineteenth by presses on both sides of the Atlantic.[5] *Bucaniers* had broad appeal far beyond the confines of England and northern Europe. The book could be found in the libraries of Robert "King" Carter of Virginia and other wealthy American colonists as well as in the Social Library of Salem, Massachusetts.[6] The fact that the Dutch printer included twelve full-page copperplate engravings in the book indicates his faith in the book's success; such images required considerable investment to produce. Given the book's quarto size (in this particular case, roughly six by eight inches), the engravers likely took at least several weeks to cut each one. Once completed, printing the images for a five hundred copy edition would have taken at least twenty-four days, according to Roger Gaskell's estimates. Altogether, each image would have cost the printer as much in labor and supplies as producing twenty-four pages of text in letterpress.[7] Ultimately, the investment of time and money was well rewarded: by any standard for the day, the *Bucaniers of America* was a best seller.

Printers were the first to advertise the book as a novel and thrilling read. A London printer confessed in the preface to his 1684 edition that he had never even heard the term *buccaneer* until reading the volume, nor had he been aware of the extent of Caribbean piracy. In recommending it, he stressed most of all that the book "informeth us (with huge novelty), of as great and bold attempts, in point of Military conduct and valour, as ever were performed by mankind; without excepting, here, either *Alexander* the Great, or *Julius Caesar*, or the rest of the *Nine Worthy's of Fame*."[8] In fact, he went so far as to describe them as English national heroes because they had so frequently outwitted the Spanish, who were cast as heavies in the London edition. Of course, this was a stretch to say the least: the term *buccaneer* originally referred to French and Dutch hunters in the Caribbean who had taken up piracy against the Spanish. More to the point, these men were so thoroughly non-national figures that one of them, Rock Bresiliaan, who apparently originated in the Low Countries, obtained his nickname Rock the Brazilian by means of a residence in Brazil.[9]

Even without the puffery, the book was an easy sell. Exquemelin used a breezy narrative style to describe his subjects' manly heroism. "After a fight of almost three hours, wherein they behaved themselves with desperate Courage, . . . they became Masters [of the city of Maracaibo, in Venezuela] having made use of no other Arms than their Swords and Pistols," he explained of François l'Olonnais's dramatic defeat of the Spanish.[10] Invariably outmanned and outgunned, his pirates managed to take Spanish ships and entire towns; they escaped from custody no matter how tight the security.

Possessed by an insatiable appetite for riches, they were prodigal with treasure once they gained it: they invariably gambled away vast sums or spent it on trifles. The pirates were not embittered by their losses, however. They seemed to view such drastic reversals as attendant to their way of life.

L'Olonnais and his men provide a case in point. After capturing Maracaibo, they stole "twenty thousand Peices of Eight, several Mules laden with Houshold-goods and Merchandize, and twenty Prisoners, between men, women, and children. Some of these Prisoners were put to the Rack, onely to made them confess where they had hidden the rest of their Goods."[11] Within weeks, the pirates threatened again to burn the town unless they received an additional ten thousand pieces of eight. They followed their threat with yet another demand for thirty thousand or else the Spaniards' homes would *"be entirely sack'd anew and burnt."*[12] Yet upon their triumphal return to Tortuga, "they made shift to lose and spend the Riches they had gotten, in much less time than they were purchased by robbing." How was the wealth redistributed? "The Taverns and Stews, according to the custom of Pirates, got the greatest part," Exquemelin remarks wryly.[13] What would such passages have meant to the book's readers? Considering that it likely was sold to elite and some middling readers involved in commerce or international politics, such readers probably read passages like these with at least some moralistic disapproval, even if it was mixed with a healthy amount of admiration or envy.[14]

To underscore the violent side of the pirates' caprice, Exquemelin liked to include extensive depictions of the grisly tortures they inflicted on unlucky victims. Indeed, the ubiquity of physical cruelty of all kinds threading through the pages of *Bucaniers of America* was unusual enough according to narrative conventions of the day that it stands out. The author explained that even when the sadistic Henry Morgan and his men occasionally decided not to put victims to the rack, they still liked "to stretch their limbs with Cords, and at the same time beat them with Sticks and other Instruments. Others had burning Matches placed betwixt their fingers, which were thus burnt alive. Others had slender Cords or Matches twisted about their heads, till their eyes bursted out of the skull." In a rare moralizing moment, the author added, "Thus all sort of inhumane Cruelties were executed upon those innocent people." Exquemelin described sexual viciousness like "insolent actions of Rape and Adultery" of "very honest women" to evoke further the corporal horrors of Caribbean piracy.[15] Indeed, his depictions of somatic cruelty veered close to a certain vein of late seventeenth-century pornographic writing that emphasized the erotic nature of flogging and the brutal ravishing of women, among other perversions.[16]

Impulsive and volatile, brave and rapacious, the pirates who came to life on the pages of *Bucaniers of America* served up an alternative model of manliness for early modern readers, and readers did not need to venture very far into Exquemelin's chapters to figure this out. Editors made sure to underscore the pirates' manliness and bravery when they composed prefaces advertising the book's pleasures. They invariably highlighted the buccaneers' "unparallel'd, if not unimitable, adventures and *Heroick* exploits," as the 1684 edition put it. "Our common *English* Highway-men ... seem guilty of Pusillamity in comparison with those [actions] of our Buccaniers," the editor continued.[17] By 1695 the London publisher had added a second volume to the *Bucaniers* with additional material on "the dangerous Voyages and bold Attempts of Capt. *Cook*, and Cap. *Sharp*, in the South-Sea." He also expanded the number of images from twelve to nineteen.[18] By 1704, the London printer heralded the book's "wondrous Actions, and daring Adventures," claiming that all but "the most stupid minds" could not help but admire them. Here the editor finessed the question of the pirates' sexual license and propensity for rape, conceding halfheartedly that these men lacked the "Justness and Regularity" that marked a Christian man, or even the "tolerable morals" of more run-of-the-mill citizens. Even taking their moral failings into account, the editor assured readers that "a bolder Race of Men both as to personal Valour and Conduct, certainly never yet appear'd" on land nor sea.[19]

London and Dublin printers reiterated these themes (and even lifted some of the same sentences) when the book reappeared in print in 1741, telling readers yet again that they ought to admire and even emulate the buccaneers for their courage and daring, particularly because some of them were English. The prefaces of various editions repeated this seemingly contradictory group of repeated themes. On the one hand, the printers held up the pirates' admirable courage and alleged Englishness. On the other hand, they noted the pirates' rejection of conventional morality and hierarchy. Combined, the prefaces depicted a dangerous, exciting mode of masculine action and behavior, and further, they *legitimized* such conduct. In none of these ways did pirates conform to prescribed models of European manliness of the time, ideals that tended to stress fiscal responsibility, sexual control, and judicious understanding of one's social place. Buccaneers did more than merely ignore such advice: they repudiated it and adopted the opposite behavior.

FIGURE 1. *Bartholomeu Portugés* from the original Dutch edition of *De Americaenesche Zee-Roovers* (1678). Courtesy of the Library of Congress.

Visualizing the Pirates in Book Illustration

If Exquemelin took a certain glee in recounting pirate adventures, the book's images underscored the pirates' ferocity and masculine brazenness. The illustrations established a visual repertoire that would influence all subsequent representations of pirates. The first of these illustrations provides a key to the images' success. Bartholomeu Português is an iconoclastic figure encompassing everything from menace to heroism. He glowers at the viewer as if annoyed, distracted from his real purpose of watching his crew destroy a harbor full of Spanish ships. His drawn sword suggests his imminent participation in the attack; his dispassionate expression and the resolute set of his jaw signals an utter disdain for the panicked men glimpsed drowning in the foreground. Indeed, the image even hints at a smile on his face, although the viewer senses that one's eyes might be fooled by the turn of his tidy mustache. His appearance is a mix of contradictions: his lack of a wig, his matted hair, and his crudely heavy brow assure the viewer that this is no gentleman, yet he wears a rich, billowing damask coat with a generous sleeve. His posture is reminiscent of Titian's portrait *A Man with a Quilted Sleeve* (c. 1510), an extraordinarily influential image that had already inspired Rembrandt's 1640 *Self Portrait at the Age of Thirty-Four*, among others. Yet Bartolomeu's facial expression is radically different from Titian's and Rembrandt's figures, evoking a thoroughgoing malice and twitchy energy.

Despite the fact that most of the sheath of Bartolomeu's drawn sword is concealed by his body, numerous details remind the viewer of its presence. All the print's movement directs the viewer's gaze up the blade, beginning with the angle of his elbow and shoulders, and mirrored in the shape of his nose, the shadow of his cheekbone, and the set of his jaw. Even the clouds of smoke from the burning Spanish ships in the distance become darkest and most ominous near the sword's tip. Bartolomeu's exposed blade encapsulates danger, ruthlessness, and prowess. Military portraiture of the period often featured men with swords and armor but virtually never with their swords drawn and erect.[20] Each of *Bucaniers of America*'s subsequent portraits, including those of Rock Bresiliaan and François l'Olonnais, provided variations on these themes: the scowl and heavy brow, drawn sword, and a detached perspective on their victims' suffering.

The images must have been potent. A series of printers reused the copperplates, at considerable expense, for nearly thirty years after their initial production. This recycling took place not simply to save money, as the costs of transport and repair of the fragile copper were substantial. It was the high quality of the images that prompted their long use in several different cities. Shortly after the book's 1678 appearance in Amsterdam, the text was translated into German and issued by a Nuremberg press in 1679. The German printer purchased the original plates and transported them over 400 miles inland. It was potentially an expensive undertaking, since transportation and escort costs, tolls, and border levies increased an item's cost considerably. For example, transport overland between Frankfurt and Nuremberg (less than half the distance from Amsterdam to Nuremberg) ballooned a book's cost on average by about 25 percent.[21]

The German printer also had to worry that the plates would be damaged in transit, since even the smallest scratch in the copper would appear in subsequent prints. Once the plates arrived unscathed, the printer then had to contract out to an engraver's workshop to find someone with the skills and equipment to print the images, as copperplates required a special press with extraordinary weight to coax the ink out of the plates' tiny, subtle cuts. In addition, the pressure imposed by a copperplate press was so extreme that the plates wore out. Depending on the quality of the copper, damage could be done after only 125 impressions. In such cases printers, incurring yet another expense, hired engravers to recut the plates by using a tool to carefully trace over their worn lines to deepen them and restore their ability to produce sharp images.[22]

The plates' travels continued after the printing in Nuremberg. By 1681 the plates had been sold yet again to appear in a Spanish-language edition produced by Lorenzo Struikman, a printer in Cologne, 250 miles from Nuremberg. Struikman sought to take advantage of eager Spanish-reading audiences willing to pay for imported books, as Spanish printing of the day did not match the high quality of northern European prints. Struikman had an engraver rub out the original Dutch caption and recalligraph it for Spanish readers. When his edition quickly sold out, Struikman reprinted it a year later, again reusing the plates.

It was the popularity of the Spanish-language edition that gained the attention of London printers.[23] When William Crooke produced his own edition, he too decided that the original engravings were so superior that he purchased them. Yet again, the plates traveled nearly 400 miles from Cologne across the Channel to London. This time the printer did a poor job reproducing the engravings, which appear worn and display the shadow of the rubbed-out Dutch caption even more clearly. But the quality of its prints did not prevent the book from selling out, and Crooke produced another edition within the year. By 1704 the plates had changed hands twice more to appear in four more London editions. Considering that the Dutch plates were ultimately used to produce nine separate editions of a consistently popular book, we might conservatively guess that at least five thousand copies of the book contained these images—and, more liberally, perhaps as many as thirty thousand—radically testing the capacity of copperplates to produce legible images.[24] As a result of this frequent reuse over decades, the images established a visual repertoire of piracy from which other engravers borrowed.

As *Bucaniers of America* circulated through Europe, one engraver after the next embroidered on the same themes of ominous danger and masculine bravado. Take the Paris printer Jacques Le Febvre, who produced four editions of Exquemelin between 1686 and 1705. With only three images in the book, he did not attempt to reproduce the visual richness of the original, but the images he commissioned nevertheless built on the themes laid out in the Dutch originals. The Dutch title page, for example, portrayed its two central pirate figures as prone to an almost whimsical violence: one jauntily keeps a hand at his waist while brandishing his sword at a prostrate Indian, while

FIGURE 2. When the plate was used
for the fifth time in 1684, the London
publisher arranged to have the caption
recut; but the shadow of the Dutch text
is easily apparent. Meanwhile, the plate
shows wear and tear from frequent reuse.
Courtesy of the John Carter Brown
Library at Brown University.

the other appears more concerned with verbally abusing his victim, who begs
for mercy. In contrast, the French engraver opted for less peripheral detail in
favor of a more focused center of action. The engraver's buccaneers are hidden by shadows, avoiding the viewer's gaze. The pirates' physical threats appear more intimidating: the swords appear ready to slash throats and pierce
breasts, and the pirates' visages are intent on inflicting harm and less inclined
to ineffective posturing.

It is significant that the elegantly dressed Spaniard who looks hopelessly
to the viewer for help is not merely about to lose his life but also receive a
serious kick to the groin—a mode of violence emblematic of how pirates
emasculated their victims. Pirates did more than render their victims prostrate (and possibly rape their wives): they also stole their goods. In doing so,
pirates exemplified a radical form of status upheaval as well as a chaotic masculine threat. According to Exquemelin, this lowly group of men rose from
obscurity and the lowest social orders to target the wealthiest ships and cities for an attack, thereby depriving Europeans of the expectation of orderly
trade and shipping. Once they had gained treasure, they famously divided it
among themselves into comparatively equal terms, cultivating a rough equal-

FIGURE 3. Illustrated title page of the original Dutch edition of Exquemelin's *De Americaensche Zee-Roovers*, 1678. Courtesy of the Library of Congress.

FIGURE 4. Illustrated title page of the Paris edition, 1688. Note how the French engraver has innovated on the Dutch images on either side of the calligraphed text. Courtesy of the John Carter Brown Library at Brown University.

ity among crewmen and a strict loyalty to one another.[25] These class inversions did not truly pose an open threat to the social order, of course; indeed, editors continued to claim that readers ought to admire these men for being "English." Still, the conquest of the ragged over the refined would have stood out to readers as a sign of the inversions of status and alternative masculinities that could exist in the imagined locale of the Caribbean.[26] It signaled that not all men needed to follow the same path.

The fact that the French engraver portrayed the pirates laying their riches at the feet of the Indian princess, the symbolic figure of America, rendered them perhaps even more dangerously capricious. This artistic decision visually suggested that they were taking from Europe to give to no one in particular—or even worse, to savages. In doing so, the image displayed the extent to which they had stepped outside the norms of European manhood. Unlike the figure of Britannia, who represented the justice and law of England, the "naked" Indian princess evoked a cruder form of order. This image characterized America as a place where riches could not be used in the rational fashion idealized by Europeans. Exquemelin's descriptions of the pirates' propensity to steal and then lose vast riches further underlined their separation from the ideals of financial moderation and manly self-control. As Peter Linebaugh and Marcus Rediker have noted, "Pirates thus stood against the brutal injustices of the merchant shipping industry, with one crew even claiming to be 'Robbin Hoods Men.'"[27]

Enhancing Textual and Visual Portrayals of Pirates

In 1724, a new, even more popular work appeared in London: *A General History of the Pyrates*.[28] Its title page proclaimed that its author was a Captain Charles Johnson, but scholars have long believed this to have been a pseudonym; the scholar Arne Bialuschewski has persuasively argued that the book was likely the work of a London journalist and bookseller named Nathaniel Mist. Whatever its true authorship, the book purported at first to offer a far different tone than Exquemelin's volume of nearly fifty years earlier. In its opening pages, the author affected a tone of stern disapproval of the pirates who had so successfully upset British trade relations for more than two decades and who had been the center of highly publicized criminal trials for several years. Such moralism was likely calculated to play well to official readers. But his subsequent narrative and the book's illustrations undermined any clear moral lesson about pirates. *A General History of the Pyrates* ultimately enhanced the narrative and visual conventions for representing piracy, especially by expanding the already-existing tendency to emphasize manliness and sexuality.

The book's emphasis on sexuality reflected a growing sophistication in visual literacy by engravers and at least some of their readers, made possible by the rapid expansion of the trade in visual prints and illustrated books during the eighteenth century.[29] Take, for example, the increasingly sexualized portrayals of pirates' display of their weapons. Exquemelin's illustrators had invariably displayed pirates with their swords unsheathed in a manner that evoked the pirates' dangerous manliness and violent proclivities. But the English engraver for the *General History*, B. Cole, exaggerated the pirates' caches of weapons to such an extent that one cannot ignore the possibility that he called forth phallic imagery. As much as Cole borrowed aspects of earlier pirate images—fierce scowls, drawn weapons, aggressive postures, and dramatic background action—he set a new pattern with his strong emphasis on "erect" swords, pistols, and hatchets.

Such images fit neatly with the text, which likewise placed heavier emphasis on the pirates' sex lives. The author explained that Edward "Blackbeard" Teach, for example, forced his "fourteenth wife" to "prostitute herself" to members of his own crew while he watched. To accompany these textual descriptions, Cole positioned Blackbeard with an extraordinary array of weapons: he holds one drawn sword "up," while no fewer than six holstered pistols are arrayed across his chest; most striking, a second sword hangs prominently between his legs.[30]

Likewise, the author describes Edward England and his crew as forcing women "in a barbarous manner to their lusts, and to requite them, destroyed their cocoa trees and fired several of their houses and churches."[31] Invariably, England was depicted in a provocative pose, displaying his hatchet arrayed in a phallic position, a posture copied in dozens of cheap editions of the book throughout the eighteenth century. But it was not merely the hatchet that guaranteed his cocky virility and manly bravado. With his hand on his hip and his body positioned in an open, frontal position to the viewer, England seems to invite viewers to see him in sexual terms. Underscoring this point, the text below the image in this edition begins, "It is very surprizing, that Men of Understanding should engage in Murder, Theft, and Rapine; and yet such was *England*." Even in a pre-Freudian Atlantic world, many readers would have seen the imagery of erect swords and angled hatchets as yoking together sexual and physical violence.

Captain Edward England, and his Crew.

IT is very surprizing, that Men of Understanding should engage in Murder, Theft, and Rapine ; and yet such was *England*, who seemed to
have

FIGURE 5. Captain Edward England
from Charles Johnson's *History and
Lives of All the Most Notorious Pirates,
and Their Crews* (London, 1725).
Courtesy of the Library of Congress.

Johnson underscored their manliness by lavishing attention on the pirates' marriages, interracial sexual liaisons, multiple children, and most of all
their perverse or barbaric sexual violence against women. He left little doubt
that a good number of the pirates' outrageous acts had been sexual. For example, Captain Henry Every and his crew moved to Madagascar, where they
"married the most beautiful of the Negro women, not one or two, but as
many as they liked . . . so that every one of them had as great a Seraglio as
the Grand Seignior at Constantinople." Meanwhile, less sedentary pirates
settled for perpetual "whoring" with women throughout the Caribbean and
elsewhere.[32] Johnson thereby established a canon of myths that would remain in print for over a century, many of which revolved around the pirates' sexuality and malevolent fearlessness. The pirates' proclivities for sexual violence called attention to their manly prowess and position as gender
outsiders, characterizations that readers might experience simultaneously as
both immoral and titillating. The sexually evocative subject matter of the text

worked in tandem with the images to suggest that the pirates inhabited a masculine subject position that was explicitly sexualized.

At this point it is worth stepping back to ask, why would books have drawn such attention to the gendered and sexual lives of the pirates? Such portrayals specifically appealed to the bourgeois and elite male readers who made up the vast majority of the consumers for such books. Reading about the exotic sexual lives of *"Heroick"* pirates would have provided a fascinating counterpoint to the more staid lives of such readers, but the stories could also cultivate male readers' identifications with the pirates by inviting them to imagine abandoning sexual self-restraint during the eighteenth century, long noted as an era during which an ethic of male sexual irresponsibility flourished in popular print media.[33] Books like Exquemelin's and Johnson's constituted rich contributions to a growing range of books—novels, travel narratives, and conduct manuals—that called forth new imaginative male identities made possible by permissive environments like the pirate ship or the Caribbean.

Although scholars have invariably used Johnson's portrayals of female pirates Anne Bonny and Mary Read to speculate about responses by female readers, these chapters also contributed significantly to wealthy men's imaginative relations to the pirates overall. Indeed, depictions of Bonny and Read display in even clearer relief how male readers might have enjoyed these books. Scholarship on popular reception of Bonny and Read frequently argues that these cross-dressing characters offered female readers new models of rebellion and female agency in matters of economics, sex, and self-protection, thereby encouraging readers to imagine far-reaching forms of personal liberation.[34] Such interpretations appear strikingly idealistic if we focus on the readers most likely to own these books: comparatively wealthy men who were already the most "free" in society and who possessed the disposable income to purchase expensive illustrated books or patronize social libraries. If such men imagined freedom by reading these accounts, we must see it far differently than that experienced by those men's female subordinates.

Above all, Johnson's book emphasizes the pleasurable titillation of Read's and Bonny's cross-dressing in a series of set pieces highlighting gender confusion and sexual behavior. In one almost Shakespearean passage, Read enters the army only to fall in love with one of her officers, leading her to risk life and limb to be near him. Distracted by her love, she neglects her duty: "It seems Mars and Venus could not be served at the same time," Johnson

FIGURE 6. Anne Bonny from the
1725 Amsterdam edition of Johnson's
Historie der Engelsche Zee-Roovers.
Courtesy of the John Carter Brown
Library at Brown University.

comments philosophically. She eventually lets her love "discover her sex" one night as they lie together in a tent. Even more risqué is the moment when Bonny and Read meet aboard the pirate ship, each in full male disguise. Taking Read "for a handsome young fellow," Bonny takes "a particular liking to her" and secretly reveals that she is a woman, presumably to solicit sex. Johnson allows the sexual confusion of the scene to transpire for his readers' enjoyment, delaying its resolution. He even indicates that Read at least considers the possibility of playing the paramour to prolong her ruse. But "knowing what she would be at" if she did not come clean, "and being very sensible for her own incapacity" to play the man for Bonny's sake, Read reveals the truth—to Bonny's "great disappointment."[35] Replete with transvestism, sex (consummated and otherwise), and a disdain for gender propriety, these biographical vignettes enhanced the themes that appeared throughout *A General History of the Pyrates*: they portrayed pirates as rejecting gender conventions and sexual decorum. The book's images further invited male readers to see these women as pleasurably dangerous sex objects. The Dutch edition of 1725, for example, displayed them in breeches, heavily armed, and

FIGURE 7. Captain Keitt from
Howard Pyle's Book of Pirates (1921),
from the collection of the author.

striking jaunty and mildly threatening poses, while their long tresses and full breasts confirm their sexual appeal and availability, as in this image of Anne Bonny. It is not hard to see that publishers intended such tales and images for male readers: their constructions of manliness via the figure of the pirate, and in cultivating male readers' enjoyment of the pirates' sexual peccadilloes, constituted a fundamental part of their subject matter.

Conclusion

If Exquemelin's and Johnson's books had been less popular or long lived, we might be skeptical that they had hit on a formula for representing pirates that would remain influential. But during the following centuries, books, plays, and eventually films continued to build on motifs established in the 1670s that emphasized manly adventure, gender transgression, erotic violence, and moral ambivalence.[36] By the time Howard Pyle began retelling a softer version of those stories alongside his evocative illustrations in magazines like *Harper's Weekly* in the 1880s, conventions for pirate representations were so accepted that it seemed obvious to him that "every boy" would "rather be a pirate captain than a Member of Parliament."[37]

These conventions had three important components that render them significant for the history of manliness in the extensive eighteenth century. First, the books explicitly touted the pirates as admirable men, describing them as "*Heroick*" and capable of "wondrous Actions, and daring Adventures." Of course, those descriptors were hardly obvious, considering the buccaneers' penchants for robbery, rape, and torture, but even if such hero worship created a degree of cognitive dissonance, these portrayals contrasted with the soberer lives of the books' readers. Illustrations of the pirates as scowling figures set against background scenes of destruction and suffering further underscored their potential for violent, dramatic action. Authors and publishers seemed to herald the alternative masculinities exemplified by the pirates and urged their readers to do the same.

Second, books by Exquemelin, Johnson, and their followers made the pirates' transgressive sexual behavior a prominent component of their masculinity that vividly encapsulated their moral ambiguity and unpredictability. Whether by discussing their interracial unions or their propensity for rape and other sexual perversions and by eventually enhancing those tales with images of weapons displayed in exaggerated phallic postures, these authors used sexuality to compound their expressed admiration of the pirates as *men*. The increasing emphasis on sexual volatility served up for male readers a titillating world of male privilege and lack of restraint and paralleled more explicitly erotic or bawdy writing of the era.

Finally, these texts located sexualized pirate masculinity in the imagined setting of the Caribbean, an American site far from established social networks, family responsibilities, or business obligations. For European and Anglo-American readers alike, its very remoteness rendered such a setting all the more available for fantasy, while its mostly Spanish settlers demanded no sympathy from northern Europeans jealous of their control over the area. The unrelenting hard work, indentured servitude, and modest desires for economic competency of Britain's mainland colonies were wholly absent from these narratives. When pirates won and lost vast fortunes on these pages, readers might enjoy the daydream of such a life. Situating those events far away in the Americas, where palm-treed harbor towns suffered the attacks of brutal buccaneers, characterized this locale as a site of dynamism, movement, and heroic action.

NOTES

For their assistance, I thank Frances Clarke, Judy Coffin, Tom Foster, Lauren Hewes, Dian Kriz, Mary Katherine Matalon, Rebecca Plant, David Rickman, the students at the University of Texas's Plan II Honors "Voltaire's Salon," and the staffs at the John Carter Brown Library, the Massachusetts Historical Society, and Harvard's Houghton Library. I am particularly grateful to *Common-Place: The Interactive Journal of Early American Life*, where I published an earlier version of this essay, "Shivering Timbers: Sexing Up the Pirates in Early Modern Print Culture," in October 2009. Images described but not displayed in the chapter can be seen at http://www .common-place.org/vol-10/no-01/eastman/. Finally, I thank Cathy Kelly: editor, mentor, friend.

1. Howard Pyle, *Howard Pyle's Book of Pirates: Fiction, Fact, and Fancy Concerning the Buccaneers and Marooners of the Spanish Main*, ed. Merle Johnson (New York: Harper and Bros., 1921), xiii, xiv.

2. See, for example, the trailer for *Captain Blood* (1935), available online at http:// www.imdb.com/video/screenplay/vi2119368729/, accessed December 15, 2009; and "The Adventures of Miles Cowperthwaite," *Saturday Night Live*, season 4, episode 18, aired May 12, 1979, the transcript of which is available at http://snltranscripts .jt.org/78/78rcowperthwaite.phtml, accessed December 15, 2009; David Cordingly's *Under the Black Flag: The Romance and the Reality of Life among the Pirates* (New York: Harcourt Brace, 1995) contrasts the long-lasting popularity of pirate lore with the original literature.

3. When this essay was originally published in 2009, it was the first scholarly treatment of the subject of manliness in pirate literature. Previous studies of pirates that incorporated gender analysis examined female pirates or the subject of same-sex sexuality on board ship. See, for example, essays by Dianne Dugaw and Marcus Rediker in *Iron Men, Wooden Women: Gender and Seafaring in the Atlantic World*, ed. Margaret Creighton and Lisa Norling (Baltimore: Johns Hopkins University Press, 1996), chaps. 1 and 2; and Hans Turley, *Rum, Sodomy, and the Lash: Piracy, Sexuality, and Masculine Identity* (New York: New York University Press, 1999).

4. Peter T. Leeson, *The Invisible Hook: The Hidden Economics of Pirates* (Princeton, N.J.: Princeton University Press, 2009), 45–81. See also Marcus Rediker, *Villains of All Nations: Atlantic Pirates in the Golden Age* (Boston: Beacon Press, 2004), 1–18; and Rediker, *Between the Devil and the Deep Blue Sea: Merchant Seamen, Pirates, and the Anglo-American Maritime World, 1700–1750* (Cambridge: Cambridge University Press, 1987), chap. 6.

5. The original translator claimed that it "was no sooner published in the *Dutch Original*, than it was snatcht up for the most curious Library's of *Holland*" before making its way around northern Europe. Alexandre Exquemelin, *Bucaniers of*

America (London: William Crooke, 1684), 1:i. Subsequent textual citations come from this edition unless otherwise noted. Crooke had the book translated from the Spanish edition, which itself was a "faithful rendering of the Dutch," by Alonzo de Bonne-Maison. Clarence Henry Haring, *Buccaneers of the West Indies in the Seventeenth Century* (New York: Methuen, 1910), 279; *A Transcript of the Registers of the Worshipful Company of Stationers; from 1640–1708 A.D.* (London: privately printed, 1914), 3:254.

6. Louis B. Wright, "The 'Gentleman's Library' in Early Virginia: The Literary Interests of the First Carters," *Huntington Library Quarterly* 1 (1937): 53; Salem Social Library, Record Book (1761), Curwen Family Manuscript Collection, box 3, folder 5, American Antiquarian Society Manuscript Collections, Worcester, Mass.

7. Roger Gaskell, "Printing House and Engraving Shop: A Mysterious Collaboration," *Book Collector* 53 (2004): 221–24.

8. Exquemelin, *Bucaniers of America*, 1:ii.

9. Leeson, *Invisible Hook*, 7.

10. Exquemelin, *Bucaniers of America*, 2:18.

11. Ibid., 2:20.

12. Ibid., 2:28–29.

13. Ibid., 2:32–33.

14. On this subject, see Robert D. Hume, "The Economics of Culture in London, 1660–1740," *Huntington Library Quarterly* 69 (2006): 487–533.

15. Exquemelin, *Bucaniers of America*, 2:98, 116–17.

16. On early modern erotic writing, see Jean Marie Goulemot, *Forbidden Texts: Erotic Literature and Its Readers in Eighteenth-Century France*, trans. James Simpson (Philadelphia: University of Pennsylvania Press, 1994); Karen Harvey, *Reading Sex in the Eighteenth Century* (New York: Cambridge University Press, 2004); Lynn Hunt, ed., *The Invention of Pornography* (New York: Zone Books, 1996); and Alexander Pettit and Patrick Speeding, eds., *Eighteenth-Century British Erotica* (London: Pickering and Chatto, 2002).

17. Exquemelin, *Bucaniers of America*, 1:ii.

18. "Advertisement: The History of the *Bucaniers of America*" (London: William Whitwood and Anthony Feltham, 1695).

19. Alexandre Exquemelin, *Bucaniers of America* (London: Tho. Newborough, John Nicholson, and Benj. Tooke, 1704), 2:ii–iii.

20. See, for example, the military portraiture of the Dutch artist Anthony van Dyck, such as his 1624 *Portrait of a Young General* and his *Portrait of a Commander in Armor, with a Red Scarf* (c. 1625), both of which evoke masculine power but not the volatility of Exquemelin's pirate images.

21. John L. Flood, "'Omnium Totius Orbis Emporiorum Compendium': The Frankfurt Fair in the Early Modern Period," in *Fairs, Markets, and the Itinerant Book*

Trade, ed. Robin Myers, Michael Harris, and Giles Mandelbrote (New Castle, Del.: Oak Knoll Press and the British Library, 2007), 3.

22. On the special requirements of copperplate printing, which include using a particularly heavy, viscous ink, dampening the paper, and meticulously wiping the plates before each impression, see Gaskell, "Printing House and Engraving Shop," 219–20.

23. The translator of the original London edition claims that English readers first learned about *Bucaniers of America* in *Weekly Memorials for the Ingenious: Or, An Account of Books Lately Set Forth in Several Languages*, a 1682–1683 journal that described new books appearing from presses throughout northern Europe.

24. Printers may have been willing to foot the bill for transporting and maintaining the plates due to the superior reputation of Dutch engravings during this era. At the same time, English engravers had quite poor reputations. I have found other book illustrations that similarly traveled throughout the region, most notably some of the grand folio-sized copperplate cuts for Cornelis de Bruyn's *Reizen*, which appeared in editions produced in Delft, London, Amsterdam, and Paris between 1698 and 1759. How many copies might be produced in a single late seventeenth-century edition is a notoriously vexed question, but it is reasonable to assume that a popular book like this one would have appeared in editions of at least five hundred copies.

25. Christopher Hill, "Radical Pirates?," in *The Origins of Anglo-American Radicalism*, ed. Margaret Jacob and James Jacob (London: Allen and Unwin, 1984), 20.

26. On this subject, see Peter Linebaugh and Marcus Rediker, *The Many-Headed Hydra: Sailors, Slaves, Commoners, and the Hidden History of the Revolutionary Atlantic* (Boston: Beacon Press, 2000), 156, 162–67.

27. Ibid., 163–64.

28. This book appeared in over one hundred editions between 1724 and 1794, in English, Dutch, German, and French, published in at least nine different European cities. Untangling the exact number is made doubly difficult not merely due to the vast number of cheap editions with variant titles but also because beginning in the 1930s some scholars attributed the book to Daniel Defoe. Subsequently, this attribution has been viewed with considerable skepticism; on this subject, see Turley, *Rum, Sodomy, and the Lash*, 159–60n8. More recently the scholar Arne Bialuschewski has persuasively argued that it was authored by Nathaniel Mist. See "Daniel Defoe, Nathaniel Mist, and the *General History of the Pyrates*," *Papers of the Bibliographical Society of America* 98 (2004): 21–38.

29. Sheila O'Connell, *The Popular Print in England, 1550–1800* (London: British Museum Press, 1999), 48–53, 109–19, and chaps. 7 and 8.

30. Even Howard Pyle's 1921 children's book insisted on making oblique reference to Blackbeard's unfortunate wife: "The life that he and his rum-crazy shipmates led her to was too terrible to be told." Pyle, *Howard Pyle's Book of Pirates*, 29.

31. Captain Charles Johnson, *A General History of the Robberies and Murders of the Most Notorious Pyrates* (1724; repr., Guilford, Conn.: Lyons Press, 2002), 93, 60–61, 198.

32. Ibid., 35.

33. The literature on this subject is vast; see especially Tim Hitchcock, *English Sexualities, 1700–1800* (London: Basingstoke, 1997), 112–14; for an overview of literature on sexuality in the eighteenth century, see Karen Harvey, "The Century of Sex? Gender, Bodies, and Sexuality in the Long Eighteenth Century," *Historical Journal* 45 (2002): 899–916.

34. Rudolf M. Dekker and Lotte C. Van de Pol, *The Tradition of Female Transvestism in Early Modern Europe* (London: Macmillan, 1989); Alfred F. Young, *Masquerade: The Life and Times of Deborah Sampson, Continental Soldier* (New York: Random House, 2004).

35. Johnson, *General History*, 116, 119, 121–22.

36. The playwright John Gay would recycle these themes of sexuality, violence, and titillation when he composed *Polly: An Opera* (1729), the sequel to his wildly popular *Beggar's Opera* (1728). In it, Polly dresses as a boy to escape white slavery and prostitution in the West Indies; after a long series of misadventures, she marries the son of a Carib chief.

37. Pyle, *Howard Pyle's Book of Pirates*, xiii. This book collects articles and images that Pyle published in *Harper's Weekly*, *Harper's Magazine*, *Collier's Weekly*, and other sources between 1887 and 1911.

A Woman Is to Blame

GENDER AND THE LITERATURE OF
ANTEBELLUM PIRATE CONFESSIONS

Matthew Taylor Raffety

C harles Gibbs, the most famous American pirate of the 1830s, blamed a fickle girlfriend for his crimes.[1] A pirate in his young days, Gibbs reformed and "lived like a gentleman" for a time until his love deceived him, and he "was made a child of . . . by her, and . . . gave way to dissipation to drown the torment," eventually returning to the bloody practices of his youth.[2] Gibbs's compatriot, Thomas Wansley, blamed his mother's infidelity, suggesting that her moral turpitude set his life on the wrong road from the moment of conception.[3] When Thomas Jones, an escaped slave and another convicted pirate, pointed the finger at the woman who had owned him before he escaped slavery for the sea, he explained, "I was not piously brought up," which led him ultimately to his life of crime.[4]

Although all these pirates engaged in their crimes in a decidedly male environment, many pointed to a woman—whether a fickle lover or an inattentive mother—as the "Eve" in the narrative of their personal falls. In the largely homosocial world of the ship, women represented a source of chaos and evil.[5] Indeed, the literary presence of women as inspiration for the misdeeds of flesh-and-blood men suggests an attempt to bring the controlling moral force of women from shore to sea by illustrating the chaos that ensues when women failed to provide moral grounding to the men who sailed.

This essay examines the roles women play in seafarers' confessional literature before the Civil War and explores the gender and sexual politics that made culturally plausible the notion that even the manliest of men—seafarers and pirates—can be turned easily into "victims" of wanton and wily women. Women enter these narratives as sirens, leading men to violence, ruin, and at worst, the gallows.

According to published confessions of convicted pirates, the murderous actions of these seafarers were, at root, some woman's fault. Of course, this is hardly a tale unique or new to the early republic. From Eve to Delilah to Guinevere to Gertrude, women have been situated literarily as the cause of men's falls. Why, then, point out this propensity among seafarers' confessions in the nineteenth century? As inhabitants of the largely homosocial world of the ship, seafarers (or whoever the "true" authors of these "true" confessions were) had to work hard to manufacture some narrative connection between women and their crimes at sea.[6] Whether essential to capture an audience, or to frame the moral explanation these cautionary tales provided, the publishers (and indeed the pirates themselves) brought women to the center of these otherwise decidedly masculine tales. Additionally, amid the rise of gendered domestic spheres, women's role as figures of the "moral" realm put additional pressure on them as the source of any moral failing in society. In doing so, these confessions reflect the rising middle-class morality that increasingly divided the world into male and female spheres, with the world of politics, commerce, and the public sphere as the domain of men, whereas home, family, and matters of morality and faith became the purview of women. Thus, for these confessions to be useful as cautionary tales warning others to "avoid bad company" (as they invariably urged), they had to be fitted into a moral universe that made sense for the readers.[7]

From Real to Paper Pirates

Although a portion of these criminal seafarers, including the respectably born Gibbs, did fall under the reach of the rising middle-class morality of the period, others, like the black seafarers Wansley and Jones, did not. Here it may be important to consider these tales not simply as articulations of the seamen's understanding of the moral world themselves but as the understandings of the confessors, publishers, and largely middling audience for these confessional pamphlets and news stories.

Gibbs and other antebellum pirates faced trial and execution a century after the golden age of Atlantic piracy ended, but public interest in the exploits of pirates had, if anything, grown even as actual piracy waned. American audiences devoured increasingly romanticized and ever more improbable true confessions of pirates during the antebellum period. Deathbed confessions like those of Gibbs, Wansley, and Jones, as well as popular compendiums of pirate tales like *The Pirates Own Book* (1837) and *The American Pirates Own Book* (1844), blossomed into an important literary subgenre and characterize a distinct period of how the public understood piracy.

In order to understand the literary and moral conventions of these confessions, it is important to contextualize such tales of maritime wrongdoing as a popular subset of a growing literature of sensationalized murder tales and confessions that had existed in various forms since early Puritan New England.[8] Whether printed as stand-alone confessional pamphlets sold at public executions by enterprising publishers or used as titillating copy by the growing number of popular news dailies in major cities, published criminal confessions were part of a rising sensationalist trend in popular entertainment that began in the late eighteenth century and culminated with the birth of "true crime" as a popular culture fixture in the 1830s.[9] The pirate tales discussed here, ranging from the 1820s to the 1840s, were produced amid the formation of the sensationalized, pathos-filled, moralizing conventions of early American crime reporting. That such gendered archetypes appeared at the flowering of crime literature, consumed by a rising northeastern middle class, suggests the importance they gave to gender roles, especially with regard to issues of morality.

Seafarers were useful as cultural tropes. They were common enough for general understanding and sufficiently exotic in their travels and appearance to be figures of adventure and fascination. They were also rugged enough to serve as paragons of masculinity, sentimental enough to be objects of ridicule and pity, and violent enough to be figures of menace. Given the popularity of maritime narratives generally, especially the reformist writings of Richard Henry Dana in *Two Years Before the Mast* (1840), and the importance of the sea as a site of American economic might and masculine identity in the first part of the nineteenth century, stories of death and mayhem at sea matched perfectly with the growing appetite for salacious tales.[10] The sea was already understood as a place of grand masculine adventure. The lure of the sea for young boys was such a problem in the early republic that federal judge Peleg Sprague of Maine complained that punishing the boys who ran away to sea "impelled by a spirit of adventure and an excited imagination" was futile, as the pull of the sea was too strong.[11] Seafarers increasingly sought to capitalize on their own stories by publishing memoirs of their adventures.[12]

Pirate tales, then, fused the growingly popular sea literature of the early republic to the equally fashionable trend for true crime reportage and literature. In particular, Charles Ellms, a Boston-based stationer and his printer and partner Samuel N. Dickenson came to define the genre.[13] Ellms began as the editor of popular almanacs in the early 1830s, then moved into true tales of the sea, first with *Shipwrecks and Disasters at Sea* (1836) before publishing his most popular work, *The Pirates Own Book*, the following year. Although Ellms marketed his sea tales as true, he "did not hesitate to embellish the lives of pirates or details about the shipwrecks."[14] Ellms and other similar publishers became important figures as disseminators of a newly rich "true" literary exploration of the meaning of pirates and piracy. Indeed, pirate tales were put to all sorts of uses in the hands of publishers and authors. Most dedicated some space to using the pirate's fate as a moral cautionary tale. Others saw opportunity to argue for criminal reform. Still others seemed more focused on moving product through telling a saucy tale. Sometimes the variety of uses competed for space in the same text. *The Record of Crimes of the United States* (1834) compiled the stories of twenty-three criminals (including pirates such as Gibbs, Wansley, and Samuel Tully) with "a brief sketch of the prominent traits and conduct of many of the most notorious malefactors who have been guilty of capital offenses" and included an introduction that, among other things, promoted the movement against public executions and trumpeted the efficacy of the emerging science of phrenology.[15]

In the hands of Ellms and his ilk, pirate confessions of the 1820s to 1840s created a literary and cultural bridge between the didactic moralizing literature that accompanied executions in earlier years and the high Victorian romanticism of Robert Louis Stevenson and *Boys Own* magazine of the later nineteenth century.[16] As such, it is important to examine the particular themes that appear in this historically distinct literary subgenre of pirate tales, even as it also made up an important piece of the new "true crime" literature developing in the new penny press of news dailies, which were catering to a rapidly expanding readership, including working- and middle-class readers.[17]

Tales of piracy, and sensationalist crime literature more generally, had far older origins but came newly into their own in the antebellum period, spurred on by the disappearance of the public execution, the rise of new outlets for journalism and reporting, and cultural shifts that made such sensationalism satisfying for an emergent literary audience.[18] "There are few subjects," the preface to the first edition of *The Pirates Own Book* intoned, "that interest and excite the curiosity of mankind generally, more than the desperate exploits, foul doings, and diabolical career of these monsters in human form."[19] Matching the rising popularity of crime stories to the growing interest in maritime tales made piracy a natural topic for market-oriented publishers trying to cater to popular taste, and these authors and publishers seem to have found their target. Gibbs's confession went through dozens of pressings; *The Pirates Own Book* sold well across several editions and even spawned knockoffs like the 1844 *The American Pirates Own Book*, which aggregated many of the confessional pamphlets from American cases in the preceding decades.[20]

From Spectacle to Narrative

Another factor contributed to the solidification of pirate confessionals as a genre in the 1820s and 1830s: the curtailment of capital punishment as a public spectacle of state power and social order. Indeed, the rise of this rich confessional literature arrived just as the theater of public execution was disappearing.[21] Gibbs's and Wansley's 1831 executions stood at the beginning of a dramatic shift away from public executions. As the executions themselves retreated from the town green to within prison walls, they ceased being part of a shared public ceremony of state authority asserting its power over the bodies of wrongdoers.[22] Thus, the popular spectacle of these events was transferred to the confessional pamphlets and true crime reportage that arose and expanded at the same time.[23]

According to a pamphlet commemorating the very public execution of Samuel Tully, a pirate hanged in Boston in 1812, the event drew "a vast multitude assembled to enjoy the edifying spectacle."[24] Indeed, approximately fifteen thousand observers came out in the Massachusetts winter to witness this pirate's demise. In Tully's case, the execution itself was the central cultural event. Broadsheets depicting his brief confession were likely posted publicly nearby and also offered for sale as grim, moralizing souvenirs.[25] Later audiences, however, experienced these pirates' ends literarily rather than viscerally. Gibbs's and Wansley's executions, for example, are described in lurid detail for those who could not attend. In contrast to Tully, Gibbs and Wansley "paid the penalty of their crimes" in relative private, with spectators assembled consisting mostly of clergy and law enforcement.[26] Absent the "vast multitude" described at Tully's leave-taking, it fell to pamphleteers to describe the punishment itself to drive home the moral lessons of these men's misspent lives. "Gibbs died hard," one account notes, explaining in detail the scene. The author describes Gibbs's last words, an entreaty for all to take a lesson from his "sad fate" and "shun the broad road of ruin, and travel in that of virtue" but went on to describe the condemned men's clothing and even the death throes themselves.[27]

Dead Men Tell Longer and Longer Tales

The transfer of executions from public to literary experience prompted the development of longer and more complex published confessions even in cases where the crime, confession, and execution were well in the past. Tully's trial and execution were memorialized in print at the time of his death in a series of broadsheets, but the brief reports of his "last words" and a letter to his father said very little about the nature of or impetus behind what led to his life of crime. Instead, Tully focused on the moral lesson to be taken from his fate, urging "my brothers and sisters will mind the company they go into; only think of me and my unfortunate end, and strive to comfort their father and mother."[28] Tully's one-page "last words" and one-page letter were expanded, however, in the hands of other authors by the 1830s; publisher H. Faxon dedicated sixteen pages of his *The Record of Crimes of the United States* to Tully's deeds in 1834.

Tully's final words continued to expand well beyond his death because although published confessions uniformly touted their veracity, their authorship was far more complex. *The Record of Crimes* boasts it was "compiled from the best authorities."[29] Even the title *The Pirates Own Book* affirms an authorial ownership on the part of the pirates themselves. Similarly, the 1824 confession of Thomas Jones is quick to point out that these were *his* words, taken at his request by a minister. Special Justice James Hopson, the author who took down Gibbs's dramatic confession, addressed the question of veracity directly, asking the accused, "Gibbs, are you going to tell me the truth, or is it to amuse me, and make me write a long story that will not amount to anything?"[30] Hopson left convinced of Gibbs's truthfulness, but at least one publisher addressed incredulous readers directly. "To correct the impression which some of our public prints have thrown out that Gibbs, like other criminals, was disposed to magnify and exaggerate his crimes," *The Record of Crimes* explains Gibbs was given, as a test of veracity, a chart of the Caribbean, on which he accurately placed the incidents and crimes he described in his confession.

The desperate attempts to reassure readers of Gibbs's truthfulness demonstrates the ways in which these confessions were complexly collaborative texts. A confession passed through numerous hands on the way to the reader. The prisoner's own narrative became interlaced with court testimony and the editorial influence of both confessor and later editors who prepared the text for publication.

By literary tradition dating to the prenational period, deathbed confessions were taken by some respectable figure to preserve the condemned man's words in the hope they would be morally edifying. This confessor was often a clergyman or court official. Once transcribed, enterprising printers and editors took the reins, selling the confessions in broadsheet or pamphlet form to an eager public. From there, other printers often performed a piracy of their own, borrowing, repackaging, and often embellishing the tales as they sought a slice of the audience for themselves.

Ultimately, whether a condemned man justifying his wrongdoing, a minister seeking to promote a moral lesson in the misdeeds of the condemned, or an editor trying to satisfy the literary tastes of the audience, everyone involved had the opportunity to shape and reshape the narrative to their own needs. Whether these tales are understood as truly the work of their putative authors or are a joint project of all hands that touched them on their way to the public is, however, perhaps beside the point. Indeed, if one accepts the notion of multiple authors in many of these cases, then the consistent need to blame women—often women at a large remove from the actual crimes—suggests that these conventions were understood and supported by authors and audience alike.

Perhaps even harder to untangle than the complex question of the authorship of confessional texts is the question of who read these stories, why they read them, and what meaning they gleaned from their readings. Readership is always contested, as readers and authors vie over a text's ultimate meaning. In the case of pirate confessions, the moral message struggled against a reading of such tales as bloody accounts of seaborne adventure and escape from the confines of polite society.[31] As with the true-crime reports in the penny newspapers that found popularity at the same time, these pirate tales at once titillated and instructed, as readers were drawn to the excitement of wild lives as much if not more than the tidy moral of repentance and condemnation.

If it can be agreed that such tales were an important part of the emerging literary and cultural landscape by the 1830s, what sorts of messages were disseminated in these stories? Certainly, such tales held important cultural meanings and operated as an important site of moral tutelage and reinforcement of social norms.[32] Yet many contemporary observers worried that market forces prompted printers to use the moral value of the confession as a mere fig leaf of respectable cover, justifying the dissemination of lurid tales to an unruly and unsophisticated readership. "The novelist, who would induce us to take the murderer and pirate to our hearts, show very plainly where their affections lie," the *North American Review* worried.[33] Similarly, *DeBow's Review* warned of the "indiscriminate reader" whose "torpid intellectual tastes" could not be trusted to understand more than "the commonplace, the superficial, the sensual, the gross, and the gaudy."[34] Indeed, the trope of ending a confession by entreating the reader to "avoid bad company" in order to escape the criminal's grim fate was so hackneyed a cliché that it was already a joke by 1812, as when William Sampson framed his anti-British pamphlet in the style of a fictional confession.[35] Sampson had his fictional British captain, who had been convicted of "murder and manstealing," pen his own, largely illegible but nevertheless familiar confession, blaming his coconspirators (though concealing their names) and pleading piety at the last:

> ***** ***** and ***** ***** and ***** ***** are d——d scoundrels, I was —— by their lying, —— and villain —— to this disgrace. If ever —— should —— that —— be hanged. I die in charity with all —— . . . mercy —— and remember —— avoid bad company.[36]

Indeed, Sampson's captain's incoherent moralizing echoes the tone of its contemporary texts such as Tully's and remains a familiar formulation through Gibbs's and beyond. While the form of such moral tutelage from the shadow of the gallows remained an essential aspect of this literature, the later texts developed far more nuanced—and decidedly more explicitly gendered—tropes and themes.

Those Sexy Rogues

Certainly the escapist allure of the pirates themselves was a meaningful part of the confessions' appeal. In many stories, the pirates are sexy rogues. The preface of *The Pirates Own Book*, for example, titillates by promising an exploration of "wild and extravagant frolics."[37] Similarly, the allure of pirates is clear in the confession of a pirate named Holmes, whose trial, the author notes, was enthusiastically attended by "a large number of the ladies who move in the fashionable circles of Philadelphia."[38] Accounts of Gibbs's trial praise the "firm, unembarrassed manner" with which he testified, and described his "iron visage" throughout the proceedings.[39] Wansley's is explicitly objectified in one account as "the perfect form of manly beauty."[40] Even after the pirates' executions, their manhood had literal and literary appeal. Gibbs's execution was accompanied by the extra horror of dissection. His "manhood" came under special focus after his death in a very literal sense, when his skull and a plaster facsimile of his penis were exhibited after his execution.[41]

By contrast, the account of pirate James Moran sought to undermine the image of sexy piratical allure. Moran played the tough throughout his 1837 trial, mocking the proceedings and "sneering" at his prosecutors, but once sentenced to death, he "became quite unmanned," according to John Perry, author of *The American Pirates Own Book*. Moran's "face was blanched to a sepulchral white—tears gushed from his eyes—and as a glass of water was handed to him, it was with a tremulous effort that he raised it to his lips."[42] In the case of Gibbs, it was not his trial that unmanned him but rather his repeated bouts with alcohol abuse. "My friends advised me to behave myself like a man . . . but the demon still haunted me, and I spurned their advice," he confessed, expressing his weakness before booze in explicitly gendered terms.[43]

Whether the manhood of the sentenced pirates was impressive enough to support posthumous exhibition, or was so tenuous that it collapsed in the face of the sentence of death, pamphleteers felt the need to reflect on these pirates as *men*, describing them in terms of "manliness" defined by both body and deed.

The women who appear in these confessions, however, take on a more symbolic character. The literary conventions of these "bad women" responsible for deeds at sea come in two large archetypes. The first is the bad mother, who failed to instill a bedrock of moral tutelage, the lack of which can be blamed for later failings. The second is the femme fatale, whose siren wiles lure men to the rocks of moral turpitude and murder.[44] In both cases, these women become the root cause of deeds that take place at a remove of years and miles from their actual presence.

Mamas, Don't Let Your Babies Grow Up to Be Pirates

Thomas Jones and Thomas Wansley both assigned culpability to maternal figures from their youth, whose inattention led to the moral failings that emerged in adulthood. Convicted of mutiny and murder in 1824, Thomas Jones, "a colored man," blamed his owner's wife for neglecting his moral education. Indeed, in the first paragraph of his confession, Jones places the blame squarely on his slavemistress, Mrs. Gatreau: "I was born a slave to Joseph Gatreau, a seafaring-man, who being oftimes from home, I was of course left under the care of his wife, a woman who did not pay that strict regard to her church she might have done; and of course I was not piously brought up."[45] After the untimely death of Mr. Gatreau, his wife "began to seek the Lord and to serve the remainder of her days in honor of her God," but it was too late. "She then began to advise me to seek religion for my future safety, but alas!" Jones wrote, "the tree was too old to be bent." Youthful petty theft and escape from slavery led ultimately to a descent to mutiny and murder, then conviction and execution. His crimes are, Jones concludes, the responsibility of the early inattention of the woman legally and ethically responsible for his moral development.[46]

For his part, Thomas Wansley, another black seafarer and coconspirator with Gibbs, placed the blame even earlier. Born to a white woman in Delaware, Wansley believed his existence was the fulfillment of a curse his grandmother had placed on his mother. Before Wansley's birth, his mother complained to her mother that her sister "lay with black men." The grandmother then wished that, for her tattling, "she should have twice as many black offspring." Wansley was one. His blackness—a manifestation of his mother's sins of gossip and adultery—was a mark against him his entire life. Facing his execution, Wansley decried the racial discrimination he suffered, but what is particularly fascinating is the way he connects even this essential aspect of his identity and the source of his suffering to his parentage, and to his mother's indiscretions. Why include, at the *beginning* of his life's reflection, the curse handed down by his grandmother? Why, in a tale with more than enough abuse and suffering to explain the hardening of his heart toward murder, did Wansley (or whoever actually crafted his narrative) situate his fate in the period even before his ill-fated conception? As much as a stretch as it was to hold women responsible, Wansley's narrative finds a way. His mere existence was a product of his mother's original sin. Both Jones and Wansley, then, feel compelled to explain their later misdeeds as originating out of their incomplete moral tutelage in youth. The failure of women resulted in their terrible crimes.

Women and Seamen: A Dangerous Combination

By contrast, Gibbs is clear in his confession that he was raised well and respectably. For him, the fall came not from the sin of inattention from his mother but from the improper or inconstant attentions of femmes fatale encountered later in life. Here, connections can be drawn between pirates' confessions and the "porno-gothic" city novels of seamy urban life popularized in the antebellum period.[47] These novels, which often focused on the seduction and abandonment of women and their descent into prostitution, paralleled the stories that seafarers such as Gibbs and Moran tell about falling for women whose fickle hearts leave them broken and ready for a life of crime. Whereas the women of the city novels turn to prostitution, similarly jilted men turn to piracy.[48] Indeed, the wrong woman's attention (or the right one's inattention) could make an otherwise good man turn pirate. Describing the protagonist's fall in Joseph Holt Ingraham's 1844 novel *The Midshipman*, Ronald and Mary Zboray note that, when he turns away from his object of affection, "he falls under the power of vice: rebelliousness, gaming and piracy."[49]

The American Pirates Own Book also framed its tales in gendered tropes. In particular, the story of James Moran, who was executed for mutiny and piracy, echoes themes of these earlier confessions. Moran notes that after he was paid out for his first voyage, alcohol and prostitution got the better of him. Alone and with money in his pocket in the strange city Liverpool, he succumbed to the "silly headlong indiscretion of youth," burning through his cash "upon the most unworthy objects": women and drink.[50]

In rarer occasions, flesh-and-blood women physically present at the scene of the crime are held liable for the men's misdeeds. Describing the 1837 dispute between George McCowen, the first mate of the *Powhattan*, and seaman John Chestnut, the New York *Daily Herald* explained, "The affray took place in consequence of the preference shown to the sailor, in spite of the mate's assiduity, by a pretty blackeyed girl, a passenger, whose good opinion each were eager to obtain."[51] When the passenger returned the affections of Chestnut, rather than the mate, McCowen found himself not only the

loser in the contest for the woman's affections but also in the precarious position of having been bested by one of the crew. According to the *Daily Herald*: "It seems, however, that the lass considered Chestnut 'the proper man,'
which excited the ire of the mate, and drove him 'into such a passion' that
he attempted to knock his rival's brains out with a large billet of wood, but
Chestnut's head, very unlike his heart, not being made of 'penetrable stuff,'
he escaped with a severe contusion."[52] The larger significance, however, is
that the story was, at least to the editors and readers of the paper, *funny*. For
them to "get it," they had to understand the gender and class dynamics at
play: the humiliation of the superior McCowen by the "pretty blackeyed girl"
prompted his violent outburst. The joke lay in McCowen's incorrect belief
that his attentions and rank meant he deserved the affections of this passenger over the lowly forecastle seaman.

Significantly, McCowen's story appeared in James Gordon Bennett's
New York *Daily Herald* the year after that paper broke the story of the Helen
Jewett murder, a salacious tale of a well-to-do man driven murderously mad
by the attention of a prostitute. The Jewett case received vast coverage in
the newspapers of the day, but it was in the pages of the *Daily Herald* that it
found its fullest and most sensational expression.[53] As the leading pioneer of
lurid (and popular) true crime stories, Bennett's paper helped form the basic architecture for such tales. Indeed, men made fools by women—whether
McCowen in this case, or the respectable Richard P. Robinson, allegedly
driven to murder by the beguiling attentions of the prostitute Jewett—was a
foundational archetype for both humor and pathos in such stories.[54] In the
use of this conceit, confessional and true crime literature merely applied to
nonfiction what was not only an ancient mythological figure, from sirens to
Salome and beyond, but a growing trend in the romantic and gothic literature of the era.[55]

Thomas Gibbs's narrative, first hastily published after his conviction in
1831, is the most sophisticated, literarily speaking, and relatedly, the most dubious in provenance. Indeed, Gibbs's confession continued to grow in both
fame and length for years after his death. The earliest published account,
Trial and Sentence of Thomas J. Wansley and Charles Gibbs (1831), stuck closely
to the specifics of the trial for the murders committed on board the *Vineyard*
for which the men faced execution. Gibbs's previous career as a privateer and
pirate was covered in a terse, appending paragraph.[56] By contrast, a version
published in 1836 had expanded that paragraph into a rollicking tale of mur-

der and mayhem. Gibbs waxes rhapsodic in a first section that amounts to an orgy of blood (he estimates a body count around four hundred) and pirate clichés ("dead men tell no tales").[57]

Although his initial (and most dramatic) series of crimes as a pirate in the Caribbean seems not to be connected to the misdeeds of a woman, the crimes that actually led Gibbs to the gallows were linked to an inconstant lover. Unlike those of Wansley and Jones, Gibbs's confession is adamant that his early crimes were not prompted by the inattentive care of his mother. Gibbs lavishes praise on his "good and affectionate parents" and wishes he had followed their "Godlike advice."[58] Indeed, Gibbs acknowledged that he was going to the gallows under a pseudonym so as not to bring shame on his undeserving, respectable family back in Rhode Island. Moreover, the editor of his confession observes that, whatever moral failings he developed later, Gibbs's upbringing had done its job, noting the surprising but "apparent readiness with which he made quotations from Scripture."[59]

In his first turn as a pirate, years before the incident on the *Vineyard* that ultimately led to his execution, Gibbs acknowledges the moral power of women in the midst of his criminal depravity. He recounts the capture of a Dutch vessel he and his compatriots seized in 1818, noting that they quickly murdered all aboard save for "a young female, about 17, who fell upon her knees and implored Gibbs to save her life." Moved by her plight, Gibbs agreed to save her, "though he knew it would lead to dangerous consequences among his crew," who feared that leaving a witness alive was too dangerous.[60] Ultimately, Gibbs's defense of this innocent girl prompted open mutiny. Gibbs even killed one of his own, shooting a fellow pirate "for daring to lay hold of her with a view of beating her brains out."[61] Ultimately, however, Gibbs acquiesced; whatever remaining moral power this young Dutch girl represented, his mutinous men ultimately undermined Gibbs's moral resolve, and he "acquiesced . . . and gave orders to have her destroyed by poison."[62] Although in the end it merely postponed her unfortunate end, the pleading of a young woman forced Gibbs to waver in his murderous resolve. At least within the confines of his confession, she represented a tenuous remaining link to a moral order Gibbs had long left behind.

In this incident (and many others) the Gibbs confession strains credibility. Perhaps even more important than its veracity, however, is the moral role this particular victim plays within the narrative. Whether or not this poor Dutch girl truly met her fate by Gibbs's order, or was a creation of Gibbs's

imagination or that of a later author, she is positioned as a moral foil, a counterpoint to the depraved world into which Gibbs and his crew had sunk. By
(temporarily) saving her, Gibbs demonstrates a hint that his original moral
tutelage remained within him, brought momentarily back to the surface by
the presence of this unnamed symbol of purity and innocence.

Gibbs's confession turns far more romantic in its second act. He claimed
to have settled in Liverpool and put his bloody past behind him. Gibbs
found love, and it was the influence of a good woman that permitted him to
live and love as an upright man. If only, however, he had actually found such
a woman! "I fell in with a woman," he explains, "who I thought was all virtue,
but she deceived me and I am sorry to say that a heart that never felt abashed
at scenes of carnage and blood, was made a child of for a time by her, and I
gave way to dissipation to drown the torment."[63] The former pirate was unmanned—made a child—by the fickle wiles of his love. He returned to the
sea and to a series of crimes that led him inevitably to the shadow of the gallows. By melodramatic coincidence, the very woman whose wavering affections turned Gibbs to drink was incarcerated in the same prison as he while
he awaited execution. He purportedly wrote her two letters, full of remorse,
repentance, and hope for everlasting salvation. At the last, it was Gibbs who,
misdeeds behind him, reversed the roles, and turned moral tutor to his former love. Although she "unmanned" him during their time in Liverpool, as
he faced execution and contemplated his past deeds, Gibbs repented and
urged her to do the same.

The highly improbable romance at the end of his tale illustrates the extent to which the author, whether Gibbs himself or another, understood the
developing gender roles of antebellum America, and how their deployment
could be used to powerful, if ham-handed, emotional effect on the audience. Gibbs's tale reads like the stuff of bad romantic literature—because
it is. The close following of developing literary conventions no doubt contributed to its decades of popularity. Matters of gender mark the key piv-
ots in Gibbs's narrative. Following a proper upbringing, he became a leg-
endary rape-and-murder pirate as a member of a hypermasculine cadre of
men whose appetites were beyond control or moral restraint. Later, once he
has reformed himself, in part through what he believed was the love of a
"virtuous" woman, he became utterly unmanned by her deceit. Finally, from
prison, their epistolary rapprochement marked his ultimate redemption. He

went to the gallows having made his peace with this world and with his maker, in part through his redemptive love for his former girlfriend and fellow prisoner.

Conclusion

Although the burgeoning literature of confessional pamphlets and true-crime stories often focused on "cases of male sexual violence against women" (which many pirate confessions also contain), the inversion—women who goad men into violence through romantic or moral inattention—is an important characteristic of these cases.[64] Blaming often-distant women for crimes that took place in the decidedly male world of the seas likens to the larger cultural project of ascribing women as responsible for the moral realm. Similarly, the rise of these tales (and the gender tropes within them) needs to be situated into the larger rise of the popular literature of the day, both fictional and nonfictional. Reading was on the rise across a wide spectrum of the population in the antebellum period.[65] As sensational tales grounded in older moralizing confessional literature, but still part of the newly emergent mass-media pioneered by Bennett and other impresarios, these narratives mark an important moment in the development of American print culture. Although women blamed for crime are hardly new literary creations, it is in part through these pirate narratives that these gender conventions took shape and became fixed in the collective culture as archetypes.

Such tales, from newspaper accounts to published deathbed confessionals, served simultaneously as titillating, prurient popular entertainment and an opportunity to reassert cultural and moral norms. In narratives like these, women represented both the early wellspring for later misdeeds as well as a physical temptation to stray beyond social boundaries. These temptations could not only send a man into a fury of passion when confronted by a sexy woman at sea but also continue to turn a man bad well after he had left her side. As such, women were presented as a consistent literary trope, representing a lingering moral power—a power that is supposed to go to sea with men to restrain their wild and dangerous natures even in the physical absence of women.

NOTES

This essay is several years in the making, and aspects of the argument herein have been drawn from several earlier presentations, especially "'He Became Quite Unmanned': The Gendering of Vice in Antebellum Seafarers' Confessions," The Hungry Ocean, John Carter Brown Library, Providence, R.I., 2011; "Sex, Seafarers, and the Sea: The Legal Literature of Maritime America," Public Lecture, California State University–Northridge, Northridge, Calif., 2010; "Pirates in Court: Performance and National Identity in Antebellum Trials," Nineteenth Century Studies Association (NCSA) Annual Meeting, Tampa, Fla., 2010; and "'I Fell in with a Woman, Who I Thought Was All Virtue': Sex and Violence in Antebellum Seafarers' Confessions," American Historical Association Annual Conference, San Diego, Calif., 2010. I owe a particular debt to the commenters and audience questioners.

1. Charles Gibbs, *Mutiny and Murder: The Confession of Charles Gibbs* (Providence: Israel Smith, 1836). On the complex history of Gibbs's narrative see also Joseph Gibbs, *Dead Men Tell No Tales: The Lives and Legends of the Pirate Charles Gibbs* (Columbia: University of South Carolina Press, 2007).

2. *The Record of Crimes of the United States, Containing a Brief Sketch of the Prominent Traits in the Characters and Conduct of Many of the Most Notorious Malefactors Who Have Ever Been Guilty of Capital Offences; and Who Have Been Detected and Convicted, Compiled from the Best Authorities* (Buffalo, N.Y.: H. Faxon, 1834), 34.

3. Thomas J. Wansley, *The Life and Confession of Thomas J. Wansley, One of the Pirates, Concerned with Charles Gibbs, Alias James Jeffers, in the Murder and Piracy Committed on Board the Brig* Vineyard (New York: Charles N. Baldwin, 1831).

4. Thomas Jones, *Life Trial and Confession of Thomas Jones (a Colored Man) Which Was Taken by a Reverend Gentleman (at Jones's Own Request) and the Account Handed over to the Keepers of the Bridewell to Which Is Added His Sentence and Last Dying Confession Convicted and Executed, June 11th: For Mutiny and Murder on Board of the Brig* Holkar (New York, 1824).

5. Margaret S. Creighton and Lisa Norling, eds., *Iron Men, Wooden Women: Gender and Seafaring in the Atlantic World, 1700–1920* (Baltimore: Johns Hopkins University Press, 1996), ix–xi.

6. Ibid., x.

7. William Sampson, *The Trial of Capt. Henry Whitby for the Murder of John Pierce, His Dying Declaration. Also, the Trial of Capt. George Crimp, for Piracy and Manslaughter* (New York: Gould, Banks, and Gould, 1812), 94.

8. See Daniel A. Cohen, *Pillars of Salt, Monuments of Grace: New England Crime Literature and the Origins of American Popular Culture, 1674–1860* (Amherst: University of Massachusetts Press, 2006).

9. Karen Halttunen, "Early American Murder Narratives: The Birth of Horror," in *The Power of Culture: Critical Essays in American History*, ed. Richard Wightman

Fox and T. J. Jackson Lears (Chicago: University of Chicago Press, 1993), 86; Cohen, *Pillars of Salt*, 31–38.

10. On the sea as a site for the forging of heroic American men in literature, see Thomas Philbrick, *James Fenimore Cooper and the Development of American Sea Fiction* (Cambridge, Mass.: Harvard University Press, 1961), 3–9.

11. Luscom v. Osgood, 1844 U.S. Dist. LEXIS 26, 15 F. Cas. 1115, 1 Sprague 92, 7 Law Rep. 132 (D. Mass., 1844).

12. Hester Blum, "Pirated Tars, Piratical Texts: Barbary Captivity and American Sea Narratives," *Early American Studies* 1 (2003): 133–58; Myra C. Glenn, "Troubled Manhood in the Early Republic: The Life and Autobiography of Sailor Horace Lane," *Journal of the Early Republic* 26 (2006): 59–93.

13. Rollo G. Silver, "Flash of the Comet: The Typographical Career of Samuel N. Dickinson," *Studies in Bibliography* 31 (1978): 85.

14. "Ellms, Charles," Searchable Sea Literature, accessed November 12, 2014, https://sites.williams.edu/searchablesealit/e/ellms-charles/. For a detailed discussion of Ellms's impact on maritime literature generally, see Paul A. Gilje, *To Swear Like a Sailor: Maritime Culture in America, 1750–1850* (New York: Cambridge University Press, 2016), 182–222.

15. *Record of Crimes*, v–xii.

16. See Bradley Deane, "Imperial Boyhood: Piracy and the Play Ethic," *Victorian Studies* 53 (2011): 689–714.

17. Daniel A. Cohen, "The Murder of Maria Bickford: Fashion, Passion, and the Birth of a Consumer Culture," *American Studies* 31 (1990): 6.

18. Joy Wiltenburg, "True Crime: The Origins of Modern Sensationalism," *American Historical Review* 109 (2004): 1377–1404.

19. Ellms, *The Pirates Own Book* (1837; repr., Mineola, N.Y.: Dover, 1993), iii.

20. "Ellms, Charles," Searchable Sea Literature; Gilje, *To Swear Like a Sailor*, 187.

21. John Cyril Barton, "William Gilmore Simms and the Literary Aesthetics of Crime and Capital Punishment," *Law and Literature* 22 (2010): 221.

22. Dwight Conquergood, "Lethal Theatre: Performance, Punishment, and the Death Penalty," *Theatre Journal* 54 (2002): 343.

23. Ibid., 344.

24. *Record of Crimes*, 232; Samuel Tully, *The Last Words of Samuel Tully: Who Was Executed for Piracy at South Boston, December 10, 1812* (Boston: N. Coverly, 1812).

25. Dennis Tatz, "Pirates in Boston: Braintree Historian Finds Poster Publicizing a Pirate Hanging in 1812," *Patriot Ledger* (Quincy, Mass.), April 16, 2009.

26. *Record of Crimes*, 29.

27. Ibid., 41.

28. Samuel Tully, *A Copy of a Letter from Samuel Tully Alias R. Heathcoate* (Boston: N. Coverly, 1812).

29. *Record of Crimes*, front cover.

30. Ibid., 28.

31. See James L. Machor, "Fiction and Informed Reading in Early Nineteenth-Century America," *Nineteenth-Century Literature* 47 (1992): 320–48; Daniel A. Cohen, "Correspondence between Daniel A. Cohen and Daniel E. Williams," *Early American Literature* 30 (1995): 88–90.

32. Halttunen, "Early American Murder Narratives," 67–78; Ann Fabian, *The Unvarnished Truth: Personal Narratives in Nineteenth-Century America* (Berkeley: University of California Press, 2000), 50, 70–75; Cohen, *Pillars of Salt*, 28–35, 98–99, 299; Patricia Cline Cohen, *The Murder of Helen Jewett* (New York: Vintage, 1999), 404–9.

33. *North American Review* 59 (October 1844): 435; Machor, "Fiction," 321.

34. *DeBow's Review* 27 (November 1859): 516; Machor, "Fiction," 329.

35. Sampson, *Trial of Capt. Henry Whitby*, 19.

36. Ibid., 94.

37. Ellms, *Pirates Own Book*, iv.

38. John B. Perry, *The American Pirates Own Book: Containing an Account of the Trial and Execution of James Moran for Mutiny and Murder—The Murder of Capt. Turley and Mr. Vanderslice, on Board of the* Braganza—*The Loss of the Ship* William Brown—*And the Execution of Spencer, Cromwell, and Small, on Board the* Somers (New York: Nafis and Cornish, 1844), 29.

39. *Record of Crimes*, 15.

40. *Lives and Trial of Gibbs and Wansley, Who Were Executed for Piracy* (Boston, 1832), 328.

41. Michael Sappol, *A Traffic in Dead Bodies: Anatomy and Embodied Social Identity in Nineteenth-Century America* (Princeton, N.J.: Princeton University Press, 2002), 290, 344.

42. Perry, *American Pirates Own Book*, 5, 20.

43. *Record of Crimes*, 34.

44. Here I am indulging in an anachronism. Although I believe the term fits what I am describing, *femme fatale* as a term of art did not exist in the era discussed. It first appeared around 1912. William and Mary Morris, *Morris Dictionary of Word and Phrase Origins*, 2nd ed. (New York: Collins, 1988).

45. Jones, *Life Trial and Confession*.

46. Ibid.

47. Karen J. Renner, "Seduction, Prostitution, and the Control of Female Desire in Popular Antebellum Fiction," *Nineteenth-Century Literature* 65 (2010): 166–91.

48. Ibid., 166–67.

49. Ronald J. Zboray and Mary Sracino Zboray, "The Romance of the Fisherwoman in Antebellum New England," *American Studies* 39 (1998): 18.

50. Perry, *American Pirates Own Book*, 4.

51. *Daily Herald* (New York), April 26, 1837.

52. Ibid.

53. Patricia Cohen, *The Murder of Helen Jewett.*

54. Ibid.; Patricia Cohen, Timothy J. Gilfoyle, and Helen Lefkowitz Horowitz, eds., *The Flash Press: Sporting Male Weeklies in 1840s New York* (Chicago: University of Chicago Press, 2008).

55. Karen J. Renner, "Seduction, Prostitution, and the Control of Female Desire in Popular Antebellum Fiction," *Nineteenth-Century Literature* 65 (2010): 166–91; Daniel Cohen, "Murder of Maria Bickford," 5–30.

56. *Trial and Sentence of Thomas J. Wansley and Charles Gibbs, for Murder and Piracy, n Board the Brig* Vineyard (New York: Christian Brown, 1831), 24.

57. Charles Gibbs, *Mutiny and Murder*, 9. The phrase *dead men tell no tales* was a common expression going back at least to 1664, where it appears in the work of English playwright James Wilson (Wilson, *Andronicus Comnenius* [London: John Stanley, 1664] 1:iv). As linked specifically to pirates, the phrase had appeared in at least one earlier confession (see Nicholas Fernandez, *Dying Declaration of Nicholas Fernandez, Who, with Nine Others Were Executed in Front of Cadiz Harbour, December 29, 1829, for Piracy and Murder on the High Seas*, trans. Ferdinand Bayer [New York: George Lambert, 1830], 10). Additionally, Gibbs's claim of participating in the murder of four hundred souls rises in later versions to five hundred (see Henry K. Brooke, *Lives and Exploits of Pirates* [Philadelphia: J. B. Perry, 1846], 156).

58. *Record of Crimes*, 34.

59. Charles Gibbs, *Mutiny and Murder*, 26.

60. *Record of Crimes*, 26–27.

61. Ibid., 27.

62. Ibid.

63. Charles Gibbs, *Mutiny and Murder*, 10.

64. Daniel A. Cohen, "The Beautiful Female Murder Victim: Literary Genres and Courtship Practices in the Origins of a Cultural Motif, 1590–1850," *Journal of Social History* 31 (1997): 211–12.

65. Machor, "Fiction," 324; Gilje, *To Swear Like a Sailor*, 188.

Pirate Ghosts and Buried Treasure

HUNTING FOR GOLD IN THE
NEW AMERICAN REPUBLIC

Adam Jortner

O ak Island, a tiny crag of rock off the coast of Nova Scotia, is home to an extraordinarily deep trough—the Money Pit—long associated with pirate lore, pirate treasure, and pirate magic, particularly relating to the notorious seventeenth-century Captain William Kidd. In 1795, three adventurers dug into its topsoil to discover layers of flagstones, charcoal, and wooden logs, "and they concluded that if Kidd had buried money it was probably here."[1] As soon as they felt something solid beneath their excavation, however, the pit filled with water, and they had to abandon their chase. As the years passed, other expeditions found themselves similarly foiled by other odd events, including subsequent untimely floods, purported booby traps, disturbing dreams, and irregular maps drawn by a man claiming an occult connection to Captain Kidd. Soon enough, stories of guardian dogs with red eyes and enormous crows became tied to the Money Pit.[2] These associations of magically protected pirate treasure wove themselves into popular culture. Leonard Nimoy's late 1970s mystery TV show *In Search of . . .* devoted an episode to the legend, and the History Channel has provided four seasons of its own related reality show, *The Curse of Oak Island.* The popular video game *Assassin's Creed III* follows its hero to Oak Island to recover the treasure, which turns out to be a magical ring that deflects bullets—useful later in the game, when the titular assassin must fight the British Redcoats.

Oak Island's folklore, fantasy, and history exemplify how the uncanny and the magical merged with pirate legends in the late eighteenth and nineteenth centuries in British North America and the early U.S. republic. By the mid-nineteenth century, tales of buried gold went as far west as Ohio and as far south as Texas. These stories connected necromancy and buried treasure, just as Christian legends had done since medieval days. In the early American republic, however, pirates crept into the mix. As Edward Kendall noted in his 1808 travelogue, "settlers in New England, indulge an unconquerable expectation of finding money buried in the earth. The money is supposed to have been buried by pirates; but the discovery of its burial-place is hoped for only from dreams."[3]

The stories of pirate treasure came out of a rich folklore developing in the United States' early republic (1775–1865). The new nation became the site of pirate treasures, secreted not in waters but beneath the earth and in the arcana of forbidden knowledge and ritual magic. In 1826, David Young noted the "prevailing opinion that vast sums of money had, at some earlier period of time, been deposited in the earth at Schooley's mountains, with an enchantment upon it; which could not be obtained without a peculiar art in legerdemain to dispel the apparitions and hobgoblins."[4] Newspapers and essays warned American treasure seekers against supernatural guardians—hobgoblins, apparitions, ghosts, an "evil spirit" who "would rise up and blast them with his vaporous breath," and in one case, an entire deceased crew "rowing the spirit of their mouldered boat."[5]

Yet the stories of pirate gold and its guardians—from Oak Island to Galveston Island—routinely cautioned against reckless pursuit of wealth. These were warning pieces about the importance of hard work. They cautioned *against* the temptation to get rich quick: "If you studied piracy while digging for the money ... old Bob Kidd buried, you should also have studied the fate of pirates," warned one particularly threatening response to New York treasure diggers.[6] Pirate legends almost all had the same moral: practice industry and play the long game. Pirates, the great plunderers of the mercantile world, became magical morality tales for emergent American capitalism.

Magic, Pirates, and Treasure

Historians and folklorists have long known about the early republican penchant for pirates and their treasure. Thirty years ago, Alan Taylor argued that treasure digging represented a response to the economic downturns of the early republic. The ability to find treasure offered a magical alternative capitalism, where inborn talent and cunning provided a way for poor farmers to beat the system—a supernatural economy to offset the disappointments of the emerging capitalist order. Treasure seeking, Taylor wrote, answered the

needs of people who felt left behind by "enhanced post-Revolutionary aspi-
rations." Other historians have linked the magic of treasure diggers to European hermetism, alchemy, and emergent Mormonism.[7]

It is possible that those who hunted for Kidd's gold believed that they
would overcome an economic system stacked against them. The stories told
about treasure hunts often had the opposite advice: searching for gold was an
immoral and costly waste of time. "Learn to make use of your time," went
one essay about a group of twenty money diggers in Vermont, lest "the evil
one . . . send you into the mountains digging for gold where there is none."[8]
One antiquarian referred to the "large holes in the vicinity" of Camel's
Hump, Vermont, as both remnants of a treasure hunt and "monuments . . . of
credulity and folly."[9]

Much of the evidence surrounding early republican treasure hunting is
folklore, collected decades after the purported events. The reliance on folklore raises the problem of "fakelore"—defined by Richard Dorson as legends
rewritten "from earlier literary and journalistic sources in an endless chain of
regurgitation."[10] Nineteenth-century antiquarian Charles Skinner, for example, included as part of his folkloric accounts of treasure hunts the story of
Mud Sam, an African American man who spotted treasure diggers at New
York's Hell Gate. Sam, of course, was a character in Washington Irving's fictional "The Money Diggers," a set of five interlocking stories that formed
the final part of *Tales of a Traveller* (1824), each involving magic, diabolism,
treasure digging, or all three. Skinner recounts the basic plot of the fictional
story of Sam as folklore in his 1896 *Myths and Legends of Our Own Land*.
Perhaps someone related the story in oral form to Skinner, or perhaps he
assumed Irving had cribbed the tale from American legends. (In fact, Irving
consciously imitated European models.)[11] In either case, Skinner's folklore
cannot be taken as anything like a biography or memoir.[12]

Yet as Neil Rennie writes in *Treasure Neverland*, the collected stories of
pirates (or in this case, their magical gold) should not be mistaken for legends of *real* pirates. As cultural and intellectual history, the reality of hidden
pirate gold (or pirate ghosts) is immaterial—no pun intended. The writings
about pirates performed different functions than did the actions of the pirates
themselves.[13] The stories and legends that spread and were shared about pirate magic might have been believed, scorned, or anything in between—but
the circulation of such stories represented a collection of ideas about magic

and pirates, and in that sense, the history of pirate magic has a real existence as intellectual and cultural history, whether or not the listeners to such stories actually went out and started digging. Shakespearean plays frequently include allusions to witchcraft, alchemy, and the occult, but that does not mean that Elizabethan audiences were preoccupied with those subjects. Rather, the presence of such concepts shows that they were part of the audience's worldview, that people of the time understood the references and were capable of participating in discourses about them.[14] Or, as Alec Ryrie has written about the magical scams and purported treasure hunts in Tudor England, "we cannot know where the boundary or boundaries between truth and fiction lie in these stories." Even if these treasure diggers never existed—and some of them certainly did—the "stories fastened on to them conjure them into significance," because they tell us what sixteenth-century England (or in this case, revolutionary America) believed about magic, treasure, and fraud.

What then was the discourse about pirate magic in the early republic? Americans heard that magic and divination were required for unearthing pirate treasure, because pirate treasure possessed a supernatural location and supernatural guardians. Pirate treasure was, in a sense, alive.[15] It was not bound to one patch of land; it could move or escape if it did not want to be found. It might sink deeper into the earth or simply fail to be in the same location from day to day. One account of an 1814 treasure hunt told readers that the effort to determine "if there was any of Kidd's money hid in these parts in the earth" failed after hours of digging when one man struck the treasure chest and cried, "Damn me, I've found it!"—whereupon the treasure vanished.[16] On a 1799 treasure quest led by Ezekiel Perry, the conjuror leading the search warned that a lack of faith or any noise whatsoever would cause the chest to move. The men worked in silence for two hours, until one of them stepped on another's toes. There was a cry of pain and exasperation, and the treasure moved.[17] Joseph Smith Jr. of upstate New York engaged in several treasure hunts; he was vilified for his searching after he became the restored prophet of Mormonism. The treasure hunted by Smith, however, had the usual fickle nature of pirate treasure. One correspondent recalled a hunt where the Smith family dug several concentric circles, but the treasure failed to materialize. Smith explained that a "spirit [had] come up to the ring and as soon as it beheld the cone which we had formed, . . . it caused the money to sink."[18] The uncanny treasure of Oak Island possessed similar transitory properties; reports in the 1860s about diggings in the 1840s claimed that the pit yielded up a few golden chain links, and then soon collapsed.[19] Some treasure hunters tried to capitalize on this fickle nature and lure the treasure like game. A small amount of money placed over the treasure might bring the gold closer to the surface. That belief formed the core of a well-known ruse of the 1780s. The con man Ransford Rogers convinced the money diggers of Morristown, New Jersey, that "they must deliver to the spirits, every man, twelve pounds, for the money could not be given up by the spirits until the sum was given to them." A little money would allow the spirits to relinquish their larger hoard and be set to rest.[20] (Rogers simply took the offerings.)

Supernatural creatures also appeared to thwart seekers. When a treasure digger known as Commodore sought treasure on Jewell Island, off the coast of Portland, Maine, he was rebuffed by "the malevolence of the devil, or evil spirit, who was put in charge of the money." The pirates who buried the treasure had killed a person or animal and poured the blood into the pit, Commodore believed, to keep the treasure secret.[21] An 1827 effort in New London was abandoned when the searchers found the chest hot to the touch, and "a giant dog peered at them from the pit mouth" and "red eyes flashed at them from the darkness." The diggers fled, and when they returned, discovered the chest had vanished.[22] Kidd's purported gold in Milford was guarded by a headless man; his cache on the Piscataqua was patrolled by a "monster horse."[23] When Winchell—a digger in eighteenth-century Vermont—discovered a "divinity" guarding the treasure, he warned that any man's lack of faith would cause the treasure to vanish (as indeed it did).[24] An 1830 effort to find Kidd's treasure on Liberty Island in New York harbor, performed with "the aid of a fortune-teller," ended when the troupe found Kidd's chest but discovered it contained "a being with wings, horns, tail, and a breath, the latter palpable in blue flames."[25] An eighteenth-century effort to find pirate gold on Deer Island on the Maine coast needed to confront "the spirits of four murdered sailors who guard it."[26] Samuel Lawrence and several comrades had begun their excavations for gold when they encountered "a large man who appeared to be eight or nine feet high" who "came and sat on the ridge of the barn, and motioned to them they must leave. They motioned back that they would not; but that they afterwards became frightened and did leave."[27]

Confronting these treasures and their guardians therefore required an appropriately skilled seeker—one with supernatural qualifications. Treasures required seers; magical dreams and magical accoutrements became the cultural currency of the treasure search. Kendall wrote that in New England, dreams were the first source to consider when seeking pirate gold, but if dreams failed, "then mineral-rods are resorted to," and after that "charms and various observances, to defeat the watchfulness of the spirits that have the treasure in charge."[28] Kendall's observation came as part of his account of the fantastic scams of Daniel Lambert of Norridgewock, Maine. In 1804, Lambert convinced his neighbors he had uncovered pirate gold, which led to a flurry of digging, because, "says the multitude, there is more money to be found in the earth; there were more pirates than one."[29] Lambert bought on credit and borrowed from neighbors on the strength of his presumed gold, and then absconded with his ill-gotten gains. What made the story plausible was not only the belief in pirate treasure but the belief in Lambert's magical abilities to recover it: "Lambert was . . . found to possess enchanted mineral-rods, which had grown in the mystic form, and been cut at the proper age of the moon," Kendall noted, and Lambert's powers were soon "vouched for by the country round."[30]

Similarly, Silas Hamilton in the 1780s kept detailed records of treasure beliefs and experiences of his fellow citizens of Whitingham, Vermont. He listed over forty references to buried treasure, such as the one that "a Pyrot hid" near Northampton, Massachusetts. Over half of the citations were to dreams, as when "Capt. Donethan Dreemed of hid money on fishers Island on mount Prospect near a Rock not the bigness of a haycock."[31] Chloe Russel, author of an 1824 treatise on dream interpretation, informed readers that she had been freed from enslavement when she dreamed of a pot of money and told the rightful owner where to dig for it. The beneficiary was so glad when he found the specie that he bought her and freed her.[32] Other efforts at preternatural sensing accompanied journeys for pirate gold. Lambert "was pronounced to be one of those fortunate persons, who, born under a certain planetary aspect, are endowed with various and extraordinary powers."[33] Several efforts to find treasure were undertaken with seer stones—supernatural pebbles by which certain individuals "could see all the lost treasure of earth and sea," as John Greenleaf Whittier wrote in 1847.[34] Seer stones granted mystical images of treasure and other distant objects to a circle of gifted visionaries.[35] In 1824, a Vermont man "carried in his hat the mystical stone in which he could see the precise locality and enormous quantity of the concealed precious metals."[36] A seer stone in Rose, New York, required no hat; the seer "held it to his eyes, and claimed the power to see through it into the earth."[37] To find pirate treasure, seekers needed a person and not a map; X did not mark the spot.

Ritual magic was also required to obtain treasure. Silas Hamilton recorded the arcane instructions for obtaining the buried treasures of his Vermonters' dreams: "Tak[e] Nine Steel Rods about ten or twelve Inches in Length Sharp or Piked to Perce in to the Earth," he wrote, "and let them Besmeared with fresh blood from a hen mixed with hogdung."[38] Commodore learned from a German tutor a series of spells to break charms and curses on mines and treasures.[39] Thurlow Weed encountered a violent ritual when he joined a hunt for Kidd's gold as a child in early nineteenth-century New York: "the throat of a black cat was cut," he recounted, and the direction of the gold "was indicated by the direction the blood spurted."[40]

The search for pirate treasure obsessed a cross-section of American society. John Greenleaf Whittier recalled a treasure search in Poplin, New Hampshire, in the 1840s involving dozens of "grown men, graduates of our 'common schools,' and liable, every mother's son of them, to be made deacons, squires, and General Court members."[41] William Bentley, a template for middle-class Yankee churchmanship, provided a Bible and psalm book to the treasure-hunting efforts of a conjuror in 1808.[42] But all kinds of people had access to pirate lore and the magical knowledge needed to find it: "Men and women without distinction of age or sex became marvellous wise in the occult sciences," according to an 1831 newspaper. "Many dreamed, and others saw visions disclosing to them, deep in the bowels of the earth, rich and shining treasures."[43] Rogers—leader of the New Jersey efforts—was "an illiterate person."[44] Mormon critics almost immediately chastised Joseph Smith's associates as "a gang of money-diggers" and "generally the dregs of the community."[45]

Christianity and Treasure Hunts

These magical traditions had deep roots in Christian Europe. Indeed, in *Hamlet*, Horatio inquires whether the ghost of Hamlet's father "hast uphoarded in thy life / Extorted treasure in the womb of earth / (For which, they say, you spirits oft walk in death.)"[46] Early modern treasure hunters in Europe understood that lucre was the devil's business; the ambivalent connection between money and morality matched with Christian beliefs that evil spirits and demons watched over buried treasure—which being secreted in the ground, was the property of the devil. In 1584, near Naples, a monk and a nun read psalms and gave to fellow treasure diggers bits of paper marked with magical symbols to disinter a demon guarding a treasure. The monk and nun were put on trial by the Inquisition. Two years later, inquisitors in Naples found another case in which a cleric had joined one of his flock who could speak to fairies, then battled demons to find the treasure the fairies had discovered.[47] A sixteenth-century treasure hunt in England required the participants to fast, pray, and give offerings to the saints.[48]

Religious impulses also haunted American treasure digging. Commodore aided his searches by reading from "the Apocrypha, where the angel Raphael exorcises the devil"—probably a reference to the Book of Tobit, in which Raphael aids in the search for secreted money and provides a charm to keep off the demon Asmodeus.[49] A history of Groton, Massachusetts, described a hunt for Kidd's gold undertaken by "pious and godly Christians, with the Bible, Prayer-book, and Pilgrim's Progress lying near them."[50] Universalist preacher Miles Wooley formed a company to dig for treasure and hired someone who, "by looking into a mysterious . . . stone, pretended to be able to discover hidden treasures." The Universalists expelled Wooley.[51] In 1789, Vermont Congregationalists fired Nathaniel Wood for the same reason.[52] An expedition to dig for Spanish gold on Deer Island, Maine, in 1824, had to pause while someone ran for a Bible "to keep the evil spirit off." When a Bible could not be procured, they used a spelling book instead. (This treasure hunt was unsuccessful.)[53]

If using a primer instead of a Bible is any indication, the religion of American treasure hunts was ambivalent at best. European antecedents shared that ambivalence. Elizabeth I had Parliament legislate against treasure digging in 1563; using magic to find treasure could net miscreants a year in jail. The same act, however, recommended the death penalty for cases of "Witchcraft, Enchantment, Charm, or Sorcery."[54] Treasure hunting was not a praiseworthy activity, but it was not *maleficium*—the evil magic supposedly performed by early modern witches. European practitioners could (and did) make a case for the Christian benefits of treasure seeking. A ghost condemned to guard a treasure had likely escaped from purgatory; finding treasure released the spirit, and thereby set a Christian soul to rest. Treasure seeking was both a morally ambiguous search for treasure and a Christian duty—even though treasure hunters openly cast spells, practiced countermagic, and used rods, mirrors, and crystals to keep demons and ghosts at bay.[55]

Whispers of witchcraft followed American treasure diggers as well. "Is your old friend a witch or a wizard?" one man asked, observing the Commodore at work. "He comes very nigh to one," was the reply.[56] Rogers's scheme in 1788 nearly came apart when the wife of a treasure seeker feared witchcraft in the harmless powder Rogers shared.[57] Joseph Smith Jr. perpetually faced accusations of "necromancy," although there was no evidence that his magic was anything beyond folk belief and traditional prayer. Yet treasure seekers rarely came under accusations of witchcraft, because treasure seeking, with its deep roots in Renaissance and Reformation Christianity, had always been something different from witchcraft.[58] The treasure seeker might "come nigh" to witchcraft, but he was not a witch: he was part exorcist, part cunning man, and part Christian servant, laying souls to rest.

The American innovation to treasure seeking was the attribution of buried treasure to pirates, though of course postrevolutionary Americans also believed that ancient seafarers, American Indians, and fleeing Tories had secreted goods that could be uncovered through dreams and divining rods. Still, Kidd's vengeance had an especial vogue for early Americans. When a skeleton washed ashore in Narragansett Bay some thirty years after the Revolution, rumors circulated that these bones had been a pirate murdered by Kidd to guard the treasure. That meant that the treasure was now unguarded by ghosts, and the shores of Rhode Island were soon covered with Americans digging for Kidd's treasure.[59]

Why pirates? In part it was no more than historical accident; pirates provided a convenient moneyed class in the same way that early modern Russian treasure tales attributed their gold to Polish and Cossack raiders. Kidd really did frequent the New England coast, and he was incarcerated in Boston before heading to trial in England. And seekers occasionally unearthed pirate treasure—or at least unusual caches of coins. Stephen Grindle stumbled across "some four or five hundred pieces of the currency of France, Spain, Spanish America, Portugal, Holland, England, and Massachusetts" on his farm in coastal Maine in the winter of 1840–41.[60] Later in the 1840s, French crowns were discovered, again on the Maine coast.[61] The *Haverhill Gazette* informed its readers that just south of Albany, Kidd had buried "50 boxes of gold, and laid upon them 13 human bodies."[62] And perhaps pirates

had particular panache in America, where the privateer navy had done surprisingly well against the British in the revolution and the War of 1812.

The Work Ethic of Treasure Stories

Yet in most stories of magical treasure, the pirates were not the heroes, nor
even the antiheroes. Stories of pirate treasure were not stories of treasure
found; they were stories of treasure lost. Stories of magical pirate treasure
had an explicit didactic function: to warn listeners against false promises that
anyone could make an end run around the normative economic values of
the emerging American economy. The belief in "buried money-chests, and
the consequent inclination to search for them," Kendall lectured his readers,
encouraged people "to depend for a living upon digging for money-chests,
rather than upon daily and ordinary labor."[63] Pirate treasure, like the magic
ring in *Assassin's Creed III*, was merely a magical MacGuffin to get to the real
point of the treasure story: the affirmation of hard work and the critique of
credulity and efforts to cheat the emerging capitalist system.

Few treasure tales of the early republic had happy endings; the seekers
usually lost, either because they were deliberately bamboozled or because
they sought instant rather than delayed gratification. An 1805 story related
the case of a miller who, believing money was buried beneath his house, bur-
rowed under the foundation and destroyed the mill on which his livelihood
depended. "Reader, do not smile at the miller's folly," warned the article, for
those who "quitting the small, but certain gains of honest industry, to grasp
imaginary riches, have plunged themselves and their families into poverty."[64]
In Irving's "The Money Diggers," the hapless Wolfert Webber dreamed of
"an immense treasure in the centre of his garden. . . . chests, wedged close
with moidores, ducats, and pistareens, yawned before his ravished eyes, and
vomited forth their glittering contents." Such dreams, of course, meant that
"Wolfert awoke a poorer man than ever."[65] Eber Howe's ferociously anti-
Mormon book *Mormonism Unvailed* used anti-Semitism to make its point
about economy and magic treasure; Howe lambasted "Joseph Smith's early
habits in searching after treasure digging" by comparing "digging after the
deposits of pirates" to imagined Jewish "over reaching in commercial, or in
other business transactions."[66] Treasure digging (and Mormonism), in this
1834 screed, was deliberately tied to the hateful association of Judaism with
usury.

Even when the treasure story did not focus on a specific seeker's misfortune, authors usually gilded the tale with affirmations of how economics *should* work. One traveler found that by 1808, Fort Stanwix, New York, had "been literally turned inside out for the purpose of discovering concealed treasure." The nearby town of Rome was meanwhile "destitute of every kind of trade, and rather on the decline."[67] The implication, of course, was that the former caused the latter. A Vermont newspaper critiqued men who dug for gold "against right reason, resting their hopes on the incantations of the magicians," and instead advised readers to "learn to make a proper use of your time, strength, and money," lest the devil tempt them with promises of easy gold.[68]

The loss of industry was the real failing of the treasure diggers, at least according to the fictionalized treasure hunts of the republic. These tales likely circulated more widely than any local legend and openly equated treasure beliefs with laziness and wisdom with industry. Thomas Forrest's *The Disappointment, or the Force of Credulity* (1767 and 1796) told the story of a treasure hoax; its principal characters were the town jokesters, intent on teaching some gullible knaves who "quit solid sense for airy golden dreams." The marks dream of improving themselves without work; the conspirators laugh about making "proselytes of half the town" as long as "credulity and love of money prevail." After learning of the imposture, the victims forgive the prank and take the moral: as one character warns (in what the author intended as a Swedish accent), "I bill take de resolution to lead a new life and follow my bid'ness wid honesty and industry." Another character concurs: "Let it be a warning to others not to listen to idle schemes and give way to vain imaginations."[69]

Similar lessons came with Irving's story of Webber in "The Money Diggers." Webber dreams three times of gold in his cabbage patch and then, awake and in pursuit, digs up the area entirely; with no crop and with creditors calling, Webber suffers the woes "common to those whose golden dreams have been disturbed by pinching realities. . . . now, when thousands of pounds had eluded his search, to be perplexed for shillings and pence was cruel in the extreme."[70]

Things grow worse when Webber meets a stranger, "an amphibious looking fellow" with a deep scar who pays for everything with "very strange outlandish coinage." Webber gleans enough from the encounter, however, to gather his own team of treasure diggers, convinced that others had failed by "not going to work at the proper time, and with the proper ceremonials."

The team locates a sign left by the pirates and commences digging, but "the loneliness of the place, and the wild stories connected with it, had their effect upon his mind."[71] Webber spots what he thinks is the ghost of a buccaneer, screams, and all hell breaks loose. Something attacks the men; Webber is beaten and his confederates race back to Manhattan. Webber is a broken man and prepares to "make my will and die," until he learns that New York "is going to run a main street through" his land. Webber instantly recovers, and his "golden dream was accomplished"; his land does yield a treasure in the form of rents paid by everyone building and living on the street that passes through what had once been his cabbage patch, with "tenants knocking at his door . . . each with a little round bellied bag of money, the golden produce of the soil." The land produces wealth—in this case, the wealth that grows from an expanding city and its economy of hard work.[72]

Not every story of pirate treasure and magic followed this precise logic; Quebecois writer Philippe-Joseph Aubert de Gaspé captured the pathos of treasure hunting in his 1837 novel *The Influence of a Book*. The plot concerns Charles Amand, an alchemist in the 1820s seeking hidden treasure in the Canadian lake country. Amand dreams of how his life would change if only he could find treasure. Flying with the spirit guardians to the moon, where "a celestial spirit sat upon a throne, exhorting him by words and gestures . . . Amand followed the spirit to the hidden side of the star where he alighted on what appeared to be a mirror made entirely of gold and rubies; it belonged to him alone. Then he returned to our globe, where everyone loved him, adulated him, envied him."[73] Edgar Allan Poe inverted the logic of the treasure story in his 1843 work "The Gold-Bug," in which a treasure hunt follows esoteric practices—and succeeds. In the story, William Legrand and his slave Jupiter drop a golden bug through the eye of skull nailed to a tree, then set up circles, scythes, and lanterns before unearthing Kidd's lost pirate treasure. Nevertheless, even in Poe's story, the crux of the matter is Legrand's superior intellect and initiative. He gains wealth through his ability and persistence, cracking a cipher to discover Kidd's gold and gems. It is "human ingenuity" alone that can solve an enigma.

Conclusion

An 1810 article complained about "the unshaken faith generally reposed in the enchantment which secures the money buried by the pirates on the sea coast of the middle states"; such beliefs were "proofs of the deep and extensive rooting of these erroneous ideas in modern society."[74] But the best defense against such errors was the story of pirate treasure itself. The language of magical pirate treasure—unlike belief in magical pirate treasure—was an exercise in exasperation. If, as Stephen Mihm has argued, capitalism depended on the idea of confidence, then the stories of pirate gold were an exercise in confidence, affirming that the wise and steady would always win out over efforts at a fast buck. The magic of pirate treasure was meant to be wondered at, but it was not meant to be believed (although it assuredly was). The danger of belief in magical treasure was the danger of piracy itself—the loss of gold, property, and honor. The pirate became not just a demon or a spirit, but a symbol and antithesis of the emerging capitalist ethos—a ghost story, in which no confidence should be placed. Tales of magical treasure were stalwarts of reliability in an unsteady world—not a reaction against capitalism, but its affirmation.

NOTES

1. Mather B. DesBrisay, *History of the County of Lunenberg* (Toronto: William Briggs), 302.

2. D'Arcy O'Connor, *The Secret Treasure of Oak Island: The Amazing True Story of a Centuries-Old Treasure Hunt* (Guilford, Conn.: Lyons, 2004), 28–30, 105, 160.

3. Edward Augustus Kendall, *Travels through the Northern Parts of the United States in the Years 1807 and 1808* (New York: Riley, 1809), 3:84.

4. David Young, *The Wonderful History of the Morristown Ghost: Thoroughly and Carefully Revised* (Newark: Benjamin Olds, 1826), 13.

5. *An Account of the Beginnings, Transactions, and Discovery of Ransford Rogers* (Newark: John Woods, 1792), 11; Clark Jillson, ed., *Green Leaves from Whittingham, Vermont* (Worcester, Mass., 1894), 122; *Nahant, and Other Places on the North-Shore* (Boston: William Chadwick, 1848), 26; *Herald of Freedom* (Boston), December 1, 1788.

6. Green Mountain Boys to Thomas C. Sharp, February 15, 1844, in *Early Mormon Documents*, ed. Dan Vogel (Salt Lake City: Signature Books, 1996), 1:597.

7. Alan Taylor, "The Early Republic's Supernatural Economy: Treasure Seeking in the American Northeast, 1780–1830," *American Quarterly* 38 (1986): 8, 19; Herbert Leventhal, *In the Shadow of the Enlightenment* (New York: New York University Press, 1976); John L. Brooke, *The Refiner's Fire: The Making of Mormon Cosmology, 1644–1844* (New York: Cambridge University Press, 1994). More recent European work on treasure digging has emphasized the long history of the practice; treasure tales are as old as the Greeks, and treasure hunts in England were associated with

demons as early as 1288. See Johannes Dillinger, *Magical Treasure Hunting in Europe and North America: A History* (New York: Palgrave, 2012), 61.

8. *Vermont Chronicle* (Bellows Falls), December 10, 1850.

9. Abby Maria Hemenway, *Vermont Historical Gazetteer* (Burlington, Vt.: Hemenway, 1867), 1:785.

10. Richard Dorson, *American Folklore and the Historian* (Chicago: University of Chicago Press, 1971), 8–9.

11. Neil Rennie, *Treasure Neverland: Real and Imaginary Pirates* (New York: Oxford University Press, 2013), 138–39, 156.

12. Charles Montgomery Skinner, *Myths and Legends of Our Own Land* (Philadelphia: J. B. Lippincott, 1896), 2:273–75.

13. Rennie, *Treasure Neverland*, v–vi.

14. James Sharpe writes about *Macbeth*: "the language of the occult, of astrology, even of alchemy is frequently to be found. This is not to say that playwrights or their audiences were obsessed with magic," but rather "that their audience would be familiar with such issues and at least some of the discourse" surrounding it. James Sharpe, *Instruments of Darkness: Witchcraft in Early Modern England* (Philadelphia: University of Pennsylvania Press, 1996).

15. Dillinger, *Magical Treasure*, 58.

16. *Gem* (Rochester, N.Y.), May 15, 1830, in Francis W. Kirkham, *A New Witness for Christ in America: The Book of Mormon* (Salt Lake City: Brigham Young University, 1959), 2:48.

17. Barnes Frisbie, *History of Middletown, Vermont, in Three Discourses* (Rutland, Vt.: Tuttle, 1867), 48–49.

18. Eber Howe, *Mormonism Unvailed* (Painesville, Ohio: Printed and Published by Author, 1834), 237–38.

19. O'Connor, *Secret Treasure of Oak Island*, 18, 22.

20. *Account of the Beginnings*, 14.

21. "History of the Divining Rod: With the Adventures of an Old Rodsman," *United States Magazine and Democratic Review* 26 (1850): 223–24.

22. Skinner, *Myths and Legends*, 2:282–83.

23. Ibid., 2:268, 270.

24. Frisbie, *History of Middletown*, 48.

25. Skinner, *Myths and Legends*, 2:273.

26. *Herald of Freedom* (Boston), December 1, 1788.

27. Kirkham, *A New Witness*, 2:378.

28. Kendall, *Travels*, 3:85.

29. Ibid., 3:88.

30. Ibid., 3:86.

31. Jillson, *Green Leaves*, 117–18.

32. Chloe Russel, *The Complete Fortune Teller and Dream Book*, in Eric Gardner, "'The Complete Fortune Teller and Dream Book': An Antebellum Text 'By Chloe Russel, a Woman of Colour,'" *New England Quarterly* 78 (2005): 272. We should not assume that Russel's autobiography was penned by Russel herself, as noted above. If we are considering the supernatural as a debate, however, the referent to this remarkable story of treasure digging yielding freedom is irrelevant. The language of magic in the early republic was the language of freedom—literally, in Russel's case.

33. Kendall, *Travels*, 3:85.

34. John Greenleaf Whittier, *The Supernaturalism of New England* (1847; repr., Baltimore: Clearfield, 1997), 65.

35. For examples of seer stones used in treasure hunts, see J. W. Hanson, *History of Gardiner, Pittston, and West Gardiner* (Gardiner, Me: William Palmer, 1852), 169; Whittier, *Supernaturalism*, 65; Skinner, *Myths and Legends*, 2:282–83; and Howe, *Mormonism Unvailed*, 237.

36. Hemenway, *Vermont Historical Gazetteer*, 1:785.

37. Quoted in D. Michael Quinn, *Early Mormonism and the Magic World View* (Salt Lake City: Signature, 1998), 40–41.

38. Hamilton's 1786 notes are reprinted in Jillson, *Green Leaves*, 119.

39. "History of the Divining Rod," 223–24.

40. Thurlow Weed, *Life of Thurlow Weed* (Boston: Houghton and Mifflin, 1884), 7.

41. Whittier, *Supernaturalism*, 57.

42. William Bentley, *Diary of William Bentley* (Salem, Mass.: Essex Institute, 1911), 3:358.

43. *Palmyra Reflector*, February 1, 1832, reprinted in Kirkham, *A New Witness*, 2:69.

44. *Account of the Beginnings*, 8.

45. Palmyra residents to *Painesville (Ohio) Telegraph*, March 12, 1831, reprinted in Dan Vogel, *Early Mormon Documents* (Salt Lake City: Signature Books, 1998), 3:8–9.

46. Dillinger, *Magical Treasure*, 61, 56, 72.

47. Ibid., 61–66.

48. Ibid., 167.

49. "History of the Divining Rod," 223–24.

50. Caleb Butler, *History of the Town of Groton* (Boston: T. R. Marvin, 1848), 256.

51. Nathaniel Stacy, *Memoirs of the Life of Nathaniel Stacy* (Columbus, Pa.: Abner Vedder, 1850), 171–72.

52. Frisbie, *History of Middletown*, 46–61.

53. *Nahant*, 26.

54. Dillinger, *Magical Treasure*, 19.

55. Ibid., 76–78, 174–91.

56. "History of the Divining Rod," 319.

57. *Account of the Beginnings*, 25.

58. Dillinger, *Magical Treasure*, 95.

59. Benjamin Albert Botkin, *A Treasury of New England Folklore: Stories, Ballads, and Traditions of the Yankee People* (New York: Crown, 1947), 532.

60. Joseph Williamson, "Castine, and the Old Coins Found There," *Collections of the Maine Historical Society*, vol. 6, ser. 1 (Portland, 1859): 107–26.

61. *Machias Union*, July 8, 1856.

62. *Haverhill Gazette*, August 15, 1823.

63. Kendall, *Travels*, 3:87.

64. *Farmers Cabinet* (Amherst, N.H.), March 3, 1805.

65. Washington Irving, "Wolfert Webber," in *Washington Irving: Bracebridge Hall, Tales of a Traveller, The Alhambra*, ed. Andrew Myers (New York: Library of America, 1991), 677.

66. Howe, *Mormonism Unvailed*, 55.

67. Christian Schultz, *Travels on an Inland Voyage . . . Performed in the Years 1807 and 1808* (New York: Riley, 1810), 16.

68. *Vermont Chronicle* (Bellows Falls), December 10, 1850.

69. Thomas Forrest, *The Disappointment, or the Force of Credulity* (Gainesville: University Press of Florida, 1976), 47, 50, 105–9.

70. Irving, "Wolfert Webber," 677, 680.

71. Ibid., 700.

72. Ibid., 698, 700, 715–16.

73. Philippe-Joseph Aubert de Gaspé, *The Influence of a Book*, trans. Claire Rothman (Toronto: Robert Davies, 1993), 35.

74. "Quitman on the Popular Prevalence of Magical Notions," *The Medical Repository of Original Essays and Intelligence*, August–October 1810, 183–84.

Conclusion

David Head

The preceding essays have shown pirates in a wide variety of lights: vectors of empire, economically rational actors, hypermasculine antiheroes, logwood cutters and intercultural brokers, private seafarers not too different from privateers, enemies of mankind and highwaymen at sea, victims of scheming women, and in the most improbable role for pirates, "magical morality tales for emergent American capitalism." The variety testifies to how pervasive, multifaceted, and enduring pirates have been in reality and fiction. Despite the depth and breadth of the contributors' work, a number of issues remain in debate. As with any scholarship, the contributors offered the latest word, not the last word.

A central point of contention has been the definition of piracy. As Carla Gardina Pestana, John A. Coakley, Kevin P. McDonald, Douglas R. Burgess, and Guy Chet demonstrate, a precise, durable definition was—and still is—hard to come by. That's a problem. If a government hoped to suppress a crime, it ought to be able to say what actions constituted the crime and where the line between legal and illegal lay. Plus, if a government were going to punish someone for piracy and hang him by the neck until dead, dead, dead, justice demanded the condemned know what he'd done wrong. For scholars, the problem is less dangerous, but it still sows confusion. How can we talk to each other if we're not sure if the same word means different things?

McDonald tackles the problem by conceptualizing piracy as a spectrum rather than a distinct category, a box into which someone either did or didn't fit. Pestana, Coakley, Burgess, and Chet echo that idea in their own ways. Someone might have engaged in a single act of theft at sea, filching a canoe, say, while others might have despoiled dozens of vessels, assaulted towns, terrorized sailors and civilians, raped and murdered. Someone might have engaged in activities such as logwood cutting, wrecking and salvaging, or simply plain old trade in violation of Spanish claims to total dominion over the New World. Someone might have robbed ships as the opportunity arose but otherwise scratched out a living from other work, such as privateering. Someone might have bought or sold stolen goods, items unavailable through other means. All of the above could have been called a pirate. Emphasizing that the definition of piracy was fluid certainly gets us closer to the lived experience of the early modern Atlantic, in which communication was difficult, administration and regulation were complicated, and attitudes toward ravaging others were more lax than we would accept today. The English cheered, Margarette Lincoln reminds us, when pirates plundered Spanish Catholics and Indian Muslims, because, presumably, as non–English Protestants they deserved it. The definition of piracy was also always a political act meant to advance an empire's interests vis-à-vis its rivals and not a value-free tool to fight crime. Nevertheless, it's possible to overstate the fluidity of piracy and in doing so enshrine piracy as relativistic, making one person's pirate another's honest jack-tar. The label then loses its meaning, swept away in a deluge of fluidity. If anything can be piracy, then nothing is.

The key to unlocking the definitional dilemma, I'd suggest, lies in emphasizing the historical context in which particular instances of piracy took place. Such an approach acknowledges that conceptions of piracy changed over time and varied from place to place, from jurisdiction to jurisdiction, while also affirming that there were limits to what might be called piracy. To cite but one example, Pestana shows that much of the maritime violence of the sixteenth and seventeenth centuries flowed directly from Spain's claim to exclusive possession of the New World and the denial of that claim by England, France, and the Netherlands. A cycle of attack and counterattack followed because Spain and its rivals had started from different premises, each plausible, about what the New World was and by what right European actions there were justified. By the eighteenth century, when the European powers had established more of a common framework for colonization of the by then not so new New World, practitioners of maritime violence were more clearly beyond the law of any nation. Hard cases remained; disputes among nations continued. But identifying a pirate in, say, 1720 was more straightforward than in 1520, because 1720 wasn't 1520. The intervening two centuries changed the historical context.

Closely related to the problem of defining piracy is the problem of defining other forms of private maritime violence, namely, privateering, reprisal, and letter-of-marque trading, not to mention the practice of naval prize, which receives little attention from scholars in the context of piracy. In the age of sail, there were many legal ways to take property from others, against their will, and transfer it to one's own use. Adding another layer of confusion was the tendency of victims of captures to call everything piracy, even if a taking was legal. "Pirate!" was the all-purpose insult of aggrieved ship owners, regardless of who took their ship.

Privateering is the activity most often discussed alongside piracy for the good reason that the two had so much in common, with a letter-of-marque often a paper-thin distinction between the two. The contestable status of privateering in the sixteenth and seventeenth centuries is understandable given that the word *privateer* did not exist in English until the seventeenth century.[1] More important than the nomenclature, however, was the uncertainty of the concept of privateering, which was still evolving from medieval ideas of sovereignty, kingship, and private violence to modern ideas of the state and its monopoly on legitimate violence. In his essay, Chet goes further. He argues that out on the water there was no meaningful difference between piracy and privateering. Lawmakers could make all the laws they wanted, with pretty legal niceties, but at sea even the most straight-laced ship owners armed their vessels for combat, war or no war, license or no license, because that's how they needed to do business. No one else could protect their ships out on the dangerous sea.[2]

It is a provocative argument and a welcome reminder that, as Chet notes, we live every day in a world of powerful government bureaucracies, visible authorities, and omnipresent regulation. Early modern people didn't. At the same time, it matters that privateering was legal and that the law recognized a privateer's prizes as different from a pirate's plunder. Privateering was a business, and it generated revenue not simply by taking enemy ships and cargoes but by securing legal title to captured goods through the adjudication of an admiralty court. With the court's stamp of approval, privateers could then sell prize property, confident that it truly belonged to them, fetching a price that reflected their unimpeachable ownership and protecting them from future legal challenges. It wasn't enough for privateers to get their hands on valuable loot. They needed the legal title, as well. Privateering provided a legitimate transfer of property. Piracy never did. Privateers could cut corners and there were certainly privateers who didn't care for the added hassle of a prize proceeding, especially in the early period when the legal apparatus of privateering was still in development. Nevertheless, despite what it shares with piracy, privateering's legal status was real. As before, the context matters, and a close attention to how privateering worked in particular times and places will go a long way to teasing out the similarities and differences between piracy and other forms of violence at sea.[3]

One certain difference between privateering and piracy is that privateering no longer exists. Most European powers abolished it in 1856, with the United States coming along a few years later, when the Confederacy attempted to initiate privateering early in the Civil War. Occasionally, some writers float privateering as a possible solution to a modern problem like global terrorism, but it is a proposal without much chance of impacting security policy.[4] Piracy, on the other hand, is still with us. To fight modern piracy, it would be useful to know what worked to suppress pirates of a previous era. As the contributors suggest, the issue has two parts: When was piracy suppressed? And what factors explain its suppression?

Most scholars point to the 1720s as the end of the golden age of piracy. Chet, however, contends that piracy continued unabated into the nineteenth century and that any decline in maritime violence was illusory, a result of calling the violence by a different name: privateering. It's clear that there was a surge in piracy in the early nineteenth century, perpetrated by figures such as Charles Gibbs, the prolific pirate of the 1830s discussed by Matthew Taylor Raffety. A decade earlier, piracy had surged around Cuba and Puerto Rico, as small boats launched from the beaches overhauled passing merchantmen. The U.S. Navy dedicated a squadron to antipiracy patrols. In the decade before that, Spanish American privateers, often condemned as pirates by Spanish merchants, Spanish diplomats, and American officials, sailed the Caribbean and Atlantic. In the decade before that, during the Napoleonic Wars, British and French privateers prowled the same waters. There was no shortage of marine predators, even in the nineteenth century.

Part of the problem of setting an endpoint for the golden age of piracy is again definitional: how little piracy does there have to be before you can say it is suppressed? An analogy to fighting infectious disease might help. Public health experts distinguish among *eradication*, meaning zero cases, the disease is totally gone, like smallpox; *elimination*, meaning no cases in a particular area, although new cases could arise, like measles in the United States, a disease that is mostly gone but has popped up again recently as some parents choose not to vaccinate their children; and *control*, meaning a disease has been reduced and managed so that it is not as bad as it once was and may be possible to eliminate over time, like malaria, which is not a problem in the United States but is found in other places in the world. Applied to piracy, it looks like piracy was controlled sometime around the 1720s and it may even have been eliminated in the eighteenth century before a new outbreak in the nineteenth. Piracy has never been eradicated, not even in the Caribbean, where the International Chamber of Commerce reports a handful of pirate attacks each year.[5]

Whatever their position on the timing of piracy suppression, the contributors agree that when identifying the cause of piracy's decline, it is best to look at changes to the underlying conditions that sustained piracy. Chet, Wilson, Burgess, Pestana, and Virginia W. Lunsford point to different factors as most important, yet they concur in rejecting the traditional emphasis on a centralized war against piracy carried out in the 1720s. That is a significant development in the historiography. Scholars as different as Marcus Rediker and Peter Earle, who don't agree on much, both bring down the curtain on their stories with a war on pirates. Now the debate is much more about which underlying factors were most important and when a turning point was reached. Once more, a close attention to historical context matters. Piracy was not suppressed because officials in London finally put their minds to the problem and the navy rounded up the bad men. Rather, many historically contingent factors changed, sometimes brought about by determined individuals but also often beyond the control or ken of anyone. Pirates came out on the losing end. As Lunsford notes, it is a lesson we would be wise to heed today.[6]

Whether or not policymakers draw lessons from the suppression of piracy, the book's contributors also have a lesson to share with students about how to use evidence in fresh ways to tell fresh stories. Lunsford and Peter T. Leeson, for example, respectively find something new in *Bucaniers of America* and *A General History of the Pyrates*, the two most enduring published sources on Golden Age pirates. Neither author discovered new evidence, a heretofore unknown journal or a cache of letters hidden in an old sea chest. Instead, they took well-known evidence and read it in a new way by applying the insights of social science to re-create pirate life in a way historians had not done previously.

The cultural histories of the book's last two sections show yet another approach to evidence. The contributors read published sources against the grain so as to glean insights the works' authors never intended to reveal. Lincoln is not concerned with the Henry Every of history, because the historical record has little to say about him. But Lincoln finds the Henry Every of popular culture is surprisingly talkative, weighing in on a host of important topics, including topics as seemingly distant from piracy as early eighteenth-century gender and marriage politics. If the ballads, books, and plays that portray a fictionalized Every were dismissed for their lack of historical validity, we would miss out on what they do have to say about the culture in which they were created. Likewise, Carolyn Eastman, Raffety, and Adam Jortner move past the accuracy of pirate books to see what message these artifacts can tell us about their readers, who were so numerous that printers and publishers turned out pirate books by the ton.

Cultural histories of books and their readers are challenging to do well. The question we would really like to have answered—what did this mean to readers?—is ultimately unknowable. We don't know why any one person enjoyed *Bucaniers of America*, *A General History of the Pyrates*, Charles Gibbs's confessions, or Washington Irving's "The Money Diggers." But as the four cultural historians indicate, we can learn about the culture of a time and place that embraced pirate stories and we can ponder what these stories encouraged readers to think about.

As creative as scholars might be at teasing meaning from the printed words of the past, there is a tension between works that depend on published accounts of piracy as a source on the actions of pirates and works that used published sources as a window onto what pirates meant in the culture. For Lunsford and Leeson, more than others, it matters if *Bucaniers of America* and *A General History of the Pyrates* describe things that happened or just spin a good tale. Both are written with such zest that historians, trained to be skeptical of the sources interrogated, are bound to raise an eyebrow. Alexandre Exquemelin was a participant in much of the action he describes, although he also liked to pass along stories he'd heard. *A General History of the Pyrates* can be sourced to newspaper articles and pamphlets, although gaps remain in what can be substantiated, and one chapter, about a utopian Madagascar community, is known to have been fabricated. The lesson is that, one last time, context matters. It is indispensable to understand how a book was published, why it was published, and what expectations the audience would have had for their reading. In the early modern period, strict accuracy was not necessarily expected while in the nineteenth century, confessions were conventional and treasure hunt stories were part of a cultural affinity for esoterica. Moreover, descriptions that strike us as shocking or beyond the pale were not necessarily gratuitous in a world where brutal violence was a way of life. If we want to understand popular books, songs, images, plays—and someday movies and video games—we need to understand the context in which they emerged.[7]

Pirates generate a lot of passion. It's fun for kids to play at buried treasure and sword fights, pretending to be little swashbucklers like they see on their shows. Adults, too, now like to act out a saltier version of pretend, dressing up, drinking up, and shouting "Arrrr!" Pirates have their own holiday, Talk Like a Pirate Day, September 19. Everyone needs a hobby, I suppose, and talking like a pirates is as good an excuse to celebrate as any other.

The contributors have pointed in a different direction. Pirates reveal a lot about how the early modern Atlantic world was built, how empires clashed, and how colonies developed. Pirates tell us about public policy and strategies to understand crime and devise methods of suppression. Pirates also reveal a lot about the cultures in which they lived and about the cultures that found them so fascinating. That process is not over. Someday, scholars of the future will look back at the late twentieth- and early twenty-first-century obsession with pirates and tell us something about ourselves.

NOTES

1. *OED Online*, s.v. "privateer, n.," accessed August 10, 2017, http://www.oed.com.

2. N. A. M. Rodger, "The Law and Language of Private Naval Warfare," *Mariner's Mirror* 100 (2014): 5–16.

3. For the importance of privateering conveying legal title, see Donald Petrie, *The Prize Game: Lawful Looting on the High Seas in the Days of Fighting Sail* (Annapolis, Md.: U.S. Naval Institute Press, 1999).

4. See, for example, Ian C. Rice and Douglas A. Borer, "Bring Back the Privateers," *National Interest*, April 22, 2015, http://nationalinterest.org/feature /bring-back-the-privateers-12695.

5. For a layman's introduction to eradication, elimination, and control, see Diane Cole, "Control, Eliminate, Eradicate a Disease: What's the Difference?" *NPR*, January 14, 2015, http://www.npr.org/sections/goatsandsoda/2015/01/14/377182067 /control-eliminate-eradicate-a-disease-whats-the-difference. For the current geography of piracy, see the icc's live piracy map: https://www.icc-ccs.org/index.php /piracy-reporting-centre/live-piracy-map.

6. Marcus Rediker, *Villains of All Nations: Atlantic Pirates in the Golden Age* (Boston: Beacon Press, 2004); Peter Earle, *The Pirate Wars* (New York: Thomas Dunne, 2005).

7. For the sources of materials in *A General History of the Pyrates*, see Manuel Schonhorn's editorial notes in his edition of the work (Mineola, N.Y.: Dover Publications, 1999). For a critical analysis of the reliability of the Blackbeard material in *General History*, see Arne Bialuschewski, "Blackbeard: The Creation of a Legend," *Topic: The Washington and Jefferson College Review* 58 (2012): 39–54.

CONTRIBUTORS

DOUGLAS R. BURGESS is a professor of history at Yeshiva University and the Benjamin Cardozo School of Law. His previous books include *The Politics of Piracy: Crime and Civil Disobedience in Colonial America* (University Press of New England, 2014) and *Engines of Empire: Steamships and the Victorian Imagination* (Stanford University Press, 2016).

GUY CHET is professor of history at the University of North Texas. His books include *Conquering the American Wilderness: The Triumph of European Warfare in the Colonial Northeast* (University of Massachusetts Press, 2003) and *The Ocean Is a Wilderness: Atlantic Piracy and the Limits of State Authority, 1688–1856* (University of Massachusetts Press, 2014).

JOHN A. COAKLEY is lecturer in history at Merrimack College in North Andover, Massachusetts. He is the author of "An Island Home: Jamaican Local Leaders in the English Imperial World" in *Newberry Essays in Medieval and Early Modern Studies*, ed. Carla Zecher and Karen Christianson (Newberry, 2013).

CAROLYN EASTMAN is associate professor of history at Virginia Commonwealth University. She is the author of the prizewinning *A Nation of Speechifiers: Making an American Public after the Revolution* (University of Chicago Press, 2009) as well as articles in *Gender and History* and the *William and Mary Quarterly*.

DAVID HEAD is lecturer of history at the University of Central Florida. He is author of *Privateers of the Americas: Spanish American Privateering from the United States in the Early Republic* (University of Georgia Press, 2015) and editor of *Encyclopedia of the Atlantic World, 1400–1900: Europe, Africa, and the Americas in an Age of Exploration, Trade, and Empires* (ABC-CLIO, 2017).

ADAM JORTNER is associate professor of history at Auburn University and the author of *The Gods of Prophetstown: The Battle of Tippecanoe and the Holy War for the American Frontier* (Oxford University Press, 2011), which won the Society for Historians of the Early American Republic's 2012 James Broussard Best First Book Prize, and *Blood from the Sky: Miracles and Politics in the Early American Republic* (University of Virginia Press, 2017).

PETER T. LEESON is the Duncan Black Professor of Economics and Law at George Mason University. He is author of the award-winning *The Invisible Hook: The Hidden Economics of Pirates* (Princeton University Press, 2009), *Anarchy Unbound: Why Self-Governance Works Better than You Think* (Cambridge University Press, 2014), and *WTF?! An Economic Tour of the Weird* (Stanford University Press, 2017).

MARGARETTE LINCOLN is a visiting fellow at Goldsmiths, University of London, and curator emeritus at the National Maritime Museum, Greenwich, London. Her books include *Naval Wives and Mistresses 1745–1815* (National Maritime Museum Publishing, 2007), *British Pirates and Society, 1680–1730* (Ashgate, 2014), and *Trading in War: London's Maritime World in the Age of Cook and Nelson* (Yale University Press, 2018).

VIRGINIA W. LUNSFORD is associate professor of history at the United States Naval Academy. She is the author of *Piracy and Privateering in the Golden Age Netherlands* (Palgrave, 2005).

KEVIN P. MCDONALD is assistant professor of history at Loyola Marymount University in Los Angeles. He is the author of *Pirates, Merchants, Settlers, and Slaves: Colonial America and the Indo-Atlantic World* (University of California Press, 2015).

CARLA GARDINA PESTANA is professor and Joyce Appleby Endowed Chair of America in the World at UCLA. She is the author of "Early English Jamaica without Pirates," *William and Mary Quarterly* (2014), and *The English Conquest of Jamaica: Oliver Cromwell's Bid for Empire* (Belknap Press, 2017).

MATTHEW TAYLOR RAFFETY is professor of history at the University of the Redlands in Redlands, California. He is the author of *The Republic Afloat: Law, Honor, and Citizenship in Maritime America* (University of Chicago Press, 2013).

DAVID WILSON is a PhD candidate at the University of Strathclyde in Scotland. He is the author of "Piracy, Patronage, and Political Economy: Captain Kidd and the East India Trade," *International Journal of Maritime History*, 2015.

INDEX

admiralty courts: colonial governors and, 81; common law and, 76, 77, 81, 115–16; jurisdiction of, 76, 81, 82, 83; procedure of, 79
American Pirates Own Book, The, 207, 209, 213, 215
Assassin's Creed III (video game), 224, 233
Atlantic Ocean: connection to Indian Ocean piracy, 28, 66, 90, 120; European claims to, 16, 18, 27, 51, 52; imperial control of, 89–90, 111–12; norms of doing business on, 114–15, 118; obstacles to suppression, 93; pervasiveness of piracy in, 15–16, 27, 29, 78, 89, 112; sites of piracy, 25, 27–28, 66; trade, 26, 40–41, 91, 94, 112, 119
Aubin, Penelope, 179–80
Aurangzeb, 78, 79, 168
Avery, Henry. *See* Every, Henry

Bahamas, 27, 28, 66, 89, 96–97, 100–101
"Ballad of Henry Every, The," 78, 167, 170. *See also* Every, Henry
Barbados, 33, 36, 52, 91, 94, 113
Bay of Campeche: buccaneers in, 59; as logwood trade site, 6, 53, 54, 64, 66; piracies in, 41, 58, 60–61, 63, 66
Bay of Honduras: as logwood trade site, 6, 54, 57, 58, 61, 63; piracy in, 60–61, 63, 66, 101; Royal Navy cruising in, 95
Baymen, 57, 63, 66
Beeston, William, 35, 44, 114
Belize (British Honduras), 6, 41, 58–59, 61, 63, 66, 67
Bennett, James Gordon, 216, 219
Bermuda, 52, 55, 57, 96–97
"Blackbeard," 3, 15, 84, 99, 101, 195
Board of Trade, 78, 80, 81, 82, 83, 84, 85, 114

Bonnet, Stede, 99, 101
Bonny, Anne, 3, 4, 84, 197
books: circulation of, 183, 191; copperplate printing of, 190–91; publication of, 184; reading habits and, 184, 186, 187. *See also American Pirates Own Book, The; Bucaniers of America; General History of the Pyrates, A; Pirates Own Book, The*
Boston, 57, 85, 98, 100, 209, 232
Brazil, 17, 18, 19, 22, 52
Bresiliaan, Rock (Rock the Brazilian), 134, 186, 190
British Honduras. *See* Belize
Bucaniers of America (Exquemelin): advertising of, 188; audience of, 185, 187, 197, 200; class inversion in, 192, 194; masculinity in, 183–86, 188, 191–92; popularity of, 185–86, 191, 197; production of images in, 190–91; publication history of, 132, 185, 186, 188; reliability of, 132, 146n12; torture depicted in, 184, 187; translations of, 186, 191; visual depictions of pirates in, 189–93, 200; written depictions of pirates in, 185–88, 200
buccaneers: attacks by, 62, 131, 132, 134–45, 142; background of, 52, 131, 132–33, 136, 139, 143; bases of operations for, 136–37; brutality of, 133–34, 136, 159; chronology of, 3, 131; group solidarity of, 138–39, 141–43; logwood cutting and, 55, 56, 59, 61, 62, 64; modern piracy and, 129, 145; numbers of, 131; organization of, 138–41, 143; origins of term, 117, 186; recruiting by, 136; support for, 137–38; suppression of, 144–45; tactics of, 142. *See also Bucaniers of America*; Exquemelin, Alexandre; l'Olonnais, Francois; Morgan, Henry

251

CPSIA information can be obtained
at www.ICGtesting.com
Printed in the USA
LVHW03s2019210618
581518LV00003B/334/P